This book is dedicated to my parents, Lynn and Jim Bartels, two American sweethearts. Thank you for raising me to appreciate the little things, for which I am forever grateful.

Love and warmth to all my family and friends, bright and big and bursting like fireworks on the Fourth of July across this funky, wild, hip country.

The
United States
ᵒᶠ Cocktails

Trident

Whiskey Ditch

Smith & Curran

Brandy Old Fashioned

Last Wo...

BAR

Colorado Bulldog

Horsefeather

BAR

Mai Tai

Tequila Sunrise

Frozen Margarita

Sazerac

Blue Hawaii Cocktail

Sourtoe

Rum Runn...

The
United
States
ᵒᶠ Cocktails

Recipes, Tales, and Traditions from All 50 States

(and the District of Columbia)

Brian Bartels

foreword by
Brad Thomas Parsons

illustrations by
Mike Burdick

Abrams Image, New York

Contents

Foreword

by Brad Thomas Parsons

BRIAN BARTELS. The name alone evokes the alliterative, all-American alter ego of a Golden Age comic book superhero, and in *The United States of Cocktails* Brian accomplishes a heroic task: crisscrossing the country like a powerful locomotive to chronicle the spirited adventures across the frontier of America's drinkways.

Brian has never met a cocktail den, tavern, corner tap, or dive bar that wasn't worthy of exploration, and his always-curious egalitarian approach to drinking, along with the stories shared every day and night behind the bar, makes him the perfect candidate to tell this story. Brian is as American as a Bruce Springsteen song, but on his version of the album cover of *Born in the U.S.A.* instead of a dusty red ball cap you'll find a well-worn Moleskine notebook tucked into the back left pocket of his Levi's 501 jeans. And he's filled those pages with the memories, observations, folklore, recipes, and a few tall tales from countless journeys. To me, Brian has always been a bartender cast from the working-class hero mold. Sure, he'll make you a perfect Daiquiri or a bespoke Boulevardier without blinking, but he also has the heart and soul of an old-school bartender. One who knows that being able to make a connection is why so many of us go to bars. Sharing a story, having a laugh, or, most importantly, just listening is a memory that will be remembered long after that glass is empty and the tab has been settled. Keeping my already well-worn copy of *The United States of Cocktails* within reach ensures that I'll always be armed with this entertaining almanac of cocktail trivia, recipes, history, and trivia—whether it's checking off a bucket list bar when I'm traveling to a new city, learning more about a regional spirit, or stirring up a delicious cocktail.

One of my biggest regrets was waiting so long to introduce myself to Brian. All those wasted years when we could have been running buddies, mixing it up in the Big City. For the past few years, whenever I found myself in New York's historic West Village neighborhood, I knew I was always within walking distance of one of Brian's bars, and posting up in a courtside seat to catch up with him, watch him work, listen to his stories, and hear that great laugh of his is one of life's greatest pleasures. My favorite wildcat is now back in Wisconsin, where he's running his own tavern, one that over the years will carry a well-earned patina of the memories and stories of everyone who passes through the doors, like many of the bars in this very book. I miss that wildcat more than you know, but I'm comforted knowing that when I find myself in Madison there will always be a bar with cold Miller High Life ponies and Marty Robbins crackling on the speakers, and we'll pick right up where we left off.

—BTP

Welcome to *The United States of Cocktails,* population: you.

MY NAME IS Brian Bartels. I have been an American my entire life, and I have been a bartender and service industry professional for more than twenty years, and I have been drinking cocktails for (*ahem*) most of my legal adulthood.

I grew up in the Midwest during the latter part of the twentieth century. From the *Choose Your Own Adventure* books of my childhood to the dreams of playing football for the Green Bay Packers to tasting my first cocktail—a brazen Jack Daniel's and Coke—as an underage college freshman, being an American is an experience I can't help but acknowledge with sustained applause.

Additionally, being a bartender is also a pretty enjoyable situation, providing me with opportunities to tell a fine story, play host to an inviting party or room, and—among many other rewards—proudly carry on the legacy of those who were doing this long before I arrived. Over the past ten years, I have been the bar director for Happy Cooking Hospitality in New York City, responsible for overseeing the spirits and cocktail programs. Beyond old-fashioned bartending tasks, I have worked shifts as an oyster shucker, ice retriever, food expediter, barista, maître d', toilet unclogger, glass polisher, juice squeezer, and everything and anything to push the service into a better place for the guests and staff.

But my nationality and professional experience aside, in many respects, I have been waiting to write this book since I turned legal drinking age and started visiting bars. I love discovering new worlds, and that happens every time we walk into a bar, where colorful characters and infinite stories await.

At Paul's Club in Madison, Wisconsin, one of my early bartending gigs, bartenders would mostly do shots of Jameson, but if we had time, and were feeling a little squirrelly, we would make Mind Erasers—vodka, Kahlua, and club soda— in rocks glasses, and we would speed-sip the cocktail through tiny straws while holding our hands behind our backs in friendly competition with the patrons. The winner got to pick which shot of shitty booze the loser, the last person who finished, had to take. This was fun, although not necessarily the best recipe for a hangover-free morning to follow. I recall thinking to myself, *Where did this cocktail come from? Who invented it? And . . . why?*

A book that explored questions like these (and more) seemed like a worthy endeavor to me, and I knew I wanted to write this book in the same way we share stories across the bar, tales that become so alive we can't wait to share them with everyone we meet. The time I have spent in bars has afforded me new perspectives on design, culture, and legacy, which have been shape-shifted by the priceless currency of social lubricants into the weirdest and most wonderful reflections of our lives and history . . . and I was fortunate enough to catalog over seven hundred different bar climates while researching this book.

ABOUT THIS BOOK

THE UNITED STATES of *Cocktails* is an exploration into the cocktails, spirits, and bar history celebrated in every state in America. This book is solely devoted to the United States and its storied cocktail traditions and idealistic sanctuaries.

And *why this national focus?* you might wonder. One easy answer is that America has produced some of the most unforgettable cocktails enjoyed by millions of drinkers throughout the world. While our first stab at American drinking was actually European-style drinking, dominated by beer, punches, cider, and Madeira wine, America welcomed a steady stream of international visitors, who brought varied influences and creativity to our shores. The first uses of the word *cocktail* were recorded here, and fruitful experimentation followed. New York gave the world the Cosmopolitan, the Bloody Mary, and the Manhattan, among many others. In the 1800s, San Francisco was leading the West Coast charge with Jerry Thomas's Blue Blazer and Pisco Punch. New Orleans alone is responsible for introducing the Sazerac, Grasshopper, Vieux Carré, Ramos Gin Fizz, French 75, Brandy Milk Punch, and many more. These are cocktails built over decades or even centuries, passed on through generations, influencing people on a global scale. And our bars, such as New Orleans's estimable Erin Rose—a must-visit destination for me every time I'm in the Pelican State—are still creating new traditions. I'm not quite sure what they put in their Irish coffee—and I might never want to know (it's probably sugar)—because I'm often too distracted by how wide I'm smiling upon my first sip whenever I taste it. Visiting New Orleans not only makes me thirsty, it inspires me.

In this book, I celebrate both our historical contributions to drinking culture and some of the most exciting things happening in American bars today. And I'm not just talking to cocktail geeks here. This book is for everyone—home bartenders with no professional experience, historians of America, culture buffs, and anyone eager to discover how differently our state-by-state traditions unfold. It is a book for people who celebrate travel, who search for the best bars in places they plan to visit. It is for the seekers of established and newly founded craft distilleries. It is for the great bartenders who have been serving people countless drinks over the years, as well as bartenders just starting out. This book is for people looking to be inspired by the creativity of unpretentious bar programs—what Tyler Davidson is doing for tiny Lewisburg, West Virginia, for instance, is worthy of celebration. And it is also for anyone who has a warm feeling for their home state, a state they used to live in, or a state they hope to visit someday.

Each state within the United States is famous for many things, but how has each affected the wider cocktail world? What obscure local delicacies are we saluting from within each state border? And how have the nation's distilleries evolved since Prohibition? And where is the future of cocktails headed? These are a few of the questions I hope to answer in the pages to follow.

There are places all over the world that have deep regional drinking traditions. In Japan, it's customary for a group of alcohol imbibers to pour drinks for one another as a gesture of companionship and respect. On the island of Crete in Greece, they play *koupa,* where someone drinks everything in their glass and then kisses the bottom for good luck. George Street in St. John's, Newfoundland, is famous for its "screech-ins": If a person is identified as a non-Newfoundlander, a screech (the colloquial term for moonshine) is presented to them, and upon drinking the shot, they offer a recitation and then kiss a cod in the face or a puffin in the ass. Because America is a cocktail of international influences and vast in scale, we have traditions as weird and wonderful as these, and more! (Just check out the Bottle Toss at Midtown Billiards in Little Rock, Arkansas, page 125 if you don't believe me.) I would argue that we have perhaps the most varied and vibrant drinking culture in the world, which has in turn influenced how people are drinking in other countries. Our traditions deserve to be celebrated.

Ernest Hemingway famously said, "If you want to know about a culture, spend a night in its bars." Bars are nothing if not cultural beacons. New ideas have spread from major cities into the smaller markets and are received by many bar programs, whether they're established cocktail parlors, ambitious upstarts, hotel bars, restaurant bars, taverns, or dive bars. When I ask Americans what they drink in their home state, they often don't just mention a specific drink, but also highlight something interesting about the people and places in question. Some might be surprised to find that a two-ounce shot called the Razorback, for example, is the unofficial Arkansas cocktail, and that Montana has "ditches" (as in "with water," so when someone orders a "Whiskey Ditch," they mean whiskey with water), or that the Horsefeather cocktail was invented in Kansas but is now more associated with Missouri.

We are a country of eclectic and adopted cultures. After all, the Razorback drink was named after the University of Arkansas Razorback mascot, which acquired its nickname in the early 1900s when a former coach claimed that the football team played "like a wild band of razorback hogs." Razorbacks were indigenous not to Arkansas but rather to western Europe and Russia. Looking a bit further into this drink reveals how we were adopting and then adapting other cultures while forging a new frontier in our homeland.

One can pretty much walk into any bar in America and order a more-than-halfway respectable Old Fashioned—and that's saying something. We've come a long way since the Old Fashioned debuted in the 1870s-1880s! But

What does a traveler do at night in a strange town when he wants conversation? In the United States, there's usually a single choice: a tavern.

—William Least Heat-Moon, *Blue Highways*

one of the reasons I wanted to write this book was Wisconsin's most famous cocktail, the Old Fashioned Press (a brandy Old Fashioned with bitters, sugar, muddled orange and cherry, and the eponymous press—half club soda and half 7Up), which is a cocktail available at just about every drinking establishment throughout the state. However, if you order this concoction anywhere outside of Wisconsin, most bartenders will pause their trajectory, flash you a wild look, and ask you to rewind what you just said, because chances are they have never heard the request for a "Press" cocktail before—and that's okay! That is why we are here. I love the fact that certain pockets of the United States get by with habits and affectations not found anywhere else. That's what makes us unique as human beings.

I hope this book encourages you, dear reader, to keep seeking the stories created by people who were here long before us, who were initiating the trends we value through today, as well as the people who are here now and starting new revolutions for the future. American nostalgia is something different to each of us. To me, it is bowling alley arcade rooms, drive-in movie theaters, and chewing bubble gum while riding a BMX bicycle. To you, it's going to be something else. No matter what your answer is, we need those memories and traditions documented in our lives. It's what makes this country so special.

THE ROLE OF THE BAR

THE UNITED STATES of Cocktails was created for much the same reason we serve cocktails in the first place: social reckoning. We are mammals, which means we were born to be interactive. I love that bars provide us with unavoidable community, and we live better when sharing our life experiences. I don't care if you're the grumpiest old geezer this side of the Mississippi; if you are out in public and ordering an Old Fashioned from a bartender aiming to make eye contact and serve you a properly made cocktail, you can cross your arms and stew all you want, but things could be way worse. There's always going to be golf and *Ghostbusters*, supper clubs and backyard barbecues, root beer floats and coffee milk (Rhode Island), Coca-Cola (Georgia) and Nike (Oregon), cocktail lounges (Bryant's in Milwaukee) and unforgettable dives (Tattooed Mom in Philadelphia), arcades and comic books, *Jeopardy!* and college football, Thanksgiving and the Fourth of July, Portsmouth and Las Vegas, pizza and cheeseburgers (born in Kentucky), and yes, there will always be Margaritas and Old Fashioneds—the sour and the sweet, offering us the option to sip and live among one another, to tolerate our differences by taking the edge off in rewarding camaraderie.

Walking into a bar and seeing people toasting and celebrating or talking and laughing can stimulate our brain cells into feeling talkative, engaging, or euphoric. There's something very sacred about the tactile, balletic nature of bars and the bottles we grab to serve our loyal and welcome patrons, friends and family members, regulars and strangers, joyful locals and weary travelers. And I saw this firsthand growing up. My grandfather owned a bar in northern Wisconsin, my father owned a liquor store for a little while, and my uncle owned and operated a bar in my hometown of Reedsburg, Wisconsin, called Larry's Drinking Establishment, a communal haven balancing etiquette and panache as well as some cold, frosty mugs of ale, where everyone knew the names of those sitting on either side. Communities were built around people like my grandfather, father, and uncle running respectable local businesses associated with communal bonding, and that tradition is equally important today to people like Gabriel Stulman and his wife, Gina, my business partners from Happy Cooking, who insist on running terrific restaurants with elevated bar programs in New York City. Camaraderie is a hard ingredient to engineer, so having a local saloon or tavern where you feel comfortable away from the confines of home is second to none. Seeing a familiar face behind the bar or sitting next to us is a pleasure we have been savoring since the early colonial days. Where else would you leave a spare set of house keys than the place you trusted with your weekly paycheck, your liver, and your kids' college tuition?

AN ABBREVIATED HISTORY OF AN AMERICAN INVENTION

THE COCKTAIL—A MIX of liquor, sugar, bitters, and usually (if one had the luxury of money), ice—was born in the early nineteenth century. In an April 1803 edition of *The Farmer's Cabinet*, a publication out of Amherst, New Hampshire, the following line appeared: "Drank a glass of cocktail—excellent for the head."

The next recording of the word *cocktail* comes from May 13, 1806, in the *Balance and Columbian Repository*, a newspaper published in Hudson, New

COCKTAIL BARS

The cocktail bars selected in each state section are featured for their exemplary measures in creating timeless cocktails. These bars continue to push their staffs to create seasonal and ever-changing menus, keeping us on our toes with creative design while honoring the classics. They are also often famous for a cocktail of their own making. Rest assured, there are far more cocktail bars than the ones featured individually in each state section, and I have made an effort to single some others out at the beginning of each chapter, so take note of all the wonderful bars across this remarkable country we call home.

STATE SPIRITS

Each chapter showcases who's been creating spirits in certain states for decades, such as the many bourbons of Kentucky; Clear Creek Distillery (Oregon); and Laird's Straight Apple Brandy (New Jersey), the oldest distillery in America. In addition, I highlight new ambassadors of America's continued journey through our beverage frontier, featuring modern distillers that are pioneering new craft trends throughout the country, such as Utah's High West Whiskey, Tito's Handmade Vodka from Texas, and Michigan's Two James. Our interest in booze has never been higher, as evidenced by the surge in craft distilleries opening since the turn of this century, largely influenced by post-Prohibition regulations that have been lifted. There were seventeen whiskey distilleries in the year 2000, and by 2016 there were more than 780, with the numbers increasing since then. It's one thing to single out the decades-old historic bourbons of Kentucky, but we must now make room for such heralded newcomers as Louisville's Copper & Kings.

History makes mixing and drinking cocktails far more interesting, and history is a crowded bar, so keep your eyes on the bartender.

—Jim Meehan, author, *Meehan's Bartender Manual* and *PDT*

York. When a reader inquired of the editor what this curious word meant, the editor replied: "Cocktail is a stimulating liquor, composed of spirits of any kind, sugar, water, and bitters—it is vulgarly called a bitter sling and is supposed to be an excellent electioneering position, inasmuch as it renders the heart stout and bold, at the same time it fuddles the head. It is said also, to be of great use to a Democratic candidate: because, a person having swallowed a glass of it, is ready to swallow anything else" (Joseph Carlin, *Cocktails: A Global History*).

The tale of the tipple gets cobbled from a few different theories. Some say the word *cocktail* was derived from a mispronunciation of the French word for "eggcup" (*coquetier*) in 1800s New Orleans. Others believe the name was created from the dregs of near-empty spirits barrels, where the "cock" was the barrel tap and the "tails" the tail-endings of said barrels. Gary "Gaz" Regan describes an interesting theory in *The Joy of Mixology* about British sailors getting "mixed drinks" in a Mexican tavern that were stirred with the root of a plant called a "cock's tail." And one of the more popular theories (from David Wondrich) of *cocktail* etymology involves animals—racehorses, specifically—who would flick their tails into the air to demonstrate they had some moxie, the same way one would behave upon sipping a spirited concoction. Though it remains an outlier theory, I am certain the word *cocktail* was at one point influenced by the way patrons in taverns attempted to outclass one another while under the influence of any so-called fog-driver, phlegm-cutter, or spur-in-the-head, since, in America, one of our greatest national treasures, often overlooked, is our ability to conjure and distribute nicknames. Spend five minutes growing up in the Bartels family household and you'll quickly grasp what I'm getting at, you little bobscotch.

As William Grimes reveals in his influential book *Straight Up or On the Rocks*, "The cocktail, a gifted but struggling amateur in the early days of the republic, came into its own with the rise of the saloon in the nineteenth century." A saloon was a place offering food and drink, music and conversation, and dry and (occasionally) comfortable shelter, and within those hallowed walls, citizens and travelers connected over society's woes and wonders, before the almighty eyes and arms of everyone's best friend, the "democratic guiding light," the bartender.

American drinking started with Native Americans sipping on pulque (similar to beer, but made with agave plants) before people started assembling in public houses, aka "pubs," and those early taverns were operating as the heart and soul of many a town. The colonial tavern was also referred to as the "ordinary" and eventually became an "establishment," performing various roles such as post office, inn, and municipal building. People saw to affairs during (and sometimes after) its business hours. Election parties and auctions were held there. Public outcry over the town government's activities was addressed there. Families gathered. Games were played. And let's not forget one of the fondest memories we could ever associate with a feel-good tavern: song and dance.

The first sentence of Susan Cheever's *Drinking in America* describes how, thanks to one simple quandary, the Pilgrims started American drinking culture in November 1620 upon landing in Massachusetts rather than the more distant Virginia: They were running out of beer. Fresh water was essential for making beer, so they broke course and latitude for fresh suds, stopping earlier than planned, as beer was essential for their daily life. From that, America

The interesting truth, untaught in most schools and unacknowledged in most written history, is that a glass of beer, a bottle of rum, a keg of hard cider, a flask of whiskey, or even a dry martini was often the silent, powerful third party to many decisions that shaped the American story from the seventeenth century to the present.

—Susan Cheever,
Drinking in America

developed into a country shaped through decisions made inside our taverns, venues that had been elevated to such heights of popularity in the 1830s that homes, town halls, and schoolhouses were said to be empty in favor of the local tavern, teeming with people of varying backgrounds. In the 1800s, even children were drinking with the enthusiasm of modern-day college coeds. Our political leaders took meetings in taverns. Thomas Jefferson began writing the Declaration of Independence inside Philadelphia's Indian Queen Tavern next to a bottomless glass of Madeira.

Taverns escalated in popularity through the 1800s, leading to the Golden Era of cocktails, from the 1890s to 1919, when some of the most iconic cocktails we still sip today were created. Bartenders were considered to be as important as some of the highest community figures. In *Roughing It*, Mark Twain's collection of travel essays, published in 1872, Twain writes that the saloon-keeper in Nevada occupied the same level in society as the lawyer, the editor, the banker, the chief desperado, and the chief gambler.

Star bartenders used their status to elevate the cocktail game in bigger cities, and a new dawn of creativity unfolded, thanks to figures such as Jerry Thomas and New York's first celebrity bartender, the City Hotel's Orsamus Willard. Orsamus's reputation of being at the famous hotel lobby bar from morning until midnight serving his famed Mint Julep is legendary. His memory was so dependable that, also according to legend, when a first-time customer abruptly left his bar to tend to his ill son, only to return five years later, Orsamus not only recognized him but asked him how his son was doing. With travel on the rise, word of mouth started spreading the good news: "If you're in Such-and-Such City [most often New York], you have to try this drink called a Manhattan. You simply must order this new cocktail known as a Martini. You have to try what they are calling a Daiquiri in Washington, D.C."

Cocktail innovation was off the charts—until Prohibition derailed it. Spirits were taken off the shelves, bars were closed, and the talented bartenders creating these delicious beverages were out of jobs. A good number left the country to bartend in Europe. Whatever creative momentum had been taking place heading into the twentieth century was clipped in 1920.

When bars reopened thirteen years later, each state had the opportunity to create new laws affecting liquor consumption and distribution. The larger cities recovered a little faster, but certain states and cities maintained statewide temperance laws long after the Twenty-First Amendment repealed the Eighteenth in 1933, which affected each state's spirit-focused evolution throughout the rest of the twentieth century.

Even today, rules for how we produce and distribute spirits have remained idiosyncratic, varying greatly from state to state. There is no taxation on alcohol in New Hampshire. "Happy Hour" does not exist in Massachusetts. Michigan and Kentucky don't allow bars to use napkins, coasters, or glassware with any logos of wine, liquor, or beer brands. In California, one can buy alcohol from 6 A.M. to 2 A.M. any day of the year, but in Minnesota, you better find a bar by 1 A.M. (or, if you're one of the lucky people having a drink on the border with Wisconsin, you can make last call there by 2 A.M.). Quirky regulations have left a unique footprint on drinking cultures, delineated by state borders.

Prohibition bred bootlegging, and bootleggers smuggled in as much illegal rum, whiskey, brandy, and other spirits as they could get their hands on, but

The cocktail is, in a word, American. It's as American as jazz, apple pie, and baseball, and as diverse, colorful, and big as America itself. Indeed, it could even be argued that the cocktail is a metaphor for the American people: It is a composite beverage, and we are a composite people.

—Dale DeGroff, aka King Cocktail, author of *The Craft of the Cocktail* and *The Essential Cocktail*, and arguably the most important bartender in the world

since none of it was regulated, there was no telling what was good or bad—and a good amount of it was bad—so people were drinking subpar product. It was enough to turn people off drinking spirits on a regular basis.

Since palates (and stomachs) were so displeased by the unpredictability of spirits, America needed a change. As such, I give you vodka. The Bloody Mary began making waves in the latter part of the 1930s, starting in New York and eventually spreading across the United States. Smirnoff Vodka was launching a new campaign in the early 1940s in California involving ginger beer and copper

BUCKET LIST BARS

A bucket list bar is the place you absolutely must visit if you find yourself traveling near a certain town or area. If you had only one bar you needed to see, the bucket list bar would be top of the list. Fair warning, some of them are not the best place to get a craft cocktail (and some barely have liquor on the shelf), but they are sacred places with a colorful history. Some of them are run by the most wonderful and unforgettable people, and when you walk into a great bucket list bar in any state in America, it should give you the feeling that something special has happened there before, or it's going to happen while you spend time there, or the bar will make you think about the space and experience long after you leave. Bucket list bars have as much character as the best cocktail bars, and whether or not they want to admit it, many cocktail bars have taken inspiration from bucket list bars, as those are often the places we visit when what we'd like most of all is a transformative experience, inspiring something nostalgic, soulful, or new to us, often capturing the sentiment of the neighborhood, city, or state where it exists.

THE OLDEST BARS

Each chapter features the oldest operating bar in the respective state. If history is available to us in the form of drinking traditions and tales, then we should pay homage to the watering holes that have stood the test of time, weather, regulars, permanently banned patrons, lease agreements, and especially changed ownerships over the years, decades, and, yes, remarkably, even centuries.

STATE BEVERAGES

In a respectful nod to the nondrinking culture, I wanted to honor the legacy of every state by offering a perspective on beverages other than the cocktails created there. I remember mixing up a cocktail or two of Kool-Aid (born in Nebraska) as a kid (and yes, my secret ingredient was always sugar!) and being fascinated by the scientific experiment of it. America is a proud culture of beverages, with or without alcohol. Most of us can appreciate what a cold bottle of Coca-Cola (created in Atlanta, Georgia) tasted like after mowing the lawn as a kid, but did you know that southerners like putting peanuts in their road Cokes? Or that Rhode Island has a predilection for coffee milk? In many places across the country, the history of our traditional nonalcoholic beverages is important, not only because they influence our palates, but because they add to the repertoire of cocktail mixers we have at our disposal.

*America,
you're getting
sloshed and saucy
On everything
I've got
But if you really
want a drink
Why not just order
A shot?*

—Tom Cruise, in the movie *Cocktail* (1988)

mugs as the company introduced the Moscow Mule (nicknamed to reflect the "kick" of the spice-forward ginger beer) to the country. As World War II ended and more people started traveling, the country began turning a corner for cocktail experimentation, which started happening mostly in hotel bars. If you wanted a specialty cocktail, you needed to visit a city's most estimable hotels.

Twenty years passed. In the 1940s and 1950s, operating a distillery in the United States required untangling miles of red tape at the federal, state, and local levels, which made it impossible or at least challenging for small producers. There were a few people taking serious cocktails seriously in the 1950s; most people were "quaffing martinis by the pitcher" as Gary Regan points out in *The Joy of Mixology*, and the Martini stayed popular for the 1950s and '60s, thanks to the Rat Pack and James Bond. Television no doubt elevated these figures into iconic status, so whatever they drank, we drank. Travel still influenced our brains, as the tiki culture started making waves, and suddenly the idea of having fruity, colorful drinks like the Blue Hawaiian, Mai Tai, and Piña Colada sounded transporting. And sweet! The only thing competing with popular syrupy drinks in the 1970s was disco.

Derek Brown, coauthor of *Spirits, Sugar, Water, Bitters: How the Cocktail Conquered the World*, captures the Dark Ages of drinking (the 1970s) very well in his authoritative guide, pointing out that the 1960s were about rebellion and rejecting conformity, and that the youth of America were disinclined to follow in their parents' footsteps, so they spurned the time-honored choices associated with their elders and more sophisticated circles such as the Martini, the Old Fashioned, and the tried-and-true Manhattan. Powdered beverages had a hold on 1970s drinking culture, with instant coffee, Kool-Aid, iced tea, and every young wannabe astronaut's cupboard go-to, Tang, waiting to take us to our own adolescent Mixology Moon. The younger drinking culture of the 1970s was restless. They wanted mind-altering drugs instead! Their palates turned to sweeter drinks. They wanted to make Whiskey Sours with low-grade sour mixes mass-produced for efficiency, but lacking rectitude. They wanted to watch *Happy Days* and make fun of all the squares. And most of all, they wanted to dance (hey, disco). Brown writes, "If you're drinking in the dark, it doesn't matter what your drink looks like. And if you're drinking on a dance floor, you're probably not very concerned with what it tastes like either." In the wake of sickly sweet cocktails, beer and wine grew in popularity, but their dominance wouldn't last forever.

BAR SNACKS

A Bar Snack will be the occasional nugget of bar factoid dispersed throughout the book. Hopefully they give you a little bit of extra credit wisdom on the beverages we share, the ingredients we use (from far away and local), and the state perspective on what makes them special. They also may shine a light on the storied history surrounding the state or explore a chapter in our drinking history and the way it affected a culture—who started what and how traditions began. Beginnings are fascinating to me. I hope you feel the same.

THE RECIPES

DARE I SAY it—cocktails are people, too. In my hope to illustrate the full canon of humanistic endeavors through the looking glass of taverns and social drinking establishments, there will be characters we meet as tart as a lime-heavy Daiquiri, as overproof as a rich Manhattan, and as stubborn as a fruit peeler trying to navigate a wet orange.

The more than one hundred recipes featured in this book were selected from and inspired by various menus of bars I've visited, publications, conversations, and email correspondence, and bring to life something special about the state in question, whether it be a local ingredient, a key moment in history, or the talents of one of the state's best bartenders working today. The recipes all remain as true to the creator's specifications as possible. With that said, I am well aware that the past can be a bit murky when recollected through the thick lenses at the bottom of bottles. Even our most celebrated cocktail and spirits historian, David Wondrich, has admitted: "Historiography is a science more or less like ballistics." We can certainly plot the outlines of the status quo, but it may be difficult to state anything as a cold, hard fact. However, I did my best to live up to my role of sleep-deprived forensic cocktail navigator, historian, and geographer through every single recipe, story, date, location, and person presented in this book, and if I have erred in my research, or forsaken someone deserving the trophy or proper recognition, I apologize. The truth is, this is a big country, with an even bigger history, but I aimed to do my best in respecting its traditions, which are much wider than the countless roads and highways covering this land.

With the recipes selected, I hope to honor the work of the many fine bartenders crafting unforgettable cocktails throughout the country where I could find them—and they are everywhere—while also incorporating some of my own creations, offering my perspective on various parts of the country, their history and local ingredients, through my own creative cocktail devices.

There are cocktails in certain states that were invented many decades ago and were the toast of the town but that are fading away, like the Rendezvous from Missouri, which was served in the 1940s at the famed Muehlebach Hotel, then published in Ted Saucier's *Bottoms Up* in 1951, but never returned or developed into cocktail menu glory. I hope to play some small part in a renewed appreciation for forgotten drinks, while also celebrating the origins of iconic ones and giving thanks for the new classics. The cocktail recipes in this book have one foot in historical regional perspective and the other in significant modern-day influences.

A Note on "Fine Strain": Fine straining (aka double straining) involves the technique of holding a tea strainer, or fine strainer, between the shaker and the glass as one pours a shaken cocktail into the glass. The strainer is a great tool for trapping ice crystals created from shaking the cocktail too hard for too long, as the ice crystals would only dilute the cocktail if they remained.

A Note on Serving Size: All of the recipes in the book are written to serve one person, unless otherwise indicated. However, simply scale up the recipes if you are having people over (or have had a tough day).

BARTENDERS AND THE RISE OF COCKTAIL CULTURE

Very much I believe in this idea of the third space. You have work, you have home, and then you have something else, where you get to be yourself, someone that is not your work self or your home self. In New York, specifically, more so than anywhere else, that place is the bar.

—Don Lee, co-owner, Existing Conditions (Manhattan, NY), in an interview with *New York* magazine

OUR MODERN-DAY BARTENDERS—THE people who pour beer and shots for locals, regulars, and tourists who want to take photos of their kids standing under the dusty bras hanging from the rafters—are all important figures in American culture today. Working with liquor, ice, and time is pure *sorcery.* Don't forget that. I can't be a child of *Lord of the Rings*, *Beastmaster*, and Dungeons and Dragons and not appreciate the wizards of wonder surrounding us—even the ones with bar towels sticking out of their scuffed Levi's. Mixologists are magicians. Just observe the classic illustration of "Professor" Jerry Thomas— the father of American mixology—mixing a Blue Blazer on the cover of David Wondrich's timeless *Imbibe!* and tell me otherwise.

I quoted Tom Cruise's character on the page 15 in one of the most obvious bar entertainment references handed down to us from 1988, when the movie *Cocktail* arrived. I bring this up to you all here and now as a way of celebrating the ups and downs we have endured as a nation. We are Americans. Some of us vote. Some gamble. Some sit up late at night and watch syndicated television shows. Some bake oatmeal raisin cookies. Some mow our lawns and pay our taxes. Some eat a probiotic diet with nothing other than raw vegetables and flavorless water filtered through the lens of *Consumer Reports* investigative research and impressionistic aggregates. Some crank Tom Petty's "American Girl" when pulling out of our driveways. Some blast Missy Elliott's "Work It." Say what you will about our reasons and rhymes, we as Americans can agree on one thing: We all have a relationship with Tom Cruise. Before. Now. And for future generations. And if you have never seen *Cocktail* before, I am not saying you need to drop what you are currently doing (though *Consumer Reports* says more than 60 percent of you should currently drop what you are doing, as 40 percent of us are loving the post-*Cocktail* viewing life) and go watch *Cocktail*. First of all, if you did that you would stop reading this book. Please don't. Continue. (The next page is *really* good! And I won't spoil what happens in the next chapter, but here's a hint: ghosts!) As US citizens, we have an obligation to appreciate the little things that make life worthwhile: root beer floats, popcorn at the movies, swimming at the lake, and Tom Cruise pouring a shot of Jim Beam whiskey in a blue neon–lit underground bar before making the "Turquoise Blue" drink all the way to the box office.

Moreover, *Cocktail* arrived at a pivotal moment. Flair bartending started trending. People were getting into craft cocktails. Before the Internet, social media was really only achieved by stations like MTV, and there, at the end of the 1980s, was Tom Cruise behind the bar, reveling in his post–*Top Gun* popularity, on the silver screen showing people how very cool it was to be a bartender. We had finally come full circle from Jerry Thomas's time as a celebrity bartender in the 1800s. It is important to remember the legacy of the most influential movie of our bartending generation, as it is inevitable that Hollywood will try to re-create it, and all I ask is they take a step back, and make it more of an indie film inspired by the bartender Sasha Petraske of the legendary New York speakeasy Milk & Honey, often credited with resuscitating the modern-day craft cocktail movement, who actually never would have enjoyed a movie about his life, which is why it would rule.

There are many heroes, each worthy of their own feature films, to thank for today's cocktail renaissance. New York's Dale DeGroff (of the estimable Rainbow Room, where he was the master mixologist for twelve years) took all the ugliness of the 1970s and '80s and put it in a shaker with house-made syrup, fresh citrus, and proper ice for dilution, and shook it all up with his trademark smile. A domino effect started happening: Angel's Share, a second-floor speakeasy in the back of an East Village Japanese restaurant, opened in New York in 1994; Blackbird's Audrey Saunders rolled up her sleeves and started slinging away, popularizing modern cocktails like the Cosmopolitan and Apple Martini alongside classic Sazeracs and Singapore Slings; and as already mentioned Sasha Petraske gained national (and then international) attention in 1999; Julie Reiner put the swank, classic cocktail–themed Flatiron Lounge in motion in 2003, the same year Gary Regan's distinguished *Joy of Mixology* found publication; and the world started paying attention to cocktails again. Saunders pioneered a new cocktail frontier with Pegu Club in 2005. It was as refreshing as knowing that the citrus juice in your cocktail was squeezed that day or to order.

Because making cocktails is a practice forever linked to tradition, it is important to recognize how many of these bartenders were incorporating pre-Prohibition cocktails back into the modern-day repertoire, all those cocktails Orsamus Willard and Jerry Thomas were slinging in the nineteenth century, making them de rigueur again, and now they are being served in every American city worth its weight in shaker tins.

I have come to know and love many bartenders in this big, bright country. They are experts of craft, be it holding a bar spoon, corkscrew, or church key. They are the attendants of our social offices, and if they are any good at what they do, they will exercise the most liberal dispositions when it comes to assembling liquid compounds for our refreshment. Tom Chiarella captures this sentiment in a *Chicago* magazine article on the Billy Goat Tavern bartender Jeff Magill in 2015:

A real bartender remembers you. He uses your name. A real bartender makes it seem as if he's been standing there all along, waiting for you. Ready for you. The bartender inhabits certain roles in the room: captain and commander, steward of arrival and departure, calm eye of a stormy night, willing servant of want, interpreter of need. He sets the tone, keeps the peace, gives a recommendation or two, makes sure the pours are fair, watches the door and the clock, monitors the most distant tables—all in service of establishing the tenor and efficiency of the joint. That's a real bartender. He elbows open the bar's hours to talk with you. He listens to you. He hears you. He studies a bit. He might come to tell you what's what or dole out advice. If he does, you remember it. And you always remember a real bartender.

I have shared this passage with all the new bartenders who have come through my bar training program. I ask that anyone starting the bartending profession capture the sentiment shared in this passage as a way of recognizing the landscape we supervise. When the bar is open, it is akin to being inside a national park: at a certain point, you are going to engage with the unpredictable wildlife, and you are the park ranger responsible for protecting the wildlife.

The spirits of choice for both cocktails and straight drinking evolved over the span of American history. When the first colonists arrived, it was brandy. When importation proved problematic, it turned to rum. Over time, we made our own native spirits: first applejack, and then American whiskies made from rye, wheat, and corn. By the beginning of the twentieth century, the crafting of rye and bourbon whiskies had become an art.

—Ted Haigh, aka Dr. Cocktail, *Vintage Spirits & Forgotten Cocktails*

TRAVEL AND TRY NEW THINGS

THERE WILL BE a fair amount of travel as we trek across the pages of this book. If the following pages are a map, I want you to be able to put your finger on a place and see what drinks are being ordered there. It's important to note that, even though we will cover charismatic and celebrated bartenders, the history of cocktails, established and heralded distilleries, bucket list bars, epic stories, and longstanding traditions in every state, *The United States of Cocktails* is also about variety. I want to capture each state in a way that celebrates the essence of what makes it so special. I traveled *everywhere* throughout the United States to corral the information you are about to read, seeing the bars, trying the cocktails, and talking to the locals about what makes each state unique.

As I share my favorite finds, I also invite you to embark on your own cocktail-fueled adventure. Put down whatever technology is distracting you, grab your keys, board a plane, train, or bus, and go see it for yourself. Get outside your routine for a weekend.

By the same token, if there is a recipe in this book that originated in New Jersey, and maybe you live in Arizona, creating it at your bar or in your home might just provide you with the inspiration to travel in new directions.

And please know that it is okay to make up new cocktails, new spirits, and new flavors yourself. That's why I wanted to create new recipes, motivated by my travels and background knowledge of various parts of the country. In the same way I am inspired by what food our kitchens are serving, there are ingredients people are using elsewhere that can be beneficial to you as a home bartender. What is collecting dust on your spice and seasoning shelf? You never know what might spark some creativity for your own cocktail-making endeavors. Sometimes that means traveling to another part of the country and seeing what other people are eating, drinking, and growing. Hatch chiles in New Mexico. Douglas fir in Oregon. Maple syrup in Vermont. Get outside your bubble and see what's under the next unturned stone. And make some mistakes. That's how we learn. Travel can be gnarly, but it's always worth changing your routine in the end. Maya Angelou famously said, "We delight in the beauty of the butterfly, but rarely admit the changes it has gone through to achieve that beauty."

But before you jump into making the cocktails, learn the first rule of bartending: How you greet the guest lays the foundation for everything. I tell my bartenders this on a regular basis: At the end of every day, the most important cocktail you have served was how you greeted everyone.

Which brings us to the beginning of our journey through *The United States of Cocktails*. In my heart of hearts, I hope you enjoy something new and wonderful on every page in front of you, and even feel that you're participating in exploring new frontiers by reading up on parts of America you have not yet experienced. I am happy to say that the United States still has so many places to visit, with many wonderful people waiting there for you when you arrive, most of them happy enough to point you in the direction of the best places to grab a drink.

With that, let's belly up.

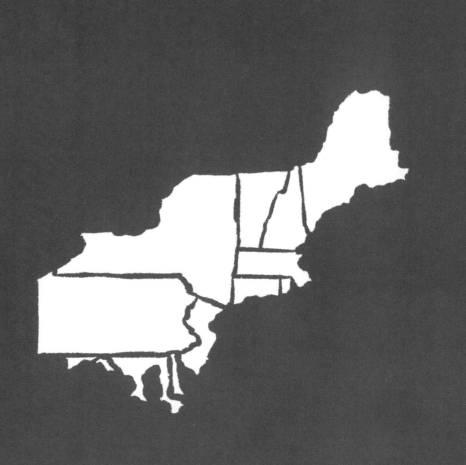

The well-made cocktail is one of the most gracious of drinks. It pleases the senses. The shared delight of those who partake in common of this refreshing nectar breaks the ice of formal reserve. Taut nerves relax; taut muscles relax; tired eyes brighten; tongues loosen; friendships deepen; the whole world becomes a better place in which to live.

—David Embury, *The Fine Art of Mixing Drinks* (1948)

The
Northeast

New York
Maine New Hampshire
Vermont Massachusetts
Rhode Island **Connecticut**
New Jersey Pennsylvania
Delaware Maryland
Washington, DC
(not really a state but the capital
of the United States, so we go for it!)

Three hundred and fifty-four steps live inside the Statue of Liberty, and Lady Liberty wears a size 879 shoe, and construction workers used more than 300 different types of tools to shape parts of the structure. Those are all easily proven facts, but it's also quite possible that bottle in her arms is New York Distilling's Dorothy Parker Gin, as everyone knows a classic lady likes her gin chilled, served up and with a twist.

New York

*The first drink
that opened my
eyes to cocktails
was PDT's Mezcal
Mule (mezcal,
lime and passion
fruit, ginger beer,
agave nectar). I
wasn't really into
cocktails until
I had that, so
being interested
in a place like
PDT was a huge
breakthrough for
me. Jim Meehan's
Mezcal Mule
cocktail was the
drink that for-
ever changed me.*

—A-K Hada,
general manager,
Existing Conditions,
(Manhattan)

FIRST THINGS FIRST. It would be uncouth and thoroughly unscrupulous to not start with New York, which has New York City within its state limits, a metropolis that has been responsible for a lot of significant firsts. The Big Apple introduced apple production to the country via its apple nurseries in Flushing, Queens, in 1730; New York opened both America's first brewery in Lower Manhattan in 1632 and its first pizzeria in 1895; and a Manhattan resident invented toilet paper in 1857, which just blows my mind. How do you invent toilet paper? But, then again, how do you not?

Not only was New York City the first capital of the United States, it was slinging some of the country's best cocktails by the end of the 19th century. New York loves a good cocktail, and it's only fitting we start this book by celebrating the place where so many of the great ones began, from the Manhattan and the Martini of the late 1800s to the post-Prohibition Bloody Mary at the King Cole Bar (inside the St. Regis Hotel, debuted by Fernand "Pete" Petiot in 1934), to the 2004 Penicillin by Sam Ross of Milk & Honey and Attaboy, and the unforgettable Death & Co.'s Oaxaca Old Fashioned, created by Phil Ward in 2007.

New York got some of its earliest cocktail credentials from Jerry Thomas, who published his first cocktail book, *How to Mix Drinks, or the Bon Vivant's Companion*, in 1862. He wore swag jewelry and worked with customized barware and made Blue Blazers—flaming whiskey poured back and forth between two mugs—while operating his saloon under Barnum's American Museum on Broadway. He could do anything. In *Imbibe!*, David Wondrich writes that at thirty-three years old, Jerry Thomas was pulling down more money per week than the vice president of the United States. Basically, he was the Prince of Bartending. All one needed to do was give the man a microphone and let him sing. Only this man's microphone was ice.

New York had its fair share of elite bartenders through the turn of the twentieth century, and though Prohibition dented the growth of cocktail culture for a healthy number of decades when and after it arrived, there were still plenty of bars in New York shaking, stirring, and swearing they were the spot to see and be seen. Though New York was one of the more resilient bar cities post-Prohibition, cocktail innovation was stagnant for the next few decades, until brunches and happy hours started getting people excited about drinking and its social vibrancy through the disco-dancing 1970s.

Sour mixes and artificial ingredients were everything in the 1980s, and the tide wasn't turned until Dale DeGroff became a student of Jerry Thomas's recipes from books published one hundred years earlier. DeGroff incorporated quality ingredients, fresh juices, and homemade syrups, bringing cocktails back to life in New York, and he began teaching his classic methods to many worthy pupils, notably Audrey Saunders, who skilled a whole new generation of eager bartenders with her and DeGroff's methods.

New York is where I discovered cocktails. I had my first true craft cocktail, a Mojito, at Sasha Petraske's Milk & Honey in 2000, and then had further craft cocktail exposure (fresh ingredients, homemade syrups, artisanal spirits, and so on) at Flatiron Lounge in 2003, thanks to owner-operator Julie Reiner.

The Long Island Bar in Brooklyn is a seemingly casual neighborhood bar with a sense of history that doesn't take itself too seriously. You can order a pilsner or have a well-crafted Boulevardier made by some of the city's finest bartenders without affectation or artifice, and have a bowl of fried cheese curds to go along with it. It's one of my favorite American bars.

—Brad Thomas Parsons, author of *Amaro, Bitters, Distillery Cats,* and *Last Call*

One of the first distillers I was ever exposed to was New York Distilling Co. Allen Katz does one hell of a job affecting people in such a positive way.

—Tobin Ludwig, Hella Bitters (Manhattan)

Flatiron Lounge was a classic example of the great New York cocktail bars we sorely needed to survive. Granted, there were other distracting bars I could have spent time in, like BED, which featured more than forty oversize Tempur-Pedic mattresses where people sipped from Champagne flutes and wore glitter on their chests, but I decided cocktails were more interesting. Flatiron Lounge—which opened the same year I moved to New York—taught me that new worlds could be discovered, and there were cocktails beyond the Buttery Nipple, the Snake Bite, and the Cement Mixer to consider, taste, and appreciate. Audrey Saunders's Pegu Club taught me civility and patience and that amazing cocktails come to those who wait.

Then in 2003 came Eben Freeman's heightened level of mixology at WD-50, a restaurant specializing in molecular gastronomy by the acclaimed chef Wylie Dufresne, where Jim Meehan and I would sit and marvel at the Rolodex of cocktail recipes Freeman had at his disposal behind the bar.

Then came Employees Only, an intimate, high-volume speakeasy run by seasoned New York bartenders (most taught under the guidance of DeGroff), an all-night party paradise where anyone staying until last call was rewarded with a cup of chicken noodle soup. Employees Only taught me to enjoy quality cocktails by a seasoned bar staff, all while the walls shook from brazen ribaldry.

Then came Death & Co., which assembled a who's who of bartending talent the likes of which modern-day New York had never seen.

Then came PDT, owned and operated by Jim Meehan, which nearly overnight went on to become one of the most important and celebrated bars in the world.

Then came Dead Rabbit and the NoMad Bar, two highly lauded bar programs showing everyone how to handle high-volume business and craft cocktail creativity with polished finesse.

Then came the ten-year New York cocktail bar avalanche, when everyone was opening a craft cocktail bar, or speakeasy, or high-volume response to try piggybacking on the previously mentioned bars and programs. And, bless their hearts, some of them succeeded, while others did not have the magic to last more than a season or two.

But everyone was eager to create better cocktails and experiences, which is exactly what Dale DeGroff had started at the Rainbow Room in the 1980s, so thank you, Dale. From all of us in and around New York and beyond.

These days, New York has as many original cocktails as it does miles of subway track (seven hundred), which snake through each of the five boroughs. Brooklyn alone has enough great bars that it deserves its own section, including Clover Club, Fort Defiance, Grand Army, Weather Up, Fresh Kills Bar, Leyenda, and my bucket list personal favorite, Long Island Bar, which is located in Brooklyn's Cobble Hill, and was resuscitated by a scholarly chap from Wisconsin who created a little cocktail called the Cosmopolitan.

People who don't live in New York often say they are terrified of its pace, its people, its sky-high buildings, and the attitudes that come with it all, but the reality could not be further from those impressions. New York City is a village. In the bar and restaurant world of the New York where I lived, it was a small village, and we are very good at taking care of one another. (But someone would always be welcome to ask landlords to take it easy on the rents.)

NEW YORK SPIRIT
DOROTHY PARKER GIN
Brooklyn

Naren Young and the work his team has done at Caffe Dante [in Manhattan's Greenwich Village] is indicative of the kind of bartender I wish I had been. I wish I understood nuance and education as well as Naren.

—Brooks Reitz, Jack Rudy Co. (Charleston, SC)

New York Distilling Company opened its doors on December 5, 2011—the anniversary of the repeal of Prohibition—in Williamsburg, Brooklyn. Distiller and founder Allen Katz is the man behind Perry's Tot navy strength gin, Ragtime rye whiskey, Mister Katz's rock and rye, and Chief Gowanus—a "Holland gin" that starts as a rye whiskey, then is pot-stilled with juniper berries and cluster hops (the oldest and most robust hops grown in the United States, used in the original 1809 variety of the Dutch gin by way of America), offering an adventurous palette of flavors. They are all toothsome-looking bottles, which are fetching behind any bar, but my personal favorite is Dorothy Parker gin. Its namesake—the famous writer and unconventional bon vivant, Dorothy Rothschild Parker—was an inspiration to many in the New York literary scene, loved gin second to none, and had a wit often unmatched. Her famous saying "I like to have a martini, two at the very most. After three I'm under the table, after four I'm under my host" has been published and posted just about everywhere Martinis and gin have been de rigueur.

STATE FACT
Though the Garibaldi cocktail (Campari and fresh orange juice) originated in Italy, New York City's Caffe Dante deserves all of the credit for making the cocktail popular in America. It is simplicity in a glass, and begs the impression of wanting another immediately after finishing the first.

In New York, we're known for taxes, assholes, and Nathan's hot dogs.

—Dermot McCormack, bartender, Spring Lounge (Manhattan)

NEW YORK'S OLDEST BAR
FRAUNCES TAVERN
Manhattan, 1762

Still kicking after all these years, Fraunces is where George Washington gave his farewell address when the Revolutionary War came to an end. There are many rooms in which to sit and have a bite or drink and soak up the history; the space doubles as a museum for good reason. There's a slipper worn by Martha Washington, and artifacts and letters written by important political figures in US history, and a display of more than two hundred historical flags. The Fraunces also has a notable cocktail, published in William Grimes's *Straight Up or On the Rocks*, called the Washington cocktail, made with dark rum, gin, Cointreau, lemon and orange juices, sugar, and a cherry.

NEW YORK BUCKET LIST BAR
McSORLEY'S ALE HOUSE
Manhattan

Known for its raw onions, crackers, and light or dark ale, McSorley's has been around since long before any of us were born (opened in 1854), and one gets the feeling it will be here long after we are gone. People loved this bar so much that the police left it alone during Prohibition. However, women left it alone as well, as the bar lifted its ban on women only in 1970. I entered its hallowed, museum-like walls on a Sunday at one o'clock in the afternoon. Knickknacks of New York history and Irish ancestry adorned the walls, glass bottles of ketchup and mustard caddies sat on the tables, sawdust covered the floor, and there was a pay phone near the front door. It is a museum and a bar at the same time. Two women with shopping bags were eating a plate of crackers and liverwurst with their beers. One of the women said: "I used to take the subway down to this neighborhood. Back when the subway was fifteen cents."

NEW YORK'S COCKTAIL BARS

As in the perfect Last Word recipe, which involves equal measures of four different ingredients, you can't stop at just one if we're talking about how to properly experience some of New York's best cocktail bars. There are many more that deserve to be included, but these four spots are just as magical as any I have visited.

PEGU CLUB
Manhattan

Pegu Club was opened in 2005 by Audrey Saunders (aka the "Libation Goddess") and has fielded some of the country's finest bartenders sculpted by Audrey's extensive cocktail and bartending prowess. It is a late-nineteenth-century Southeast Asia–inspired gin palace located on West Houston ("house-ton"), one of New York's most iconic streets. *Noble* is a word often associated with Pegu Club and the bartenders who have spent time working there, each influenced by Audrey, who was a pupil of Dale DeGroff in her early career. Everything assembled here is done meticulously, flawlessly, and with exemplary sophistication.

CLOVER CLUB
Brooklyn

Julie Reiner opened Clover Club in 2008 on Smith Street in Cobble Hill, Brooklyn. The Prohibition-themed cocktail bar was an instant success, and has lived up to its neighborhood go-to destination reputation ever since. They make exquisite cocktails, serve tasty food, and provide exemplary service with a cozy ambiance (the back room, complete with fireplace, is still one of my favorite places to grab a drink in the colder months). Pick a classic cocktail or one of their modern selections. There is no wrong choice here.

PDT
Manhattan

When a tiny little bar with fewer seats than a picnic bench is reaching audiences in Tulsa, we know we're on to something. PDT (Please Don't Tell) opened on May 24, 2007, and the East Village in Manhattan was never the same. Jim Meehan put craft cocktails on his shoulders and helped usher in a new cocktail resurgence throughout the United States, so much that friends who were visiting New York couldn't claim to have properly experienced the city unless they'd had a chance to drink at PDT. PDT's famous entrance is through a phone booth. One enters, dials the number, and—if lucky enough—is guided into a realm of cocktail wonder by its many talented bartenders.

ATTABOY
Manhattan

Attaboy took over for an unforgettable cocktail bar called Milk & Honey, opened by Sasha Petraske on New Year's Eve in 1999. It has no menu. You simply tell the bartender what spirit you are considering, and a conversation is ignited on flavor profile, and what you may be inspired to taste. Open since 2013, founders Sam Ross and Michael McIlroy, former Milk & Honey bartenders, had the goal to make things simple, but impress anyone passing through with their ability to create based on mood. They operate in a space responsible for some remarkable modern classic cocktails, such as the Gold Rush, the Paper Plane, and the Greenpoint. Ross created the Penicillin cocktail (Scotch, honey, lemon, ginger), which catapulted him into modern-day notoriety for making a wide audience fall for Scotch, which is an extremely difficult thing to do.

I tell everyone to visit Leyenda in Brooklyn. It's the type of place you could sit at for hours and never be bored. Great people. Great spirits. Great neighborhood. It has just about all the boxes checked.

—Jared Sadoian, bar manager, the Hawthorne (Boston, MA)

My dad had a Jack Daniel's on the rocks every night. One grandmother always had a Dubonnet on the rocks. And my grandmother who loved spirits always had a Campari on the rocks. My sister had all the Absolut ads tacked to her wall as a teenager. And every bar I can think of in my childhood had J&B Scotch on the bar.

—Allen Katz, owner and head distiller, New York Distilling Company (Williamsburg, Brooklyn)

The American cocktail bar I tell everyone to visit? PDT.

—Gary "Gaz" Regan, cocktail and spirits historian, author of *The Joy of Mixology* and *The Negroni*

McSorley's is the single most important bar in America. There's nothing like it. It's friggin' old. All those layers and layers of history, and it hasn't sold out, and it's still got its character, and it still serves only two different kinds of beer. It's going back in history and it shows you how Americans used to drink, and it's not clichéd, or gimmicky, or a tourist trap, it's an actual fucking bar, and it's the greatest bar in New York, and it's the greatest bar in America.

—Robert Simonson, author of *The Martini*, *A Proper Drink*, *The Old Fashioned*, and *3-Ingredient Cocktails* (Brooklyn)

MANHATTAN
Brian Bartels

Sad but true: No one quite knows when or who started the Manhattan on its course of history—though many point to the Manhattan Club in 1874. Feel free to get creative with how you tweak the original recipe. I personally enjoy rye whiskey as the default option, given its spices—not to mention origins: The default spirit associated with early recipes reflects rye whiskey.

2 ounces rye whiskey
    (I am a fan of Ragtime rye, from New York Distilling Company)

¾ ounce Italian sweet vermouth

3 dashes Angostura bitters

Garnish: 1 brandied cherry

Stir the ingredients with ice until chilled; strain into a chilled cocktail glass and serve up, garnished with the cherry.

COSMOPOLITAN
Toby Cecchini

Some modern cocktail enthusiasts might chortle at this submission, but it's too important to ignore, as it helped to break the staid fashion of shitty cocktails in the 1980s. In 1987, Toby Cecchini was making it rain pink on West Broadway at Keith McNally's breakout restaurant the Odeon and the movement was strong enough that it eventually stretched across America. Toby's Cosmopolitan was built with fresh lime juice, and the level of popularity for that singular cocktail reverberated through and beyond the *Sex and the City* era, and dominated the end of our century.

1½ ounces Absolut Citron vodka

¾ ounce Cointreau

¾ ounce cranberry juice

¾ ounce fresh lime juice

Garnish: lemon twist

Combine the ingredients and shake with ice; strain into a chilled cocktail glass and serve up, garnished with the lemon.

FITTY-FITTY MARTINI
Audrey Saunders, Pegu Club, Manhattan

The classic Martini (which must always be associated with gin, and never vodka, and shame on you, 1980s) does not have a name associated with its origin—which occurred somewhere in New York in the late 1800s—but I am more than happy to applaud Audrey Saunders, aka the "Libation Goddess," as the creator of the marvelous Fitty-Fitty. It's not as booze-heavy as a full-blown Martini, and it's one of the most elegant sipping cocktails I have come to know. Audrey was on to something here: It's hard to not smile when enjoying this remarkable potion.

1½ ounces Plymouth gin

1½ ounces dry vermouth (preferably Dolin)

1 to 2 dashes orange bitters

Garnish: lemon twist

Stir the ingredients with ice in a mixing glass until chilled; strain into a chilled cocktail glass and serve up, garnished with the lemon.

BLACK SQUIRREL OLD FASHIONED
Brian Bartels, Fedora, Manhattan

What does every American bar need? A knowledgeable, personable, humble bartender willing to educate and introduce new things to their guests and a stocked bar with all of the basics—reference Jim Meehan's PDT book if you need a little help with that.

—Leishla Maldonado, bar manager, Courtland Club (Providence, RI)

When Happy Cooking Hospitality reopened Fedora in a historic part of the West Village in January 2011, my mind was buzzing with cocktail ideas for the menu. At that time there were few Old Fashioneds on cocktail menus, and the only one I was inspired by was Damon Boelte's at Prime Meats in Carroll Gardens, Brooklyn, which was made with homemade seckel pear bitters grown in the restaurant's backyard. So I decided to try a variation with another unique bitters—pecan. When considering the name for this nut-influenced variation, I couldn't help but think of the supper clubs from my Wisconsin heritage (for more on this, see page 163). The Black Squirrel Lounge is a supper club bar in my small hometown of Reedsburg, Wisconsin, beloved by my family as a sentimental destination for reunions and get-togethers. (Reedsburg is famous for many things, but one of its notable highlights is having an unusually large black squirrel population.) I'm told I have ruined other Old Fashioneds for people because of this cocktail, but honestly, the day I felt I had created something special was when someone told me they got off a plane from a long flight, and took a cab directly to Fedora before dropping their bags off at home, because they missed the Black Squirrel. Nuts.

2 ounces Four Roses bourbon (or Maker's Mark, Jim Beam, or Buffalo Trace)

¼ ounce Cherry Heering (or Cherry liqueur)

¼ ounce maple syrup

3 dashes Miracle Mile Toasted Pecan bitters (Angostura is okay to substitute)

Garnish: orange peel

Stir the ingredients (except bitters) with ice in a mixing glass until chilled. Strain into a chilled rocks glass with fresh ice, top with the bitters, and express with the orange peel before garnishing.

NORTH SEA OIL
Leo Robitschek, NoMad Bar, Manhattan

One part smoky, one part citrusy, and one part gentle earthy notes—but all-encompassing layers of joy. When I sip on this drink, I can close my eyes and imagine I am visiting Iceland—and I have never been to Iceland! This drink gives me goose bumps. Whenever I think about how happy it makes me, I have to figure out a time when I can sip it again. I had deliberately refused to ask Leo how to re-create it at home until now, for fear of drinking it too often, but now you have it, which means I had to track it down, even after Pietro Collina, who worked at the NoMad, rattled the recipe off to me once in Washington, DC, and I was trying to plug my ears and sing, "La la la . . . I am not listening to you, Jeffrey," like Eddie Murphy in *Beverly Hills Cop*. Damn it.

1½ ounces Linie Aquavit

¾ ounce Cocchi Americano

½ ounce Laphroaig 10-Year Islay Scotch whiskey

¼ ounce Combier triple sec

Garnish: grapefruit peel

Stir the ingredients with ice until chilled; strain over fresh ice into a chilled rocks glass. Garnish with the grapefruit.

Mainers have their own vernacular, naturally. I learned they use the word "hosey" when it comes to securing seats or a table. For example, "We saw a beach chair available to sit, but Stephen King dressed up in a lobster outfit and hoseyed it before we got there."

Maine

At one point I did the math and for every seven bottles of anything spiritous sold in Maine, one bottle was Allen's. My favorite nickname for Allen's itself (not the cocktails made with it) is the Lily of the Tundra, as across the snowmobile trails in northern Maine, riders will toss bottles in the fields as they machine along, and the snow will bury the bottles. Come spring, as the snow melts, the necks of all the discarded bottles of Allen's will slowly bloom in the barren fields.

—Andrew Volk, owner, Hunt + Alpine Club (Portland)

MAINE, THE TIPPY-TOP-MOST state in the United States, produces the largest number of blueberries, toothpicks, and books by Stephen King in the entire country. It also has lots of wintergreen and pine trees. The license plates say "Vacationland," and the state motto is *Dirigo*, Latin for "I direct."

Neal Dow is regarded as the father of Prohibition. As mayor of Portland, Dow helped initiate a law making Maine the first dry state way back in 1851 (though he was called out for hypocrisy in allowing the city to secretly buy alcohol for "medicinal purposes").

Today, Maine does penance for its role in Prohibition by fully embracing alcohol in all its forms. Throughout the state, one can find craft beer bars sprouting everywhere, bed-and-breakfasts with artisanal wine offerings, and even a drinking town or three with an antiques problem (basically anywhere along Highway 1). If you're in the southern part of the state, do yourself a favor and drop by the Wallingford Dram, which is easy to find, as it is one of only a few bars in the tiny village of Kittery. Wallingford specializes in well-crafted cocktails and specialty shots, a nice highbrow-lowbrow balance one doesn't often see on menus. I arrived at 6:30 P.M. and ordered a Boat Cowboy cocktail, made with reposado tequila, bourbon, pineapple, lime, and bird's-eye Thai chile; an older woman approached the bar next to me and ordered a Moscow Mule, a Mai Tai, and two Pickleback shots to start (or end?) her evening. With this convivial establishment, Maine also gets the award for best cocktail bar on a state border, as the Wallingford Dram is just steps from the New Hampshire state line.

Beyond notable craft beers such as Allagash Brewing, Maine Beer Company, and Barreled Souls, along with a healthy amount of breweries in and around the great city of Portland, Maine has also developed a nascent reputation as a craft cocktail and spirits destination, featuring up-and-coming cocktail-focused companies such as Coastal Root Bitters (based in Portland, and featuring such flavors as coffee, tamarind lime, and pine bitters), Ass Over Teakettle Bloody Mary mix (a mother-daughter company out of Cornville), and distilleries such as Sweetgrass Farms, Maine Craft Distilling, and Round Turn Distilling, responsible for Bimini Gin, a modern American liquor using classic gin botanicals, such as juniper and citrus, along with hops and coriander seed.

BAR SNACK
Patients could obtain whiskey during Prohibition with a doctor's prescription. This can't help but remind me of Maine's approach to marijuana: Medical marijuana was legalized in 1999, and eventually in 2016 it became legal for any adult over twenty-one to possess, consume, and cultivate marijuana for personal use. I'm not saying I'm an advocate for anything, but wouldn't it be more awesome if we all just got along? Munchies for thought.

MAINE'S OLDEST BAR
JAMESON TAVERN
Freeport, 1779

The Jameson Tavern sits right next to the L.L.Bean factory and has reportedly been haunted for many, many years—not by one ghost, but by several. Clientele began seeing a little girl named Emily as she made her way through the dining room, always seeming to disappear right when someone would try to catch her, and others have experienced unprovoked flying toothpicks and felt ghostly auras on a weekly basis. But don't let that stop you from coming on by for the lobster stew and fish and chips, best washed down with an Allagash brew. They also have a happy hour starting at 2:30 P.M. every day. *A happy hour at 2:30 P.M. every day?!* Next door to a twenty-four-hour factory making fleece and flannel? Hell, I might start hauntin' that place!

MAINE BUCKET LIST BAR
ROLLIE'S BAR AND GRILL
Belfast

Rollie's shares the name of my paternal grandfather. I *had* to check it out. A charming, *Cheers*-esque spot on a sloping street, Belfast's Rollie's serves up the goods, as evidenced by the locals sitting at the bar and the families dining at the tables. There is something for everyone here: friendly staff, vintage benches, big-screen TVs for all the games, upscale pub food, and . . . *gigantic* bottles of booze. I had never seen anything like it! Half-gallon 1.75 ml bottles (or "handles," as many selections are known to have glass handles) festoon the back bar. The bartenders pour from these gigantic handles into—wait for it—*gigantic* cocktail glasses. When one orders at Rollie's, one does not receive a teeny cocktail but rather a drink fit for a giant, or a burly lumberjack at least, which seems apt in the state where Paul Bunyan was supposedly born.

In my college days in cold central Maine, we played a game called Stump. It consisted of a stump that everyone stood around (holding their drinks, naturally) and each person tapped a nail into the top of the stump until it was just standing. Then a hammer was passed around. Each player had to toss the hammer in the air so it made a full rotation, grab it, and swing it toward your nail in one swift motion. Everything that could go wrong was penalized with a drink (and often small amounts of blood), and everything that could go well was rewarded by telling others to drink.

—Andrew Volk, owner, Portland Hunt + Alpine Club (Portland)

MAINE COCKTAIL BAR
VENA'S FIZZ HOUSE
Portland

Vena's Fizz House opened in July 2013 in Portland's Old Port, a neighborhood that sports cobblestoned streets, nineteenth-century brick buildings, and fishing piers as well as new restaurants, boutique shops, and bars of all shapes and sizes. This soda bar and cocktail shop is owned and operated by the hospitable wife-and-husband team of Johanna and Steve Corman. The first time I visited Vena's, Johanna greeted me as though I were a family member arriving home for the holidays.

The first two rooms hold books, various bar ingredients, antique bar memorabilia, and a welcome wagon of barware, bitters, syrups, tinctures, and infusions all for sale, curated for the novice home bartender and professionals alike. The elevated bar area, featuring specialty cocktails and mocktails, is in the back and from every seat offers a view of the apothecary's playground.

MAINE SPIRIT
ALLEN'S COFFEE FLAVORED BRANDY
Somerville, Massachusetts

Allen's is a neutral citrus-based liqueur made with Arabica bean coffee extract. It has a textured, rich dryness and natural sugars, elevating its coffeepot mouthwash quality. Of the 130,000 Massachusetts-produced cases sold annually, more than 96,000 are purchased in Maine. Though I haven't been able to verify this fact by physical inspection, Allen's Coffee Flavored Brandy clearly lives inside the liquor cabinet of every Maine home and every fishing boat.

THE SOMBRERO
Brian Bartels

An original Sombrero is made with Kahlúa and cream or milk. For Mainers, whether you've just come in from chopping wood, hunting, or fishing around the coast, the Sombrero seems to be the cocktail waiting for you—albeit made with Allen's in place of Kahlúa. Many Mainers believe the Sombrero's popularity arose from fishermen pouring a little Allen's into their morning coffee as they took to the boats, or toasting a long day after trawling the seas. The Sombrero goes by several nicknames that sound like those of characters in an Adam Sandler movie: the Down East Panty Dropper, Jackman Martini, Bitch's Martini, Moose Milk, Biddeford Martini, and Fatass in a Glass. Just fun-loving names for any well-adjusted family, really. You can be as creative with this recipe as you like. Instead of regular milk, use a nut milk such as almond or oat milk, or head to the tropics with some coconut milk.

2 ounces whole milk or heavy cream

2 ounces Allen's Coffee Flavored Brandy

Pour the ingredients into a chilled rocks glass filled with ice. Stir to combine.

WHITE NOISE
Briana and Andrew Volk,
Portland Hunt + Alpine Club, Portland

Andrew Volk and his wife, Briana, have been nestled in the downtown Portland community for a healthy amount of time. If there is a craft cocktail movement happening in that area, it can be attributed to the Volks' efforts at the Portland Hunt + Alpine Club and Little Giant, and they are both must-visit spots. This recipe—which is a great large-format cocktail* for anyone hosting a party, as it's easy to build, refreshing, and low in alcohol—comes from *Northern Hospitality with the Portland Hunt + Alpine Club*, Briana and Andrew's celebrated book on how they met in Portland, Oregon, and moved across the country to Portland, Maine. Hunt + Alpine also has one of my favorite menu introductions:

If you're going to lie, lie to save a friend
If you're going to cheat, cheat death
If you're going to steal, steal a pretty girl's heart
And if you're going to drink, drink with me

1½ ounces Cocchi Americano

1 ounce St. Germain elderflower liqueur

2 ounces club soda

Garnish: grapefruit twist

Pour the Cocchi Americano and elderflower liqueur into a chilled double Old Fashioned glass. Fill the glass with ice, and then top with the club soda. Stir gently to combine. Hold the grapefruit twist with both hands between your thumb and forefinger. Twist the peel over the cocktail. Rub the peel on the rim of the glass for extra flavor. Drop the peel into the glass.

*The large-format version of White Noise can easily be made in a pitcher. Pour 9 ounces Cocchi Americano and 6 ounces St. Germain into a 64-ounce pitcher, fill with ice, then top with 12 ounces club soda. Stir gently to combine and garnish with several grapefruit twists. To serve, pour gently from the pitcher, making sure to spoon in some ice along with the liquid. Do not allow the drink to sit too long before serving, as the ice will melt and dilute it.

Operating machinery is illegal
on Sundays in New Hampshire,
but operating a Bloody Mary bar
at 9 A.M. is perfectly acceptable.

New Hampshire

NEW HAMPSHIRE IS a state that has not received enough love. There are beautifully named towns such as Beecher Falls, West Swanzey, and Holderness. There are rolling hills and mountains to be climbed, and places near and far where some of the friendliest people in the United States are waiting to welcome you into their drinking establishments, homes away from home.

The first American potato was planted in 1719 in New Hampshire, the first alarm clock invented in Concord in 1787; the first free public library was established in Peterborough in 1833 (yay books!); the motto "Live Free or Die" comes from a letter by General John Stark (no relation to the *Game of Thrones* character) in remembrance of the victorious Battle of Bennington; Newport's Sarah Josepha Hale wrote a poem called "Mary Had a Little Lamb" in 1830; one of the best American plays, *Our Town*, by Thornton Wilder, a play-within-a-play, takes place in Grover's Corners, a fictional town on the eastern side of the state; and the White Mountain State owns the title of one of my favorite US lakes to say out loud and proud, "Lake Winnipesaukee."

There's a little something for everyone in New Hampshire's cocktail scene, but especially if you like mead. Get your mead on with mead-forward cocktails at Sap House Meadery in Center Ossipee, 815 and the Birch in Manchester, and Chuck's BARbershop in Concord, a gorgeous speakeasy inside a barbershop playing music from the 1920s and serving a wide variety of cocktails—just don't forget the secret code for entry.

New Hampshire also has a historic sign featuring alien abduction, on Highway 3 near Lincoln. On the evening of September 19, 1961, Betty and Barney Hill "lost" time while driving home to Portsmouth. No word on whether or not they'd had a few Brandy Alexanders before getting in their car, but their watches stopped working after the encounter.

> *"Portsmouth wasn't founded on religion, like a lot of other American towns. It was founded on commerce. This was a brothel town. Imagine that," he said, and pointed to the building in front of our car. "At one point long ago, that was the tallest building in America."*
>
> —Uber driver (Portsmouth)

> *You got nice long legs so I'm sure you got no problem walking into town.*
>
> —Hotel concierge (Portsmouth)

BAR SNACK

Vodka can be made from apples. One catch: It takes three hundred apples to make a single bottle of vodka.

BAR SNACK

Mead is one of the oldest beverages in the world, dating back more than seven thousand years to the ancient Egyptians. We make beer from grains and wine from grapes, but mead is made with honey. Simply combine water, wine yeast, and honey, and once the ingredients begin fermentation, the yeast begins eating the sugars in the honey, which converts the ingredients into alcohol and CO_2. Though the world of alcohol has many rules, there are no rules for mead. It can be imbibed at any temperature, at any time of day, and even around complete strangers.

NEW HAMPSHIRE'S OLDEST BAR
THE HANCOCK INN
Hancock, 1789

Part bed-and-breakfast, part tavern, and all romance (it says so on their website—hubba hubba), the historic Hancock Inn has been welcoming travelers since the Revolutionary War, when the first roads in the area were still being built and rum was being passed from town to town. It's the kind of cozy roadside inn that has a fireplace with a dog lounging nearby, and a classic cocktail waiting for you at the Fox Tavern, which is located inside the Hancock Inn. Pretty nice place to relax after easy-hiking at nearby Mount Monadnock, with resplendent views of surrounding New England.

NEW HAMPSHIRE SPIRIT
BANANA-INFUSED JAMESON
Cork, Ireland

I live an hour away from Portsmouth, but this is where the best business for me comes from. It's great, too, except when someone gets sick in my car—but that's okay, too, because the surcharge is two hundred bucks when someone gets sick in my car. I mean, I can't work again that night, but I take a photo of the mess, send it in to Uber, go clean the car, and by the time I get home, Uber's put the money in my bank account. Are you kidding me? That's great!

—Uber driver (Portsmouth)

No joke. I personally saw enough banana-infused Jameson on cocktail menus in New Hampshire to officially link the state with this concoction. If I had to guess why it was so popular, I would say banana-infused Jameson does a fine job of tasting like actual bananas were used in the creation of this delicious liquid, and that's the truth. If it were artificially flavored, everyone (or me, at least) would be angry. It's great on the rocks, in an Old Fashioned or Whiskey Sour, and can even be quite a-peeling (yes, I had to) (you haven't met a collector of puns until you have met my father) in punches. And it's easy to create. Pour one 750-millimeter bottle of Jameson into a large nonreactive container with three peeled and sliced ripe bananas. Let them infuse for at least three days, ideally at room temperature and in the shade. Strain out the bananas with a fine strainer and return the Jameson to its rightful place in the bottle. (Incidentally, the next time you peel a banana, try peeling it from the bottom instead of the stem end. It's always easier. That's how the monkeys do it, Curious George.)

NEW HAMPSHIRE BUCKET LIST BAR
EARTH EAGLE BREWINGS
Portsmouth

What makes Earth Eagle so great is that not only does it deliver on the tasty beer selection, it also features a substantial cocktail menu and health-conscious food options, like hummus (or, as I like to call it, "the new nachos"). The staff greets you with a resounding "Hello" and "How are you doing, friend?" as you walk through the doors. It's rejuvenating to be in a room where the staff is hustling like that and yet maintaining healthy levels of hospitality for everyone involved, all while cranking Led Zeppelin. And if you're nice back to the staff, the bartender might give you a sticker, the same way they used to give you a lollipop when you went to the bank with your parents as a kid. ☺

NEW HAMPSHIRE BEVERAGE
APPLE CIDER

Following the petition of a group of fourth-graders from Jaffrey, the New Hampshire General Court passed a bill in 2010 to adopt apple cider as the state beverage. Not only that, David Goodell, who would become governor of New Hampshire in 1889, is credited with inventing the "Lightning apple parer" in 1864, though I often call the modern-day version "that knife from the drawer." The Lightning apple parer was a stationary device that allowed an apple to be held in place while one turned a crank, which allowed a peeler to easily strip the apple's skin. Voilà. It's off to the apple races.

NEW HAMPSHIRE COCKTAIL BAR
THE WILDER
Portsmouth

Inside the Wilder, bartenders pour creative cocktails with smiles in a space decorated with art from very talented locals. Once you settle in, it's evident that every other person is drinking an Espresso Nitro Martini on draft, which is delicious enough to destroy us all. "How many of these do you make in a night?" I asked the bartender. "A million," he said, expressionless. It takes two seconds to pour into a glass and another two seconds to top off the rich coffee-flavored cocktail with Bailey's whipped cream, giving it a nicely sweetened crown and making you think you're having a Guinness Cocktail. You're not. You're having an Espresso Martini. And after you're done having one, you're having another. And is that a pinball machine in the corner . . . ?

ESPRESSO MARTINI
Brian Bartels

Espresso Martinis have been popping up on cocktail menus throughout the country, but I saw an abundance in New Hampshire bars. Many classic recipes call for vodka, coffee liqueur, simple syrup, and espresso, but I prefer to use cold brew, as it's often more readily available and less expensive to produce than homemade espresso, and avoiding hot espresso is ideal, as it dilutes the ice too fast, which would make celebrated cocktail mad scientist and specialty ice enthusiast Dave Arnold (author of *Liquid Intelligence*) sad, and we can't have that, kids.

1½ ounces Absolut vodka

¾ ounce St. George NOLA
coffee liqueur

½ ounce simple syrup
(1:1 sugar to water)

1 ounce cold brew coffee
(store-bought, or see below
for homemade concentrate
recipe)

Shake the ingredients well with ice; strain into a chilled cocktail glass and serve up.

Cold Brew Coffee Concentrate

Makes about 2⅔ cups concentrate

3 ounces coarsely ground
coffee beans (from about
¾ cup whole coffee beans,
which have been ground to
yield 1½ cups)

3 cups water (filtered,
if possible)

Combine the ingredients in a Mason jar or nonreactive container and stir well. Cover and let steep at room temperature for 12 hours. Strain through a thin paper coffee filter and allow time for all the cold brew to pass through the strainer. What has passed through your paper strainer is your concentrate. Powerful stuff. Best to dilute with equal parts water (e.g., 4 ounces cold brew concentrate to 4 ounces water for each serving). Seal and keep refrigerated for up to 1 week. <u>Note</u>: In recipes asking for cold brew, dilute with 1:1 cold brew concentrate to water.

HULK SMASH
Sarah Maillet, 815, Manchester

The speakeasy 815 is located in the heart of Manchester, New Hampshire's capital. They create a lot of their own liqueurs and infusions and have one of the best whiskey selections in the area. Hulk Smash is a spin on the Whiskey Smash, and the rye's spice matches nicely with the herb-driven green Chartreuse. Once you add some mint to the mix, it's time to Hulk out.

8 fresh mint leaves

½ ounce fresh lime juice

½ ounce fresh lemon juice

½ ounce simple syrup
(1:1 sugar to water)

1½ ounces High West double
rye

½ ounce green Chartreuse

3 dashes Fee Brothers mint
bitters

Garnish: fresh mint leaf

Lightly muddle the mint, lime and lemon juices, and syrup in a shaker for 5 to 10 seconds. Add the rye, Chartreuse, and ice and shake well until chilled; fine strain into a chilled coupe glass and top with the bitters. Serve up, garnished with the mint.

Vermont

Maple syrup might be the hardest-working sweetener in show business, and Vermont happens to lead the country in maple syrup production, which means people in Vermont probably have stronger bones, as there's more calcium in maple syrup than milk. It takes approximately forty gallons of sap to make one gallon of maple syrup, and it's important to make sure you're using 100% pure maple syrup, as some popular brands use high fructose corn syrup, which can lead to madness and convulsions.

VERMONT WAS THE first state to allow partial voting rights for women, the first state to abolish slavery, and the first state to legalize same-sex marriages. The only thing you can't do in Vermont is put up a billboard advertising anything, as that is not allowed. So, in a huge way, thank you for being a real human being, Vermont.

Vermont is famous for maple syrup, trees, the jam band Phish, covered bridges, IBM, artisanal cheese, Bernie Sanders, and teddy bears, as the Vermont Teddy Bear Company is one of the largest handmade teddy bear producers in America. And let's not forget: Ben & Jerry's was created in Vermont. I'm told the employees receive a free pint of ice cream every day, which is why I can never work there.

Nevertheless, all Vermont roads lead to maple. I know Vermont claims that milk is their state beverage, but maple syrup is where it's at. One of my friends once told me his eight-year-old son was keen on sneaking a small glass of maple syrup when his parents were not looking. Even my good friend Jim McDuffee has claimed, "I honestly think I order pancakes just so I get a chance to drink maple syrup." Good maple syrup can be *great* when applied to the right situation.

Montpelier, the largest producer of maple syrup, is also the smallest capital in the United States, holding strong with a population of fewer than eight

It's always fun to find a dive bar in a town you've never been to and start up a conversation with the cranky bartender who's probably worked there for sixteen years and only makes Vodka Sodas, Jack and Cokes, and cracks open PBRs, eavesdropping on regulars chatting over nothing at the bar. That is what I love about dive bars.

—Jocelyn Smith, bar manager, the Mule Bar (Winooski)

Favorite American bartenders: I have many and it's hard to pick. I would say for bartending technique and general "This is how I live my life and rock at it": Natasha David from Nitecap in New York. She is wonderful and fluid behind the bar and she is a WOMAN who owns a bar and has a family. I really am in awe of her. The other is Hunky Dory's Claire Sprouse (Brooklyn). What she has done with her focus on sustainability is incredibly admirable.

—Ivy Mix (born and raised in Vermont), cofounder, Speed Rack, co-owner, Leyenda (Brooklyn, NY)

thousand people. It is also the only US capital without a McDonald's. The go-to cocktail spot in Montpelier is Kismet, which provides a nice balance of classic cocktails and a worthwhile list of Bloody Marys, which may be a key reason why they can claim to offer one of the most popular brunches in Vermont.

Winooski, a small village just outside Burlington, holds two very special bars worth visiting: the Mule Bar and Misery Loves Co., a farm-to-table restaurant with seasonal cocktails.

Burlington, the state's most populous city, provided some memorable cocktails tasted at some of its many worthwhile destinations: the Light Club Lamp Shop is not only the spot in town to see live music (among endless festooning lights and lampshades, no less), it is a surprisingly welcome cocktail haven; Juniper, at the Hotel Vermont, offers a cocktail menu with mostly Vermont-based spirits, beers, and ciders, including its own line of bourbon, vodka, and gin; and the Archives (which tugged at this author's heartstrings of nostalgia, reminding him of days when he had a pocketful of quarters) brings vintage arcade games and elevated cocktails together. I had the Baked Alaska cocktail when I visited, a gin-based sour with CBD*.

One standout cocktail that is quickly becoming adopted as a Vermont cocktail is the Bee's Knees, a gin sour sweetened with honey. "The bee's knees" was a phrase used during Prohibition to mean "the best" version of a drink, often using a sweetener and citrus to cover up the nasty flavors of bathtub gin. Bee colonies and our ecosystem require more attention, so the bartending world has adopted the Bee's Knees cocktail and a myriad of variations as a conduit for awareness. Vermont's honeybees are a major contributor to the state's agricultural welfare, so the Vermont distillery Barr Hill introduced Bee's Knee's Week, in late September, which raises awareness and some modest funds to maintain colonies for beekeepers.

Saxtons Distillery, Smugglers' Notch Distillery, Dunc's Mill, WhistlePig, and Stonecutter Spirits are some well-known distilleries making waves in Maple Country. Stonecutter does a cocktail scavenger hunt every fall to celebrate the laundry list of great cocktail places throughout the state, which is always a great way to get familiar with what's new and game-changing in the Vermont cocktail world and beyond.

*Cannabidiol (CBD) has been popping up everywhere in the past couple of years. We now find it in syrups, sodas, and coffee products as a non-psychoactive way of relieving aches, pains, anxiety, and all other things we suffer on a daily basis, like people who walk in horizontal groups down narrow sidewalks (share the road, man!). Some bartenders have embraced it, and some have felt there is no need to have it, as alcohol itself does a pretty good job of relieving all aforementioned ailments. Just ask my old high school English teacher.

BAR SNACK

Speed Rack, a nationwide bartending competition featuring badass female bartenders in a number of cities, which gives 100 percent of its proceeds to breast cancer research and prevention, was co-founded by Ivy Mix, a superhero from Tunbridge, Vermont, famous for its annual World's Fair festival, held every September, featuring pig races, tractor pulls, and 4-H agricultural arts and crafts competitions. "Speed Rack" is a reference to the shelf below the bar where bartenders store liquor for faster cocktails.

VERMONT SPIRIT
BARR HILL
Hardwick

Ivy Mix is my favorite. Ivy has accomplished such a great amount in such a small amount of time. Bartending since the age of seventeen, she has moved up along the tough ranks in NYC. With her devotion to the craft and passion, it's contagious and inspiring. But to me, her most important achievement has been Speed Rack. WOW.

—Amy Kovalchick, bartender, Fedora (Manhattan, NY)

The very first cocktail I had was Vodka and Coke. At a house party one town over from Tunbridge when I was like eleven. Gross!

—Ivy Mix (born and raised in Vermont), cofounder, Speed Rack, co-owner, Leyenda (Brooklyn, NY)

Barr Hill has been operating under the Caledonia Spirits umbrella since 2012, when a longtime Vermont beekeeper decided to bring raw honey into the distillation process. The distillery makes vodka, rye whiskey, and one of my favorite spirits, Tom Cat gin, which is their raw honey gin aged in Vermont white oak barrels for three months, and it belongs on your shelf. In addition, they started Bee's Knees Week, an annual program devoted to helping sustain and rebuild bee colonies through Bee Cause, a nationwide organization (thebeecause.org) connected with more than three hundred schools in every state.

VERMONT'S OLDEST BAR
YE OLDE TAVERN
Manchester, 1890

Manchester is a tiny little town of four thousand people, tucked away in the Green Mountains. The Tavern was opened in 1890 and has an old stagecoach vibe from the front entrance, beautifully restored in the recent past. The inside features abundant knick-knacks on the walls, a quaint six-seat bar, antiques that will make Grandma jealous, and uneven doors. Stop by for a Manhattan and have some cranberry fritters with Vermont maple butter. The place is also famous for having the first telephone line in Manchester.

Every bar absolutely needs an amaro program. It allows you to expose people to things they never knew they needed in their life! Or at least Fernet.

—Jocelyn Smith, bar manager, the Mule Bar (Winooski)

VERMONT BUCKET LIST BAR
THE MULE BAR
Winooski

I was at the Mule Bar on a Sunday night at 8 P.M., which felt like the best place in the world at that moment, given the conviviality. Look around and every other person is enjoying the Gin and Tonic featuring house-made tonic made with quinine syrup. Whether or not it is the first place you visit, it is always the last place you end up. But no matter when you visit, try the breakfast sandwiches, which are served all day and night. On top of all this, the bar has the most comfortable stools I have sat on in recent memory, which means a lot to this little keister. (And yes, I used the word *keister*. You try being raised by a German-Irish family from northern Wisconsin.)

VERMONT COCKTAIL BAR
DELI/126
Burlington

One enters Deli/126 through what seems like an unmarked meat locker front door, into a cozy cocktail lounge that features live jazz a few nights during the week. Bar director Emily Morton applies the right balance of Prohibition-era influence while modernizing the mood with shout-outs to industry legends (Jim Meehan's Center City Swizzle from 2010, George Kappeler's Widow Kiss from 1895, and varying recipes from Deli/126 bartenders of recent years past). What stands out most, however, is the innate desire to continue building stronger philanthropic endeavors. Morton is connected to the community and values the relationships of bartenders and service industry people near and far.

OLD VERMONT
Brian Bartels

Jim Meehan is very influential to me. When I was given the opportunity in late 2017 to design my own bar, the liquid was important, but the experience was crucial. I spent weeks of my life curating every detail of Deli/126's experience, from using 1920s ingredients in every cocktail, to orienting the room toward the bar or musicians, to designing unique spaces to enjoy a drink within the bar, and to providing education for the curious drinker. Meehan's Bartender Manual *validated that effort.*

—Emily Morton, bar director, Deli/126 (Burlington)

Though the origin of this drink isn't clear, it has been around for quite some time, and I wanted to add it as a precursor to Emily's cocktail. They're both great!

- 1½ ounces gin
- ½ ounce grade B Vermont maple syrup
- ½ ounce fresh lemon juice
- 2 dashes Angostura bitters
- Garnish: orange peel

Shake the ingredients with ice until chilled; strain into a chilled cocktail glass and serve up, garnished with the orange.

THE (NEW) OLD VERMONT COCKTAIL
Emily Morton, Deli/126, Burlington

Emily Morton is one of the nicest, most hospitable, and most passionate cocktail and hospitality professionals I met through researching this book. The excitement in her eyes when she made this drink said everything about people being proud of their heritage. Emily offers her take on this classic cocktail and of course uses two of the best Vermont products (Barr Hill gin and maple syrup).

- 2 ounces Barr Hill Tom Cat bourbon barrel–aged gin
- 1 ounce London Dry gin (Deli/126 uses Beefeater)
- ¼ ounce Vermont maple syrup (the darker the better)
- 1 teaspoon fresh orange juice
- 1 teaspoon fresh lemon juice
- 4 dashes Regan's orange bitters
- 2 dashes Angostura bitters
- Garnish: orange peel

Stir the ingredients with ice until chilled. Strain into a chilled coupe glass. Express the orange peel a few inches over the top of the drink and then add it to the drink.

STONE FENCE
Brian Bartels

In 1775, Ethan Allen and the Green Mountain Boys were a-drinkin' at the Remington Tavern in Castleton. Since they were preparing to stage a revolution at Fort Ticonderoga, they wanted to toast the unknown, and the local liquid in their glasses was none other than rum and hard cider, which, served cold or hot, adds up to the same results when sipped: victory.

- 2 ounces rye whiskey (apple brandy, Scotch, rum, or bourbon also work)
- 4 ounces fresh-pressed apple cider
- ¼ ounce fresh lemon juice
- 1 dash Angostura bitters

Pour the ingredients over ice, briefly stir, and live forever.

Massachusetts

Though happy hours are against the law in Boston, there was a good chance colonials were genuinely happy enough to sip a few from Cole's Inn, which opened the first licensed New England tavern in Boston on March 4th, 1634 (the same year Boston Common opened as America's first public park). Samuel Cole was responsible for New England's first drinking establishment, which served the likes of lords, Native American chiefs, politicians, and poets (e.g. Henry Wadsworth Longfellow).

MASSACHUSETTS HOLDS A lot of records. It opened the first American lighthouse in 1716, invented basketball in 1891, and claims the longest-named lake in the world, Lake Chargoggagoggmanchauggagoggchaubunagungamaugg (try that at your next spelling bee competition) in *Webster's*. The Fig Newton was born in Cambridgeport, the first zip code in the United States (01001) was assigned to Agawam, the first chocolate factory in the United States was opened in Dorchester, the first chocolate chip cookie was made in Whitman in the 1930s, and Harvard was the first college established in North America. There are so many tourist destinations throughout the Bay State and we haven't even reached Boston. Boston is one of my favorite cities to walk in, given its rich history and New England–style colonial architecture—and its incredible cocktail dens.

Did you know Boston Common is the oldest public park in the United States? I didn't. Or that the city's cream pie was created there in the late nineteenth century? Did you know happy hours have not been allowed since 1984? I actually did know that! The list of notable events that have occurred in Boston goes on and on, and the bars and taverns associated with its history deserve continued praise. There are many fine drinking establishments in this city, which pretty much commands my full attention in terms of Massachusetts cocktail influence, a torch lit and carried by influential figures such as Jackson Cannon, Misty Kalkofen, and Josh Childs, who co-owns Silvertone Bar & Grill, Parlor Sports, and Trina's Starlight Lounge. Childs is referred to as a "godfather" by many Boston industry folk. And Brother Cleve, a longtime Boston cocktail historian and mentor, might be standing nearby in a fedora, nodding in agreement.

MASSACHUSETTS OLDEST BAR
THE WARREN TAVERN
Charlestown, 1780

It's not very often one can say they had a drink at the same bar as George Washington (see Fraunces Tavern, page 27). The Warren Tavern is named after Dr. Joseph Warren, who not only practiced medicine but was a general at the Battle of Bunker Hill in 1775. Back then, taverns were essentially inns with a communal dynamic. People stayed upstairs and ate and drank downstairs. The building housing the Warren is in great shape for one born in the eighteenth century, thanks to a restoration project in 1975. Stop by for some oysters, clam chowder, and the opportunity to sit in a space full of American history.

MASSACHUSETTS SPIRIT
PRIVATEER RUM
Ipswich

Though I have been to Boston and can confirm it is rich in Jameson bottles on every shelf in every bar, rum is now the spirit I often associate with Massachusetts. Privateer, which began distilling in 2011, does a remarkable job of resuscitating the historic legacy of rum in New England. They produce a silver reserve label, an amber rum, an annual gin, cask-strength rums (Navy Yard and Queen's Share), and Distiller's Drawer, which are special one-time-only rotating releases of unique bottlings. Oh, also: every Privateer spirit by head distiller Maggie Campbell has received a four-star rating from F. Paul Pacult's *Spirit Journal*. #nobiggie

BAR SNACK

Jackson Cannon penned a beautiful essay titled "Letter to a Young Bartender," which should be read by everyone looking to be better at work, life, and being a well-rounded human. If you are an industry professional, and you truly care about serving others, and feel disillusioned, weary, or unfulfilled after endless closes and thankless moments where you were trying your best to take care of everyone in the room, please read the letter. It's online and easy to find. You'll start feeling better. It's a healthy reminder we are not machines; we have limits, and that's okay, but never forget the almighty power of patience and tolerance when we share space with different human beings and— let's call out the cute little elephant in the room—alcohol.

MASSACHUSETTS BEVERAGE
CRANBERRY JUICE

Cranberries have been growing in Massachusetts for centuries, with the first recorded cranberry cultivation happening in the early 1800s, and the state still produces more than 30 percent of our country's cranberries. Cranberry got its momentum with Ocean Spray lifting off in 1930, which I believe coincides exactly with the time people started living longer. The juice market skyrocketed in the 1980s, which heightened demand for cranberry juice, followed by more published scientific studies attributing vitamins to the little red berry. Cranberries are credited with having nutrients and antioxidants aiding in stomach disorders, urinary tract infections, kidney stones, preventing tooth decay, and fighting off colds. Yep. When you know all that, drinking a vodka cranberry seems practically medicinal.

MASSACHUSETTS
BUCKET LIST BAR
BACKBAR
Boston

Backbar was opened by Sam Treadway, one of Boston's cocktail Jedi. On top of well-crafted potables, the Star Wars geek in me swoons for a Bananakin Skywalker, made with Scotch, pineapple, lime, Cappelletti, banana, and Angostura, and served in a tiki mug. Along with pun-licious names such as Kale-ing Out Your Name, Raw Vegan Pirate Diet, and the McConaughaissance, I celebrate the Bartender's Choice option, which reads: *We would love to have a conversation in order to find the cocktail that best fits your taste.* The bartender serving me said he'd moved to Boston one year earlier. "I only wanted to work here, but they didn't have an opening, so I became a regular, because I love this place so much. Eventually, they had a job opening." If you're there late enough, they'll hand out small plates of spicy caramel popcorn. I recommend sticking around.

MASSACHUSETTS
COCKTAIL BAR
THE HAWTHORNE
Boston

If you love cocktails, talking about cocktails, sharing a cocktail or two with someone in your life, seeking inspiration from the annals of cocktail history, and having those cocktails be something you think about for the rest of the week, then, wonderful people of Planet Earth, there is a place in Boston, Massachusetts, and it is called the Hawthorne. Everyone who works there moves purposefully, with the right amount of nimble dexterity. Heed their website's masthead:

WELCOME FRIENDS!
We believe in the transformative power of conviviality and the idea that art, music and strong drink can lubricate our consciousness for new possibilities. Our endeavor is to be a part of the continuum of bar, saloon, and tavern as a hot bed of revolution, intellectual discourse and romantic pursuit. Welcome to The Hawthorne and to the time-honored rituals of communion, revelry and the strengthening of the bonds of family and friendship. Cheers!

The Hawthorne is at the ready. One simply has a conversation with their bartender and, through that majestic, timeless interface no tablet, kiosk, or iPad can replace, a special bond is formed. Humans. Speaking to each other. Whoa.

The Vodka Red Bull is my least favorite American cocktail to make. Because it makes me feel like a drug dealer.

—Sam Treadway, co-owner, Backbar (Boston)

CAPE COD
Brian Bartels

This straightforward cocktail actually tastes like vacation near a warm, sunny beach, and hopefully this is currently where you are enjoying one, near a plate of freshly cut watermelon, an endless bowl of salty pretzels, and some bottles of seltzer—which is a recipe option in Trader Vic's 1972 *Bartender's Guide Revised*, which contains the first published recipe for a Cape Codder. The seltzer does a nice job of cutting some tartness and adding everyone's party favorite: bubbles.

1½ ounces Absolut vodka

4 ounces cranberry juice

½ ounce fresh lime juice

Club soda (optional)

Garnish: lime wedge

Pour the vodka into a chilled highball glass with ice, then top with the cranberry and lime juices, and the club soda, if desired. Garnish with the lime.

WARD EIGHT
Brian Bartels

A Ward Eight Boston bartender allegedly created this cocktail in 1898 in honor of the politician Martin "the Mahatma" Lomasney, who never drank but abhorred the thought of Prohibition, knew how to rock a mustache, and famously said, "Don't write when you can talk; don't talk when you can nod your head." If you love Whiskey Sours, and Tom Brady, and Boston history, this is your cup of (*ahem*) mahatma tea.

2 ounces rye whiskey

¾ ounce fresh lemon juice

¾ ounce fresh orange juice

1 teaspoon grenadine

Garnish: orange peel

Shake the ingredients with ice until chilled; strain into a chilled cocktail glass and serve up, garnished with the orange.

PERIODISTA
Jackson Cannon

I came across the Periodista in a *New York Times* article by Robert Simonson, so I owe fellow New Yorker by way of Wisconsinite Mr. Simonson a proper amount of debt for this recipe. (Next round of cheese curds are on me, sir.) The Boston Periodista was introduced in the mid-1990s by the bartender Joe McGuirk of the now-defunct Chez Henri, and has become a commonly shared cocktail throughout the Boston craft cocktail crowd. McGuirk found a recipe in a liquor company's handbook for its Latin-themed menu, and though that original recipe contained dark rum, Mr. Cannon prefers the lighter rum version. It's important to get the facts right, right? Which brings us to etymology: *Periodista* means "journalist" in Spanish.

1½ ounces white rum

½ ounce Cointreau (or Combier)

½ ounce apricot liqueur (Rothman & Winter Orchard is great)

½ ounce fresh lime juice

Shake the ingredients with ice until chilled; strain into a chilled cocktail glass and serve up.

There is plenty of oceanfront property along the shores of Rhode Island—384 miles, in fact, and that includes its thirty-five different islands. One version of how it got named is that Dutch explorer Adrian Block called it "Roodt Eylandt," or "red island," due to all the red clay accumulating on the shoreline. One thing's for sure, the state still holds the record for longest official name: "State of Rhode Island and Providence Plantations."

Rhode Island

Rum is definitely associated with Rhode Island. It harkens back to the olden days of rum distilling and rum running from Colonial times all the way through Prohibition. In many respects, I would say our unofficial state cocktail is the Dark and Stormy (dark rum and ginger beer with lime).

—Chris Bender, director of operations, Stoneacre Brasserie (Newport)

WE HAVE REACHED the smallest state in the entire United States. I hope you're happy. For being so small, Rhode Island has a long and layered role in American history. Did you know the first circus was in Newport in 1774? Additionally, the first US Open golf tournament was in 1895, the first speeding ticket punishable by jail time was issued in 1904 in Newport (for driving fifteen miles per hour!), the Industrial Revolution started in Pawtucket in 1790, and the Redwood Library in Newport is America's oldest library.

Newport has the Great Chowder Cook-Off in early summer, the annual Jazz Festival in late summer, and Winter Festival in February, featuring ten days of music, food, and fun for the *Family Guy* in all of us. (*Family Guy* creator Seth MacFarlane attended the Rhode Island School of Design, and the show takes place in the fictional town of Quahog.) Glendale holds the world's oldest penny arcade, Pelham Street in Newport was the first gaslit street in America, and there are more donut shops per capita in Providence than anywhere else in the country.

Rhode Island is also known for its attempts at Guinness World Records. One of my favorite US recordholders is Blake Rodgers, of Cranston, who managed to acquire 3,131 high fives in a twenty-four-hour period at the Dunkin' Donuts Center in Providence. Somebody buy that man his next cocktail!

Providence is one of America's oldest cities, and deserves more attention from the general masses due to its historic buildings and contemporary outdoor art, featuring full-building paintings and images from renowned artists through the Avenue Concept project.

It's worth noting that the Hope State was one of the wettest states during Prohibition, and places like Eddy in downtown Providence (a favorite of many local bartenders who enjoy drinking there on days off) should make people very happy today with their cocktail offerings, like the Orange Julius Caesar, made with Plantation 3 Stars rum, Bols yogurt liqueur, lime, vanilla, and Bittermens orange cream citrate.

The first Providence bar I visited was the Dean Bar, a hidden gem inside the Dean Hotel in downtown Providence. The bartender greeted me by saying, "Welcome to the weekend!" as I ordered the Traveling Man cocktail, a shaken cocktail made with Maker's Mark bourbon, amaro, Grand Marnier, yellow Chartreuse, and lemon juice. I marveled in appreciation at the pour as Bob Dylan started singing, "Well, it ain't no use to sit and wonder why, babe . . ."

BAR SNACK

In ye olden days, "grog" was a sailor's daily ration of rum diluted with water. Sailors would line up and collect their allotted amount of liquid courage and then commence a hearty "scuttlebutt" of chatter—which brings us to the word *scuttlebutt*: A "butt" was the name of a large wine barrel aboard the ship, and the liquid inside the butt was "scuttled" (full of water). Thankfully, "buttscuttle" didn't have the same staying power.

RHODE ISLAND SPIRIT
NEWPORT CRAFT BREWING & DISTILLING COMPANY
Newport

In 2006, Newport Craft Brewing & Distilling Co. became the first Rhode Island distillery in more than 135 years. Newport Craft produces a wide variety of creative craft spirits, including a barrel-aged amaro made with hops, an overproof blackstrap molasses white rum, a peat-forward seven-year-old whiskey, and pure moonshine, distilled from the traditional methods practiced in Newport in the late 1800s. Copper pot still rum production was quite popular in late-1600s Rhode Island, and Thomas Tew, a privateer and sailor known as the "Rhode Island Pirate," once nicknamed the area "Rogue's Island" for its reputation of harboring pirates and other licentious ne'er-do-wells.

RHODE ISLAND BUCKET LIST BAR
NICK-A-NEES
Providence

One gets the sense that Nick-A-Nees is a regular haunt for everyone looking to socialize, and do it between rounds of cold beer, laid-back cocktails, shooting pool, and listening to music. The location could be the opening scene in a Scorsese film, where people congregate over the ups and downs of a given day, watch some old folks shoot pool and play shuffleboard, and hear a quality cover of the Georgia Satellites' "Keep Your Hands to Yourself" once in a while.

RHODE ISLAND BEVERAGE
COFFEE MILK

Though people do imbibe their fair share of Del's frozen lemonade (especially if there's vodka and a beach nearby), more people in Rhode Island go for coffee milk. It looks like chocolate milk made with a small amount of chocolate syrup. But the key ingredient is a sweetened coffee concentrate. Most people use Autocrat coffee syrup, born in Lincoln, Rhode Island, in the 1940s, to make the sweet magic happen. Use 2 tablespoons coffee syrup for every 8 to 10 ounces cold milk. Add coffee syrup to ice cream and you've got a Coffee Cabinet, which non–Rhode Islanders would call a "milkshake."

RHODE ISLAND'S OLDEST BAR
THE WHITE HORSE TAVERN
Newport, 1673

Though there are other White Horse Taverns in other parts of the United States, this White Horse Tavern—which ironically looks like a big red barn—is said to be the oldest standing bar in America, constructed in 1652 and converted into a tavern in 1673. It hosted many a colonist, soldier, and pirate in its heyday, and still stands out for its local ingredients, such as artisan cheeses, locally sourced honey, and oysters fresh off the boat from Narragansett Bay. Just remember some dining rules: Jackets are not required but collared shirts are expected, remove your hats, keep off your cell phones, and be nice to all human beings (I particularly like the last two).

RHODE ISLAND COCKTAIL BAR
COURTLAND CLUB
Providence

Courtland sits in the middle of a block and has a small parking area next to its unlabeled exterior. Their most famous cocktail, Mother Theresa, is made with mezcal, beets, cassis, and rosé. It arrives in a stainless-steel soup cup on top of a plate, and the ice cubes sticking out of the glass have tiny gold-flecked stars. I asked the bartender if she felt annoyed having to make so many Mother Theresas. "Mother Theresa is too important for me to not appreciate the drink," she said. "And it also means all the beets I juiced are not going to waste."

If you're only in Providence for one night, try and make it over to Captain Seaweed's. It is a true dive bar that ain't gonna do you wrong. And you know it's gonna be good, cuz they don't have a website. If you have a website, you're no longer a dive bar.

—Bartender at the Dean Bar (Providence)

Rhode Island is big on coffee milk. So, if you're not drinking coffee milk, were you even in Rhode Island?

—Leishla Maldonado, bar manager, Courtland Club (Providence)

NEWPORT 75

Chris Bender, Stoneacre Brasserie, Newport

On Wednesdays I head to the most amazing jazz bar in Providence, called the Acacia Club. It's behind and underneath a masonry—the second-oldest black-owned masonry in the country. Rum and Cokes, soulful jazz, and fried chicken are the way to go.

—Leishla Maldonado, bar manager, Courtland Club (Providence)

This is a riff on the classic French 75 cocktail, which often features Champagne, gin, lemon, and sugar. Chris "the Knight of Newport" Bender's version is more fruit-forward, and goes well with any live music, as Newport is famous for its jazz and folk festivals, founded in the 1950s.

½ ounce Newport gin

½ ounce Aperol

½ ounce St. Germain elderflower liqueur

½ ounce fresh lemon juice

½ ounce fresh grapefruit juice

½ ounce fresh orange juice

2 ounces dry sparkling wine

Garnish: fresh mint sprig

Shake the gin, Aperol, St. Germain, and juices with ice until chilled. Strain over ice in a white wine glass. Top with the wine and serve, garnished with the mint.

GREEN APPLE MULE

Leishla Maldonado, Courtland Club, Providence

Moscow Mule variations have been quite popular over the years, but this particular one has been wowing patrons at Courtland Club since they put it on the menu in 2018. There are commercial green apple juices and smoothies available, but if you have a juicer, you're all aces.

2 ounces Bully Boy vodka (or
your favorite vodka)

½ cup green apple granita
(recipe follows)

3 ounces Fever-Tree ginger
beer

Garnish: crushed black pep-
percorns, dehydrated apple
chip, and a Japanese maple
leaf (optional)

Combine the ingredients in a chilled rocks glass. There's no need for ice if your granita is nice and frozen.

Green Apple Granita

Makes about 2½ cups

8 ounces green apple juice
(Snapple has a great
option if you don't have
a commercial juicer)

5½ ounces ginger syrup
(recipe follows)

4 ounces fino sherry

1 ounce fresh lemon juice

Combine all the ingredients and freeze for 2 hours. Use a fork and scrape into flaky crystals. Repeat this process every hour until the granita is the desired consistency. Cover tightly and store in the freezer for up to 2 months. (Make it at least 1 day in advance of serving.)

Ginger Syrup

Makes about 1½ cups

½ cup sugar

½ cup boiling water

½ cup chopped peeled ginger

Combine the sugar, boiling water, and ginger in a blender and blend until smooth. Strain through a cheesecloth or fine strainer into an airtight container. Store in the refrigerator for up to 2 weeks.

Connecticut

I believe this was the first Dean of Admissions at Yale University, who not only played a mean flute, but mastered the art of never needing a plastic straw. It's true what they say: Yale University produces innovative talent.

AFTER PASSING THE first automobile law to set a speed limit, at twelve miles per hour, in 1901, Connecticut was off to the races, putting license plates on cars in 1905 and establishing more towns ending with -bury, -ford, and -ton than anywhere else in America. But let's not forget one of the most important American inventions of all time: the bicycle, which was the Columbia Bicycle, first manufactured in Hartford in 1878. Kickstart my heart.

Connecticut son Paul Newman started Newman's Own Foundation in 1982, which donates 100 percent of its after-tax profits to organizations in need, such as those serving children with disabilities or poverty-stricken areas of the world, groups working to improve nutrition in schools and lower-income communities, and countless other philanthropic endeavors. But our favorite Connecticut birth must always be our great-great-great-grandpappy, Jerry Thomas, born in New Haven in 1825, who apprenticed as an assistant to a principal bartender in a New Haven tavern, learning the bar trade at a time when America's drinking game began to evolve, and who, after traveling, training, and working in some of the best programs throughout the country, subsequently became the most popular and important bartender in America.

Foxon Park, in East Haven, is a family-run soda company that's been providing the state with flavorful nonalcoholic beverages since 1922. The company's white birch beer, flavored with Alaskan birch and wintergreen, is a state favorite. Definitely a worthwhile accompaniment when munching on New Haven's famous coal-fired, cracker-thin pizza (aka "apizza").

New craft cocktail bars are sprouting up throughout the state: Hartford's Little River Restoratives, specializing in pre-Prohibition cocktails and punches, and New Haven's 116 Crown, which offers cocktail classes in addition to top-notch food and cocktail pairings, and Elm City Social, featuring a popular peanut butter and jelly Old Fashioned (peanut-infused bourbon and strawberry syrup are marvelous pals), are standouts.

Litchfield Distillery is producing some fine product in northwest Connecticut, honoring the local farming community. Early farmers were called "batchers" and made their living with hard-earned agricultural sustenance. I salute the distillery's "Batchers Manifesto": "Take Pride in Your Work: Nothing exceptional ever comes easy. We honor good old-fashioned, roll-up-your-sleeves effort and remain steadfast in our belief that hard work is the only path to greatness."

And of course let's not forget (or forgive) Billy Wilson's Ageing Still bar in Norwich for creating the Car Bomb (equal parts Irish whiskey and Irish cream liqueur, dropped into a pint of Guinness and slammed) in 1979. Relating the story surrounding this cocktail would be unnecessary, as the tale of how it came to be named is 100 percent disrespectful to victims of terrorism and violence, not only from the IRA days of the late 1970s but throughout the world in all times. In my heart of hearts, I hope this cocktail is never served or asked for ever again.

CONNECTICUT BUCKET LIST BAR
ORDINARY
New Haven

Ordinary sits on hallowed ground, as the space was New Haven's first town tavern back in 1659. Connected to the historic Taft Hotel on a corner of New Haven Green, it has gone through a few different names since it began. The current owners restored the baroque, oak-paneled interior; revamped the restaurant, sourcing ingredients from local farmers; and returned the property to its original glory. They serve a nice variety of punches and keep Yale students from studying—and using their *Webster's* dictionaries, a useful irony, as Noah Webster, creator of the first American English dictionary, was born in West Hartford, and famously visited the Ordinary in 1775, standing and playing a fife with one hundred Yale students waiting to escort George Washington to the Continental Army in Cambridge. And they say nothing good happens outside of bars.

CONNECTICUT SPIRIT
VODKA
Everywhere

Vodka, you may be surprised to learn, was once considered vile. In the 1930s, John Gilbert Martin became vice president of Heublein, based in Hartford, and purchased Smirnoff vodka shortly thereafter, originally marketing it as "white whiskey." Imagine telling a modern-day vodka connoisseur they're really into white whiskey, then imagine them not being your friend. When World War II ended, in 1945, people were looking for more excuses to share a drink, and the Moscow Mule, Bloody Mary, Screwdriver, and Vodkatini started gaining notoriety, which catapulted the sales of vodka into the stratosphere.

> ### STATE FACT
> Police are allowed to pull you over if you're traveling sixty-five miles an hour on your bicycle.

CONNECTICUT
BEVERAGE
CLUB SODA

In the early 1800s, one of the first soda water fountains opened in New Haven, introduced by Benjamin Silliman, a Yale chemistry professor. "Soda fountains" specialized in carbonating water to replicate mineral water that bubbled up from the earth, creating a product that many at the time believed prevented or cured diseases and absolved dyspepsia or indigestion. By 1836, it was estimated that New York alone had more than 670 soda draft fountains throughout the city, and though working with pressurized beverages certainly didn't come without its accidents (exploding equipment, broken glassware, innocent people flying across the room), the beverage only continued becoming more popular, with flavored syrups eventually catching on. Druggists and chemists were using bicarbonate soda and having a dandy of a time figuring out what to call their creations. "Carbonade"? "Charged water"? "Mephitic gas"? "Oxygenated water"? In the end, three different options overruled the rest: seltzer, soda water, and soda pop. And depending on what part of the country you lived in, you were ultimately going to call it something else. In Wisconsin, most people call it *soda*, while just over the border in northern Illinois, you're getting *pop*, and if that's not odd enough, a small percentage of people in New England call it *tonic*. Egad!

CONNECTICUT
COCKTAIL BAR
CONSPIRACY
Middletown

Champions of art, culture, time travel, and all things craft cocktail, Conspiracy deftly employs the best parts of iconic American influences, serving classic cocktails in vintage glassware in a relaxing room of leather chairs, booths, and banquettes. Conspiracy's menu reads as a beautifully balanced reflection of classic cocktails done right, with pre-Prohibition cocktail influences, along with modern variations on classics, like the Campfire Old Fashioned (bourbon, smoked maple syrup, and bitters, served with a toasted marshmallow). Don't have just one, and don't skip Tiki Mondays.

CONNECTICUT'S
OLDEST BAR
GRISWOLD INN
Essex, 1776

One of the oldest bars in America is also one of the most charming. Like many of the longstanding taverns in the Northeast, the Griswold also operates as an inn, with thirty-three rooms, multiple dining rooms, a wine bar, and a pub for weary travelers. Put a little popcorn machine in the corner and you've got yourself a place to camp until they give last call. I can envision a *Vacation* movie taking place there in the future, which might upset Chevy Chase, Maryland.

Rum was once very popular in this part of Connecticut. New England rum had the reputation of being very, uh…assertive. Gotta make it through those tough winters somehow, I guess.

—Mark Sabo, bar owner, Conspiracy (Middletown)

BAR SNACK
In seventeenth-century Connecticut, it was illegal to drink for more than thirty minutes at a time, or to finish more than half a bottle of wine in one sitting. My aunt Yvonne would have spent the rest of her days behind bars.

YALE FENCE
Brian Bartels

This recipe hails from David Embury's *The Fine Art of Mixing Drinks*. In the same book, he also features a Greenwich cocktail, which is similar, but uses crème de cacao instead of vermouth for a rich, chocolaty profile. Yale University, founded in 1701, is famous for its music and drama programs (hey there, Meryl Streep). It's hard to get into Yale. But it's easy to get into this cocktail.

1 ounce gin

1 ounce applejack

1 ounce sweet vermouth

Garnish: lemon twist

Combine the ingredients with ice and stir until cold; strain into a chilled cocktail glass and serve up, garnished with the lemon.

CIDER CUP #1
Jen and Mark Sabo, Middletown

This lower-ABV (alcohol by volume) tipple is a welcome addition to any fall menu. Orleans are low-alcohol cider-based aperitifs from Eden Specialty Ciders in next-door-neighbor Vermont, featuring herbs and roots and no artificial sweeteners or flavoring agents. Like apples, they can be used in a multiplicity of ways.

¾ ounce Orleans Bitter

¾ ounce Orleans Herbal

½ ounce Calvados syrup (recipe follows)

½ ounce fresh lemon juice

1 teaspoon quince paste

1 ounce apple cider

Garnish: seasonal fruit (sliced apples are always a good move)

Combine the Orleans, Calvados syrup, lemon juice, and quince paste and shake with ice until chilled. Strain over crushed ice in a chilled double rocks glass (Conspiracy uses a camping cup). Top with the apple cider and garnish with fruit.

Calvados Syrup

Makes about 2 cups

1 cup Calvados

1 cup sugar

1 teaspoon ground cloves

2 star anise pods

1 teaspoon allspice berries

1 cardamom pod

2 cinnamon sticks

Combine the ingredients in a saucepan. Warm on the stove over medium-high heat. Remove from the heat at the first crack of a boil. Let cool and further infuse. When the mixture is at room temperature, strain out the spices and refrigerate for up to 2 weeks in an airtight container.

Yes, it's true. I stole my high school brother's Springsteen Pink Cadillac tour T-shirt for my fourth-grade picture-day photo. Even though it draped down to my knees, I. Still. Felt. Like. A. Boss.

New Jersey

New Jersey is famous for many things. Weird New Jersey (look it up), Snookie, arguments between Pork Roll and Taylor Ham, fast and excellent driving, and applejack.

—Aaron Polsky, bar consultant, Los Angeles (raised in New Jersey)

THE GARDEN STATE doesn't get enough credit for serving us some wonderful seashores, four-mile-long boardwalks, seven major shopping malls in a twenty-five-square-mile radius, and countless diners—it's often called the Diner Capital of the World.

America's first baseball game was played in Hoboken, its first drive-in movie theater was in Camden, and in Paterson's Lambert Castle there is the New Jersey Spoon Museum, featuring more than five thousand spoons from every state and from countries throughout the world.

Thomas Edison, one of my favorite Americans of all time, lived in West Orange until he died, in 1931. Edison invented the light bulb, the phonograph (that's a record player to you millennials), and the motion picture projector in his Menlo Park laboratory, and tours are available at the Thomas Edison National Historic Park, which has been preserved since his passing.

We all know Atlantic City is the all-gambling, all-in, alcohol-is-available twenty-four-hours-a-day East Coast Las Vegas, but did you know that Ocean City is a dry town, and has never allowed alcohol? Tell that to North Caldwell's Tony Soprano, who was more of a Scotch-on-the-rocks guy than a cocktail fan. (Tony didn't like to wait. But then again, you were always halfway there, livin' on a prayer, with Perth Amboy's Bon Jovi.)

Today, there are plenty of worthy cocktail choices throughout New Jersey. For instance, I recommend hitting up Jersey City's South House—a fun and lively space with quality southern fare and cocktails—and the Farm and Fisherman Tavern in Cherry City, known for its house Manhattan and Bee's Knees, and Francis Schott's cocktail programs at Stage Left Steak and Catherine Lombardi, celebrated New Brunswick destinations.

When Bruce Springsteen released *Greetings from Asbury Park, N.J.* in 1973, it was a wake-up call that every kid in America got a chance to answer, because he was that kid in America telling us life was not going to be easy, but there's nothing wrong with being on fire, and all it takes is using the tools surrounding us to play and sing like there was nothing to lose, and with that declaration of independence, coupled with unbridled freedom, the United States would never be the same again.

BAR SNACK
Thomas Edison was responsible for getting Alexander Graham Bell, inventor of the telephone, to consider an alternative to "Ahoy" every time we answer the phone: "Hello?"

My first cocktail was a gin Martini. I was in high school, on the floor of Caesar's Atlantic City. In the late '80s, the casinos were notorious for not scrutinizing fake IDs. I walked up to a bar that had a bunch of digital poker screens and, not being able to think of anything else, ordered a Martini. I was pulling my money out while the bartender gave me a blank stare. Finally, he pointed to the poker screen and said, "Shithead, the drink is free, so long as you play $1 poker." I was introduced to buybacks, gambling, and hard liquor in one fell swoop.

—Dermot McCormack, bartender, Spring Lounge (Manhattan, NY)

NEW JERSEY SPIRIT
LAIRD'S APPLE BRANDY
Eatontown

In 1698, applejack was the first distilled spirit in what would become the United States, and we have William Laird to thank for keeping the tradition alive through today. Applejack is bottled at 80 proof and bonded is bottled at 100, and, crazy as it may sound, Laird's Bonded Apple was MISSING around the turn of this century. So let us first send an endless round of applause to New York's Audrey Saunders for being a hero to the bonded apple brandy legion of followers. She kept reaching out to the Laird's family (now run by William Laird's ninth-generation granddaughter, Lisa Laird Dunn) in hopes they would resuscitate their production of Laird's Apple Bonded brandy and they eventually succumbed to her pleas. As a result, we all get to celebrate. The future is female, indeed, and she's holding a Jack Rose cocktail (Laird's Applejack, grenadine, and citrus), or maybe we should rename it Jane Rose.

NEW JERSEY'S OLDEST BAR
BARNSBORO INN
Sewell, 1776

It's not every day a tavern declares itself open for business in the same year America claims its independence, but New Jersey is the lucky winner of this national treasure. Located inside a cedar log cabin, it was previously known as the Spread Eagle, the Crooked Billet Inn, and the Barnsboro Hotel before becoming the Barnsboro Inn, now known for great food (hey, Cajun calamari), good prices, and family—an important distinction, as current owner Tom Budd is a descendent of John Budd, who built the original log cabin where the Barnsboro resides.

NEW JERSEY BUCKET LIST BAR
DULLBOY
Jersey City

If you love cocktails and the written word, Dullboy is your archetypal destination. Vintage typewriters are mounted above their tables, along with meaningful quotes from books captured in frames, while another wall is plastered with different book covers: Tom Wolfe's *The Painted Word*, Philip Roth's *Goodbye, Columbus*, and William Faulkner's *The Sound and the Fury*, among others. The bar opened in 2015 and has a very nice variety of spirits, along with a classic cocktail menu and an original cocktail menu, all featuring names of literary women (the Reyna, the Eva, the Vanessa, and so on). The space captures the romanticism surrounding writing and drinking, inviting visitors to sit and talk about their favorite books all night long.

NEW JERSEY COCKTAIL BAR
THE ARCHER
Jersey City

I visited the Archer over the holidays, when they were featuring some terrific themed cocktails such as Miracle on Newark Avenue, Jingle All the Way (an Old Fashioned variation using peppermint tea–infused bourbon), and Triple Dog Dare, using New Jersey apple brandy and cinnamon spice. It's a big, lively space, and the Archer can build a crowd, which is a testament to their well-oiled cocktail program. The number of cocktails being made and the speed and efficiency at which the bartenders were producing said cocktails was a rewarding sight to behold, which is why I recommend sitting at the bar.

> **STATE FACT**
> Atlantic City is where the street names for the Monopoly board game originated.

For American distillers to watch, I love what comes out of St. George; Tuthilltown, for their incredible work in changing the craft whiskey landscape; and Ventura Spirits, for their innovative use of waste fruit from supermarkets.

—Aaron Polsky, bar consultant, Los Angeles (raised in New Jersey)

TUXEDO
Brian Bartels

The Tuxedo Club, a social club for recreation and sanctuary for wealthy New Yorkers (basically the Hamptons before the Hamptons became popular), opened in Jersey City on June 16, 1886. The original Tuxedo cocktail is without question a variation on the Martini, and would also be interesting should one feel compelled to switch fino sherry with manzanilla or, dare I be a nutty ne'er-do-well myself, some amontillado. Please note there is a Tuxedo #2 cocktail as well, which is made with gin, blanc vermouth, maraschino, and extra dashes of orange bitters, with an absinthe rinse.

2 ounces dry gin

1 ounce fino sherry

1 dash orange bitters

Stir the ingredients with ice for approximately 15 seconds; strain into a chilled cocktail glass and serve up.

JACK ROSE
Brian Bartels

The Jack Rose was allegedly created at Gene Sullivan's Café in Jersey City by bartender Frank J. May, aka Jack Rose, but opposing theories point to the Waldorf Astoria in New York, restaurateur Joseph Rose from Newark, or Harvey's in Washington, DC, and it even makes an appearance in Hemingway's *The Sun Also Rises*. Wherever it began, at least we can agree this cocktail is easy to make, easy to drink, and easy to order another.

2 ounces Laird's apple brandy

¾ ounce fresh lemon juice (or fresh lime juice, if you're feeling sprightly)

½ ounce grenadine (ideally homemade or something artisanal)

Garnish: lemon peel

Shake the ingredients with ice until chilled; strain into a chilled cocktail glass and serve up, garnished with the lemon.

BAR SNACK
One of the favorite drinks in colonial-era New Jersey taverns was "scotchem," a mixture of applejack, boiling water, and a dab of mustard, because when I think of delicious apple drinks, I think of mustard.

There are 72 "Rocky steps" in front of the Philadelphia Museum of Art, and there are approximately 446 bridges in Pittsburgh (aka "The City of Bridges"), and there is only one Punxsutawney Phil, just like there is only one Amy Kovalchick (page 64). If you're ever lucky enough to sit at her bar you'll know what I'm talking about.

Pennsylvania

PENNSYLVANIA IS GIGANTIC. Good golly! Anyone who says otherwise has not driven through it, from east to west, or vice versa. How did Taylor Swift get discovered in such a large state?

I can't predict the weather as well as Punxsutawney Phil, the celebrity groundhog of every February 2, Groundhog Day, whose prognostication has been a Pennsylvania and American tradition since the mid-1800s, but I can guarantee that there are wonderful bars, people, and things to do all throughout Pennsylvania, with or without a cheesesteak in one of your hands, and whether or not you decide to climb the *Rocky* steps at the Philadelphia Museum of Art.

The state has a rich history as far as booze is concerned. Between 1717 and 1776, a quarter million Scottish and Irish people traveled from the opposite side of the Atlantic, settling in places like Pennsylvania, where the land was bountiful, the government liberal, and the spirits made from rye as the de facto grain, instead of barley. In and around Pittsburgh in 1790, there were 570 verified distilleries making "Monongahela Rye," using water from the local Monongahela River and distilling with one of two different methods: "pure rye," which used an unadulterated mash of rye and barley malt, or "all rye," which was 100 percent rye. Americans were so thirsty for the Monongohela rye that the distilleries served the early versions white and unaged, as the demand quickly outgrew supply.

Western Pennsylvania played a big part in the development of Kentucky bourbon, as poor farmers refused to pay taxes suggested by Alexander Hamilton, the first secretary of the treasury, on their spirits to help fund our Revolutionary War debts—a controversy that flared up into the Whiskey Rebellion of the 1790s. Many farmers pulled up stakes and moved to Kentucky, a less taxed state.

Though rum was the most popular spirit in the United States in the late 1700s, it was largely brought in through our relationship with the British, which had turned sour after the Revolutionary War. So whiskey in general and bourbon in particular soon became our American spirit, and it was produced and consumed with local pride.

We owe Pennsylvania many thanks, not only for its early role in the American bourbon phenomenon, but also and especially for Fred Waring and the Pennsylvanians, a talented musical outfit from the 1930s. Waring wasn't satisfied to be just a bandleader, and sought the opportunity to showcase his Miracle Mixer (aka blender) at the National Restaurant Show in 1937 in Chicago, and that product, later renamed the Waring Mixer, forever changed

---

BAR SNACK

Ever had a Boilermaker? You have nineteenth-century Pennsylvania steelworkers to thank for that truly American drink combination. Steelwork itself was never a glamorous job, and that option of having a little dram of whiskey paired with a beer to burn off the harsh reality of a long, hard day's work became a social benchmark for the blue-collar heroes of yesteryear.

frozen drinks—Margaritas, Piña Coladas, and, yes, the frozé you are currently avoiding—as it became simple to take liquid and ice and blend them into a smooth, lip-numbing, brain-freezing phenomenon.

Yinz (what some people in Pittsburgh say to each other instead of "y'all" or "you all") are salt-of-the-earth people, and Pennsylvania deserves a lot of recognition for its cocktail history. Consult the book *Pittsburgh Drinks*, by Cody McDevitt and Sean Enright, for a terrific account of Pittsburgh's footprint in the world of cocktails and bartending. To quote Enright: "Pittsburgh has a close-knit community where sharing ideas and techniques are essential to growth. We discuss, debate, and argue, but also—always—we listen. This sort of respectful camaraderie makes drinks, bars, and cities better." Pittsburgh is a terrific example of a vibrant cocktail culture that is generating some exciting innovations, cultivated and inspired by the sage counsel of people like Sean Enright, and worthy cocktail destinations, such as Butcher and the Rye, Acacia, and Enright's Spork.

PENNSYLVANIA BUCKET LIST BAR
KELLY'S BAR & LOUNGE
Pittsburgh

In addition to sporting the best neon bar sign in Pittsburgh, Kelly's has an enormous food and cocktail menu. I picked up on the unofficial rules pretty fast: Be kind to the staff—don't get too lippy, and have your money ready, and don't look them in the eyes, and speak up, and don't move too fast, and if you don't like the Steelers there's something wrong with you. Get the mini mac and cheese and just try not to smile while eating every bite. Kelly's is the epitome of a neighborhood bar and lounge celebrating its own way of walking through the world, and what's more—it doesn't even have a website. Take that, Internet.

PENNSYLVANIA BEVERAGE
FRANK'S BLACK CHERRY WISHNIAK

Okay, first of all, what is a "wishniak" ("wish-NEE-ack")? A wishniak is a Russian cordial made with sugar, cherries, and vodka. As a childhood fanatic of anything with black cherry and soda, I salute this legacy—especially since Frank's was in danger of discontinuing in the 1990s. Frank's has been around Philadelphia since the 1950s, and is required sipping next to one of their infamous cheesesteaks (Gino's or Pat's, who ya got?). As the can says, "It's the best," and as the slogan goes, "Is it Frank's? Thanks!"

BAR SNACK
If one has never had (or heard of) Boilo, it is a warm holiday punch cocktail made by simmering ingredients such as raspberry ginger ale, honey, raisins, oranges, lemons, cinnamon, and cloves, and then adding whiskey (and possibly Everclear for good measure). It is often shared between friends and families outside Philadelphia, in Coal Country.

STATE FACT
The term speakeasy originated in Pennsylvania. Allegedly, Kate Hester, owner of an unlicensed bar in 1880s McKeesport, told her customers to "speak easy" about attending. The rest, as they say, is herstory.

PENNSYLVANIA COCKTAIL BAR
CHARLIE WAS A SINNER.
Philadelphia

Rye whiskey was once the jewel of the Monongahela region. It's making a comeback now, but will probably never reach the glory it held before the distillers were run out of Pennsylvania to avoid what they saw as unfair taxation.

—Sean Enright, co-author, *Pittsburgh Drinks*, owner of Spork (Pittsburgh)

No matter who you ask about Charlie, the response is always, "We don't talk about Charlie." I know. I found the unconventional bar name and lack of information about Charlie to be odd. No one knows the background of Charlie or if he or she still remains and what he or she did to be labeled a sinner, but the cocktails served at Charlie are mischievous enough to cause anyone to examine their own sins and those of everyone else in the room. This hip lounge could easily have been created by Dorothy Parker and Tim Burton, had they gone into business together—a high compliment to the room's cinematic, turn-of-the-century bordello vibe.

BAR SNACK

A Philadelphia Fish House Punch is the stuff of pre-Prohibition legend. Before cocktails became de rigueur, punches were the cocktails, and the Philadelphia Fish House became a noteworthy punch, created by a group of colonial Americans consisting of fishermen, politicians, and proud Philadelphia citizens seeking a proper sanctuary from all the pre-Revolution noise of the world. Author and cocktail historian David Wondrich argues that the Fish House cocktail "deserves to be protected by law, taught in the schools, and made a mandatory part of every Fourth of July celebration." The punch, which includes dark rum, Cognac, and peach brandy, was created by the State in Schuylkill ("skoo-kil") Fishing Company, a confusing-sounding social club founded in 1732. Its founding members would hang out at their wooden clubhouse headquarters (dubbed "the castle"), fish for perch, don white aprons, fry fish on outdoor grills, and drink rum punch. Take one down, pass it around. (The punch. Not the fish.) According to the legend, George Washington once enjoyed so much Fish House Punch he could not write in his journal for three days.

PENNSYLVANIA SPIRIT
JANNAMICO SUPER PUNCH
Abruzzo, Italy

Is it punch? Not really. Is it amaro? Well, no. Who is drinking it? Actually, lots of people in Pittsburgh. Should I bring it as a gift when meeting my girlfriend's parents for the first time? No. What makes it super? Jannamico gets labeled as a relative of Jägermeister, which I think is only partly accurate. The Italian American population of Pittsburgh has celebrated this syrupy-sweet cult beverage for decades, with Steel City claiming over 80 percent of its sales on an annual basis. Super Punch often gets categorized as an amaro, but it's actually sweeter than most amari, so it's a nice addition to coffee or ice cream, or something to secretly purchase for your friend's midnight birthday party as a gag: Jannamico is like wrestling an alligator-sized octopus, or in other words, it is an acquired taste.

PENNSYLVANIA'S OLDEST BAR
McGILLIN'S OLDE ALE HOUSE
Philadelphia, 1860

Opened in 1860, some years after the Liberty Bell cracked and just before Abraham Lincoln became our sixteenth president, McGillin's has hosted some notable luminaries during its tenure, such as Tennessee Williams, Ethel Merman, and Will Ferrell. I had a drink at McGillin's recently; it hosts a fair number of bachelorette parties, Corona flags, and some colorful locals, who are happy to speak to you about the Phillies' chances of making the playoffs, or to speak out loud in a way that makes it clear that your presence near them is irrelevant. As Ma Bartels is apt to say, some people are just looking for the right kind of language out loud.

There is a small hole-in-the-wall in the town of Blawnox. Bob's Garage. It's about ten minutes from where I grew up. The staff decorates the whole bar in amazing Christmas lights that stay up throughout the year. They change them up a bit for the different holidays. And…they have a jukebox and karaoke nights! Need I say more?!

—Amy Kovalchick (born in Pittsburgh),
bartender, Fedora (Manhattan, NY)

BAR SNACK

The taverns of yesteryear were all-too-often frequented and operated by males. Bars were infamous for banning women, not serving women, or not employing women. Pittsburgh banned female bartenders from 1941 to 1967. To me, those would have been boring years to be drinking in Pittsburgh. Today, thankfully, women are a driving force in cocktail culture in the city. LUPEC (Ladies United for the Preservation of Endangered Cocktails) was founded in Pittsburgh in 2001 to preserve classic cocktails that might otherwise be forgotten. These ladies celebrate the history of women's involvement in bartending and cocktails by showcasing their recipes on their respective menus and conducting regular meetings to contest the tyranny of patriarchy in the bar world. The future is female for a very good reason: We males have a lot to make up for, a lot to listen to, and a lot to remember.

CLOVER CLUB
Julie Reiner

My first cocktail was a whiskey sour. I was at a cousin's wedding. I can't remember which cousin, though. Maybe it was from all those sours. But I would say, outside of Mr. Rogers, Andy Warhol, and flaming Dr Pepper shots from college, a Jack Daniel's and Iron City Beer was my recollection of growing up around Pittsburgh.

—Amy Kovalchick (born in Pittsburgh), bartender, Fedora (Manhattan, NY)

Created in the late 1800s at the hallowed Clover Club inside the Bellevue-Stratford Hotel in Philadelphia, the Clover Club cocktail has been a modern-day workaholic on bar menus across the country. Superwoman Julie Reiner resuscitated the famous cocktail created in a men's club when opening her very own Clover Club, one of the best bars in New York.

1½ ounces Plymouth gin

½ ounce Dolin dry vermouth

½ ounce fresh lemon juice

½ ounce raspberry syrup (recipe follows)*

¼ ounce egg white

Garnish: fresh raspberries

Shake the ingredients with ice until chilled. Strain into a separate mixing glass, then dry shake (no ice) for a good 10 seconds. Pour the drink into a chilled cocktail glass and garnish with the raspberries.

*The cocktail can also be made by replacing the raspberry syrup with a ½ ounce rich simple syrup (2:1 sugar to water) and muddled or shaken hard with 3 or 4 fresh raspberries in the shaker.

Raspberry Syrup

Makes approximately 2½ cups

½ cup fresh raspberries

1 cup sugar

½ cup water

½ cup vodka

Smash the raspberries and mix them thoroughly with the sugar. Allow them to macerate for 30 minutes. Heat the water—but do not boil—and pour it over the fruit mixture, stirring until the sugar has dissolved. Strain the mixture through a chinois and add the vodka. Store in an airtight container in the refrigerator for up to 2 weeks.

WILLIE STARGELL
Brian Bartels

Pittsburgh Drinks, a terrific book on Pittsburgh drinking history by Cody McDevitt and Sean Enright, highlights how Whiskey Sours were very popular post-Prohibition—almost as popular as the beloved Pittsburgh Pirates baseball team. The 1970s Pittsburgh baseball legend Willie Stargell famously said, "When they start the game, they don't say 'Work ball!' They say, 'Play ball!'" I created this sour cocktail in honor of the late baseball season and the heart of autumn, when I'm craving cherries, maple syrup, and something ginger y but still refreshing. Drink up and play ball.

1½ ounces whiskey (if you have Wigle's Rivers and Mountains whiskey, huzzah, but any whiskey will do)

¾ ounce Cherry Heering

¾ ounce fresh lemon juice

1 ounce Fever-Tree ginger beer

Garnish: lemon slice

Combine the whiskey, Cherry Heering, and lemon juice and shake until chilled; strain over ice in a chilled rocks glass. Top with the ginger beer, lightly stir, and garnish with the lemon.

Dogfish Head opened in 1995 as the smallest craft brewery in America and developed into one of the most sought-after and talked about breweries at the turn of the century, before beginning to distill spirits in 2002. The ladybug is the official state bug of Delaware. This is where she lives. The house is unlisted because, well, duh. You'd probably go there and take a bunch of photos, psycho.

Delaware

We opened Comegys in Wilmington over thirty years ago. There wasn't really anything around this neighborhood, and it was just me and my two brothers. We never had any experience and had no idea what we were doing and had no understanding of how to run a bar. But we knew the community, and we could talk to people. And now, here we are, thirty years later, and that's my daughter, Candace, behind the bar, and she's happy. Things seem to be working out.

—Fred Comegys, owner, Comegys Pub (Wilmington)

WHEN I TOLD people I was going to Delaware, they had a pretty consistent response: "The only thing I know about Delaware is from that part in *Wayne's World* where they say, 'Hi . . . I am in . . . Delaware . . .'"

Turns out that Delaware is a fun and fascinating state—albeit small. It is forty-ninth in size, measuring 96 miles long and 9 to 35 miles wide.

Did you know Delaware was the first state to ratify the Constitution, in 1787? Additionally, the log cabin arrived in the 1600s with Finnish settlers who brought their craftsmanship to Delaware, hopefully enjoying the bounty of American holly trees. A group of second-graders petitioned to have the ladybug be the state insect in 1974, which was when Bob Marley—yes, reggae god Bob Marley—was living in Delaware. Nowadays, people flock to the coast for summer beach weather and Fisher's caramel popcorn, while celebrating the state's absence of a sales tax and the fact they have the highest-speed Internet service in the country. Who wouldn't drink to that?

The state isn't defined only by its wonderful Dogfish Head Brewery—which opened in 1995 as the smallest craft brewery in America and developed into one of the most sought-after and talked-about breweries at the turn of the century. Along the Atlantic Ocean shoreline, you'll find radioactive-looking Red Bull drinks and a host of beach-friendly summertime cocktails, colorful slushies, salty Margaritas, and spritzes. There are also plenty of great restaurants elevating their cocktail menus to match the delicious food, such as Wilmington's Domaine Hudson and Hockessin's House of William & Merry, and if you're passing through Smyrna on your way to the beach, "lively up yourself," as Bob Marley would say, to a Diamond State libation and a small-batch bottle at Painted Stave Distilling.

I went to Delaware because I celebrate the underdogs in life, and if most people were going to claim they did not have an idea of what made our second-smallest state famous or unique, I was going to find it and carry the torch over every late-night bar conversation I would have moving forward. I am happy to report there is a place called Comegys. It is a bucket list bar worth its weight in Orange Crushes (popular not only in Delaware but also widely celebrated on the beaches in Maryland) and wonderful people.

DELAWARE
BUCKET LIST BAR
COMEGYS PUB
Wilmington

Go to Comegys next. It's the best bar in town. Tell them Nora Wallace's kid sent ya!

—Erin Wallace, co-owner, The Copper Dram (Greenville) (I did in fact meet mom Nora, who was just as kind as everyone else in Comegys)

Comegys has iconic photography covering its barroom walls, all thanks to legendary local photographer and owner Fred Comegys, who started taking photos when he was seventeen and photographed such figures as Muhammad Ali, Joe Frazier, Prince, Bruce Springsteen, and many more. "Ali was one of the nicest human beings on the planet," Fred told me. Fred opened his bar with his two brothers more than thirty years ago.

I was lucky enough to be there on a Friday night in September, among familiar faces though I'd only just met them—it's a home away from home. Even though I have been there only once, I still remember every detail, which is why it's such a special place. If you don't believe me, just take a look at the pub's Instagram: endless pictures of friends with smiles on their faces, no place they would rather be.

DELAWARE'S OLDEST BAR
JESSOP'S TAVERN
New Castle, 1724

At Jessop's, one of the oldest taverns in America, the staff all wear colonial attire and patrons can look forward to a lively evening, especially if you're seated next to a group of pesky ghosts trying to bum some of your beer. Jessop's focuses on Belgian beer with Dutch-, English-, and Swedish-influenced cuisine. Make sure you try the fish and chips and, as always, save room for the bread pudding.

DELAWARE
COCKTAIL BAR
THE COPPER DRAM
Greenville

Entering this bar made me feel like I had just walked into a cozy little cabin in the Adirondacks, surrounded by fellow travelers all looking for some solace after a demanding day. UB40's "Red Red Wine" was playing. There are paintings of women on the walls evoking the Victorian era, but my favorite part of this bar's aesthetic might be the pennies. Pennies cover the bar face, the back bar, and the bathroom tiles. Copper Dram's cocktails are creative and feature a wide variety of house-made tinctures and syrups. Try Conner the Barbarian. It's named after Conner, the young son of owners Erin and Tom, a spirit-forward concoction wielding Famous Grouse Scotch, Drambuie, gunpowder-green oleo-saccharum, and black ash ice.

DELAWARE SPIRIT
DOGFISH HEAD DISTILLING CO.
Milton

I know, right? I, too, thought Dogfish Head made only beer! Well, it just so happens they also make spirits, and not only spirits but lots of different kinds of spirits. Flavors from every corner of the world. Roasted Peanut vodka, Barrel Honey rum, and Sonic Archeology—a Prohibition-era bottled cocktail combining Dogfish Head whiskey, rum, and apple brandy with honey, lemon, and pomegranate juices. The spirits are unfortunately limited to select states on the Eastern seaboard, but who knows what the future holds.

STATE FACT
Thomas Jefferson nicknamed Delaware the "Diamond State" because he felt it was a little jewel in the midst of a sprawling eastern seaboard.

DU PONT
Brian Bartels

Located in downtown Wilmington, the Hotel Du Pont has always been associated with sophistication, and its cocktails are no exception. This recipe was originally published in Ted Saucier's *Bottoms Up*, but the original specs have been updated to reflect a little more woo-woo, and by "woo-woo" I mean flavor. Though I enjoyed the original Du Pont recipe, I feel this modern take elevates the complexity. Bertoux (a California brandy from Jeff Bell, bar director at New York's PDT) is a great spirit to take a drink to a more seductive level.

1½ ounces American brandy (preferably Bertoux or Copper & Kings)

1½ ounces manzanilla (or amontillado) sherry

2 dashes Angostura bitters

Garnish: orange twist

Stir the ingredients with ice until chilled; strain into a chilled cocktail glass and serve up, garnished with the orange.

ANALOG COCONUT COOLER
Dogfish Head Distilling Co., Milton

Dogfish Head opened in 1995, but they did not start distilling spirits until 2002, and though they are available only in a limited number of northeastern states, I hope Dogfish Head keeps spreading the goodness across the country (and yes, that is sort of a pun, but sort of not, on Dogfish Head Peanut Butter vodka). I am a fan of coconut water in cocktails, but it's not as easy to mix with other ingredients as one might think—and this drink uses it to perfection. The Analog is a fairly simple drink to build, so you can get right back to your Frisbee toss on that sunny Rehoboth Beach, with your Bluetooth playing "Summertime" by DJ Jazzy Jeff & the Fresh Prince.

2 ounces Analog vodka (or another American vodka, such as Tito's)

2 ounces coconut water

1 ounce fresh lime juice

½ ounce simple syrup (1:1 sugar to water)

¼ cup whole fresh cilantro leaves

Garnish: fresh cilantro sprigs or coconut shavings

Combine the ingredients and shake with ice; strain and pour over fresh ice in a chilled highball glass. Sprinkle the glass with a garnish of cilantro or coconut.

Maryland

Patron of Seven Stars Tavern in Maryland, Edgar Allan Poe will forever be remembered as one of America's most innovative authors, responsible for numerous essays, book reviews, a novel, short stories, a book of scientific theory, and poems, most notably his famous "The Raven," which was originally supposed to be about a parrot who apparently (aparrotly?) loved Chartreuse.

BEFORE I VISITED Maryland I was told people do only shots of pretzel-infused spirits and Pinnacle Whipped vodka while vacationing on the state's endless beaches. These seem like unusual beverages to consume not only in hundred-degree weather but in general, anywhere in the world, unless one loses a bet. I am happy to report that this is not the case, unless one is vacationing on the eastern end of oddly shaped Maryland, most likely in Ocean City, a tiny little town with a clean white-sand beach that, with amusement parks, carnivals, and arcades stretching over two miles of boardwalk, gets plenty of summer traffic.

Baltimore, aka Charm City, has its fair share of American history and notable figures: Edgar Allan Poe frequented the Seven Stars Tavern on Water Street; Francis Scott Key wrote "The Star-Spangled Banner" in 1814 at the Fountain Inn, setting his meters to the tune of an old drinking song; and Billie Holiday grew up playing hooky on the streets of Fells Point before becoming the greatest jazz singer in the world. Today, Charm City wields a galaxy of wonderful cocktail destinations, and one would be happy to visit some of their marvelous halls. Step inside sophistication at the venerable Rye, get schooled at the Bookmakers Cocktail Club, or climb some steps to cocktail heaven at Bluebird Cocktail Room in Hampden, a lively neighborhood with great restaurant options.

And if you're wondering, no, I have still not seen *The Wire*, but yes, it does sound like the most amazing television show ever!

MARYLAND SPIRIT
CHARTREUSE
Grenoble, France

There's only one Chartreuse in the world, which is comforting, as there is really only one bar where people know crab cakes, football, and Chartreuse better than anywhere else in the United States, and it's in Baltimore, and it's called the Idle Hour. The owners are Brendan Finnerty and Randall Etheridge, and they run a pretty nifty corner neighborhood bar with nightly vinyl sessions, cold bottles of National Bohemian lager (aka "Natty Boh," a Maryland staple), and shot glasses festooning the bar filled with a greenish liquid, making one think we are not in Kansas anymore. There are more than 130 herbs and plants involved in making the hypnotic-looking green version of Chartreuse, wielding flavors of mint, basil, and hyssop; the green Chartreuse is less sweet than the yellow, and balances a Boilermaker out a little better. Idle Hour goes through enough of it that they might rename Baltimore "Chartreuse City."

MARYLAND BUCKET LIST BAR
MOUNT ROYAL TAVERN
Baltimore

Inside this legendary bar, there will be regulars, semi-regulars, guys sipping cheap tap beer and singing "Wild Horses" out loud and wearing sunglasses at night, art students from the Maryland Institute College of Art, painters, roughnecks, fire-dancers, writers, and people not necessarily looking to fight, but certainly happy to "exercise their confrontation skills." The space is the Vatican City of dive bars, only the pope is a female bartender wearing a tank top, her arms are covered in tats, and she is ranting about all the fights that broke out at the bar the night before. There is even a Rubenesque Baroque-era painting of four females with bare backsides and arms locked in solidarity. But if you don't look up, you'll miss the real spectacle, which is a painted replica of the Sistine Chapel ceiling—one reason why the bar earned the nickname "the Dirt Church." Take a brief moment and survey the roomful of characters, which can make you feel like you've just walked into a scene in a Tarantino film, and that suddenly your life might be in a little bit of danger. It's just lawless enough to keep you honest. Or is it?

BAR SNACK
The Hungerford Tavern, in Rockville, Maryland, was regarded as one of America's first true taverns. George Washington, Benjamin Franklin, and Thomas Jefferson met there to discuss strategies to defeat the British during Revolutionary times. In 1774, the call to freedom was heard from the Hungerford Tavern, and legend has it that Washington spent a night at the Hungerford around this time, and the tavern owner, a staunch loyalist, attempted to assassinate him.

STATE FACT
The Old Line State gave up some of its land to form Washington, DC. My older brothers used to break off candy bars and always gave me the bigger half, so I appreciate your mercy, Maryland.

BAR SNACK
The inventor William Painter was born in Ireland, but spent a good amount of time in America creating patents, founding Crown Holdings in Baltimore in the late 1800s. He claimed eighty-five patent inventions, but his most famous would have to be one of the most essential bartools: the bottle opener.

MARYLAND COCKTAIL BAR
RYE
Baltimore

My introduction to rye whiskey and Manhattans was Pikesville rye at the Belvedere Hotel with my grandmother. I was seventeen years old. Maryland was a haven for rye whiskey when it was dwindling in nearly every other part of the country. In that part of the country, you could go to any liquor store, or any package store, and find Pikesville rye. And I would ask, "Why is Pikesville on the label, Dad?" And he would say, "Your grandfather drank that, your great-uncle drank that, your great-grandfather drank Pikesville rye." That was tradition.

—Allen Katz (born and raised in Baltimore), owner and head distiller, New York Distilling Company (Brooklyn, NY)

Recognized as one of *Esquire*'s Best Bars in America after opening in 2011, Rye incorporates a healthy dose of amaro in their cocktail menu, but what ultimately captured my heart was the well-named Until Mars Was an Afternoon Forest, a Calvados-based drink with grapefruit, walnut orgeat, D'Aristi xtabentun ("eesh-teh-bentoon," an anise liqueur from Mexico flavored with honey), and fennel. The name references a passage from Ray Bradbury's *The Martian Chronicles*, documenting a young man's desire to see Mars grow into a fully habitable planet, with trees and air and "a whole sky universe to climb and hang from; an architecture of food and pleasure, that was a tree." Rye is in the Fells Point neighborhood, which can be quite a lively area on weekend evenings; it's not so much an afternoon forest, but certainly may give the impression that there are some Martians walking about.

MARYLAND BEVERAGE
DARK RUM
Privateer True American Amber or Queen's Share, Gosling's, or Diplomatico Riserva Exclusiva

The Chesapeake Bay is a haven for rum drinkers. Ask any grizzled regular at the Boatyard Bar & Grill in historic Annapolis, and if they feel like talking, they'll tell you the same. Most Chesapeakers like to drink rum, and not just rum, but dark, molasses-y rum; the kind where you don't know if you should take another sip, or pour it over ice cream, or put it in your car to get you to the next gas station, you old sailor, you.

MARYLAND'S OLDEST BAR
REYNOLDS TAVERN
Annapolis, 1747

William Reynolds opened his "ordinary" (an old word for tavern) in 1747, and it continued to be a Reynolds family operation into the 1800s. It served diners and drinkers, took messages for people, sold theater tickets and hats, and rented rooms, stabled horses, and provided friendly yet competitive games of chess and backgammon until 1935, when a group of far-sighted Annapolitans proposed that trust fund residuals from the Female Orphan Society be used to purchase and convert the structure into the Annapolis Public Library. Luckily for us, though, the power of the written word prevailed, and the library eventually outgrew the building. In 1984, the space was restored and became the Reynolds Tavern once again, named after the original owners and boasting a bar, a restaurant, a three-room hotel, and a basement bar where the hat shop used to be. Summers are ideal for their beer garden, which features weekly Shakespeare performances next to an old magnolia tree. What a legacy.

MARYLAND BEVERAGE
BLACK-EYED SUSAN

The Black-Eyed Susan is the official drink of the famous Preakness Stakes horse race in Baltimore. The first published recipe came out in 1985, featuring vodka, rum, and triple sec, and mixed with orange and pineapple juices, and though we have found multiple variations since the original debuted, I applaud author David Solmonson's approach, which is to eliminate vodka, as it's essentially flavorless, and celebrate something Maryland was known for back in the early days of distilling, such as rye, or a dash or two or bitters.

ORANGE CRUSH
Brian Bartels

Invented in 1995 at the Harborside Bar & Grill in Ocean City, the non-orange soda alcohol version of Orange Crush has been picked up and reproduced by many an Eastern Seaboard shanty and shebeen, as it feels like an automatic latter-day replacement for a Mimosa, but with a little more kick, and served in a chilled pint glass instead of a flute. Here's to Maryland, ambassadors of all things vitamin C.

2 ounces vodka

1 ounce triple sec

2 ounces fresh orange juice
(1 orange will yield 3 to 4
ounces juice)

2 ounces lemon-lime soda

Garnish: orange wedge

Stir the ingredients with ice in a chilled pint glass. Garnish with the orange.

TIKA TIKA
Ryan Sparks, Regal Beagle, Baltimore

The Regal Beagle was the name of the neighborhood watering hole in the once-popular 1980s sitcom *Three's Company*. These days, the Beagle serves much better cocktails than the ones served on TV in the 1980s. This tiki-inspired cocktail is not only refreshing, it features some unique ingredients—curry and yuzu, a sour Japanese citrus, and Two James whiskey out of Detroit, Michigan, Ryan's home state. If you don't have access to Two James whiskey, which has smoky tea notes, try Corsair Triple Smoke single malt from Kentucky, High West Campfire out of Utah, or Westland peated single malt out of Washington.

1 ounce Two James Johnny
Smoking Gun whiskey (or
sub Maryland's Lyon Rye)

1 ounce Avuá Amburana
cachaça

1 ounce coconut milk

1 ounce yellow curry syrup
(recipe follows)

½ ounce fresh yuzu juice

Garnish: pineapple slice and
Thai basil sprig (optional)

Shake the ingredients with ice until chilled. Dirty dump ("dirty" means to pour the shaken ice into the finished glass instead of using fresh ice in the glass) into a chilled tiki mug or highball glass and garnish with the pineapple and basil, if desired.

Yellow Curry Syrup

Makes 1 pint

1 pint simple syrup (1:1 sugar
to water)

2 tablespoons curry powder

Combine the ingredients in a medium saucepan and bring to a simmer (do not boil), then remove from the heat and let cool. Transfer to a clean container, cover, and store in the refrigerator for up to 2 weeks.

The bald eagle was chosen as an emblem of the United States on June 20, 1782. The eagle is a symbol of freedom, and has endured a legacy through its depiction on currency, documents, flags, public buildings, and varying government-related correspondence. One sees "E Pluribus Unum" attached to many references surrounding the United States, which is our country's motto. It translates to "Out of many, one," which means the United States was one nation, made out of many colonies, and united as one. Speaking of one, I believe this particular eagle may have had more than one Gin Rickey.

Washington, DC

My favorite unique drinking tradition is the shots bartenders use as a handshake. These are the drinks that no one pays for and are sent out as a courtesy, one bartender to another. When I started it was Irish Mist, then Gran Ma (Grand Marnier), then Jameson, then Old Overholt, and now it's amaros.

—Derek Brown, president, Drink Company, owner, Columbia Room (Washington, DC), co-author, *Spirits, Sugar, Water, Bitters: How the Cocktail Conquered the World*

THOUGH NOT TECHNICALLY a state (and only sixty-eight square miles!), the District of Columbia is the capital of the United States, and given its cocktail growth over the past few years (and the fact that the Daiquiri—though created in Cuba in 1896—debuted in DC's Army and Navy Club circa 1909), it deserves some praise. For example, bar owner Derek Brown has been busy keeping the District of Cocktails' citizens inspired by quality beverages and exemplary service—which is all in the family, as his great-grandfather was DC's police chief. Columbia Room, Brown's seminal DC cocktail bar, which opened in 2010, is a must-visit for cocktail fans, offering a menu of originals, with Old Fashioned variations, vintage spirits (not many other bars are serving Napoleon Cognac from 1811), Highballs, and no-proof cocktails.

DC has written a new Declaration of Cocktails in the past few years, with places like 2 Birds 1 Stone, offering weekly revised cocktail menus with new illustrations; 12 Stories Bar (try the "super-chilled" Grey Goose Martini); José Andrés's Barmini restaurant and bar, with each cocktail served in a different style of glass, making each presentation unique; and Hank's Cocktail Bar, housed in a former church, featuring cocktails with repurposed ingredients to cut down on waste and, as a result, brand-new "Hallelujahs!".

In addition to DC's cocktail scene, there is plenty to appreciate. The Lincoln Memorial is a wonderful place to stand and take in a very important part of our nation's history, overlooking the Reflecting Pool and Washington Monument in the distance. Knowing that Martin Luther King, Jr., delivered his "I have a dream" speech on the steps of the Lincoln Memorial in 1963 makes me a proud and humble American. I encourage you, dear traveler, to go visit the free museums, the sprawling, lush parks, the cobblestoned streets of Georgetown, the unforgettably named Foggy Bottom neighborhood, Embassy Row, and the cherry trees that blossom in springtime, and then celebrate your efforts with a sip or three of a Gin Rickey.

The Gin Rickey started as bourbon-based "Joe" Rickey, but gin was in full swing in the late nineteenth century, especially at Shoemaker's Saloon (aka the "third room of Congress") on Pennsylvania Avenue, where the drink was created by request for the lobbyist Colonel Joe Rickey. It's a simple mixer, as this formula can work wonders with any base spirit, and my belief is that one should always lean on the citrus over the sugar. Don't let your bartender skimp on the lime juice by adding only a couple of weak drops of lime into the drink. And don't forget to vote.

Dan's Cafe has been around DC for as long as I can remember and is the epitome of a dive bar. When you order a Highball (that's all you should order here, by the way), they give you a glass, a bucket of ice, a bottle of your mixer, and pour a pint bottle of your choice into a squeeze bottle and give it to you. You're pretty well set for three or four rounds. I've always said it's safe to start drinking here, but never to finish.

—Brian Nixon, owner and bartender, Truxton Inn and McClellan's Retreat (Washington, DC)

WASHINGTON, DC, SPIRIT
DON CICCIO & FIGLI
Ivy City

Don Ciccio opened a distillery in 2012, but the spirit-making family has been producing for generations. Their portfolio, exceeding twenty different liqueurs, is everywhere in DC cocktail bars and restaurants with elevated bar programs, and has gradually started spreading throughout the United States. If you ever see the Amaro delle Sirene on a menu, give it a try to experience the thyme, eucalyptus, and licorice notes that complement the bittersweet profile. And visit the Bar Sirenis, inside the expanded distillery, featuring art deco design from the influential Italian architect Gio Ponti, with a choose-your-own-adventure spirit-to-cocktail menu.

WASHINGTON, DC, OLDEST BAR
THE ROUND ROBIN BAR
1847

The actual bar at the Round Robin is, in fact, round, and located in the historic Willard Hotel (now the Willard InterContinental). The legendary bartender Jim Hewes has seen more than five presidents and one reality television goon take office, and hosts educational happy hours involving spirited discussions surrounding the history of the Willard Hotel or about US intelligence and espionage in the twentieth century, and one called "Holidays at the White House: A Season of Stories." In 1904, as the hatchet-toting prohibitionist Carrie Nation raged against drink, a sign in the Round Robin went up: "All Nations Welcome—Except Carrie."

WASHINGTON, DC, BUCKET LIST BAR
OLD EBBITT GRILL

Talk to anyone who has lived in or visited DC, and they have been to or heard of the Old Ebbitt Grill. Though it is not factually the oldest bar in DC, it is always the most referenced. The place—open for breakfast, lunch, dinner, and Martinis—is always busy. Its raw bar and oyster game is one of the most well known in DC, and is a nice accompaniment to drinks while sitting at the beautiful mahogany bar, just spitting distance from the White House.

WASHINGTON, DC, COCKTAIL BAR
A RAKE'S BAR

A Rake's Bar is a run, don't walk experience when it comes to design, innovation, and staff education. They use seasonal, hyperlocal ingredients and spirits, meaning they are regional. There is no tequila, Scotch, pisco, or Cognac. They serve only what is local, and what is not being wasted. The bar staff—knowledgeable and passionate while behind the stick—are some of the most informed I have come across. Not many other places do this and accomplish it with such panache. It's worth the visit to experience the creative sustainability, which is a practice more bars should be applying.

The cocktail is delicious. It is something we should love too—after all, we invented it.

—Derek Brown, president, Drink Company, owner, Columbia Room (Washington, DC), co-author, *Spirits, Sugar, Water, Bitters: How the Cocktail Conquered the World*

THE BELMONT

Brian Nixon, McClellan's and Truxton Inn, Washington, DC

This popular cocktail has been around for a couple of years, featured on the "Tried-and-True" menu at McClellan's, a popular bar in Dupont Circle, just north of downtown and the White House. The Belmont was created when Brian Nixon hosted a party and someone bartender challenged him to make a drink that "tastes like autumn." This drink accomplishes just that, with some nice chocolate spice and orange oil for a first-place finish.

¾ ounce Rittenhouse rye

¾ ounce Boomsma Claerkampster Cloosterbitter (or green Chartreuse, if that's closer to ya)

¾ ounce Angostura amaro

2 dashes Fee Brothers Aztec chocolate bitters

Garnish: orange peel

Stir the ingredients with ice for 10 to 15 seconds until chilled; strain over fresh ice in a chilled Old Fashioned glass. Express the orange peel over the drink and run it around the rim of the glass. Rest the peel on the edge of the glass.

THE GETAWAY

Derek Brown

The first person anyone thinks of when it comes to DC's cocktail movement is Derek Brown. His most celebrated bar is Columbia Room, which seems to win an award every year for its outstanding cocktail program. He was named *Imbibe*'s Bartender of the Year in 2015, the same year he was appointed chief spirits adviser to the National Archives Foundation, and serves on the board of the Museum of the American Cocktail. Brown's first book, *Spirits, Sugar, Water, Bitters: How the Cocktail Conquered the World*, documenting the history of notable people responsible for shaping the world of cocktails as we know them today, was published in 2019, and is a welcoming guide to the history of our cocktail world at large.

1 ounce Blackstrap rum

½ ounce Cynar amaro

1 ounce fresh lemon juice

½ ounce simple syrup (1:1 sugar to water)

Shake the ingredients with ice until chilled; strain into a chilled cocktail glass and serve up.

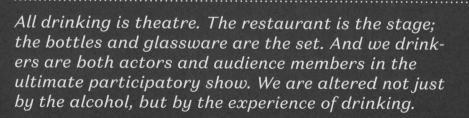

All drinking is theatre. The restaurant is the stage; the bottles and glassware are the set. And we drinkers are both actors and audience members in the ultimate participatory show. We are altered not just by the alcohol, but by the experience of drinking.

—Anne Zimmerman, in *PUNCH*

The
South

Virginia *West Virginia*
Kentucky *Tennessee*
North Carolina South Carolina
Georgia *Florida*
Alabama **Mississippi**
Arkansas *Louisiana*
Oklahoma *Texas*

The famous bronze King Neptune statue in Virginia Beach was created in 2005 and named after the mythological god Neptune, the Roman god of the sea, who has long defended well-balanced cocktails with fresh ingredients. And though the "Virginia is for Lovers" sign was created over fifty years ago, we decided to give it a little cocktail moxie to make the Atlantic Ocean happy.

Virginia

KNOWN AS "THE birthplace of the nation," Virginia was never one to settle. Yes, the first peanut plantation in America started here. As a lifelong fan of peanut butter, let's get that established. But so did Thanksgiving in 1619 and the first female-run bank in 1906. Virginia is the home of the annual Chincoteague pony swim, and is famous for the Chesapeake Bay Bridge, an engineering masterpiece and the world's largest bridge-tunnel complex.

Early legislation made it difficult for there to be more than two taverns per county in Virginia, which meant that in 1677 you could live like a queen or king if you served alcohol. Even today, bars need to maintain a certain percentage of food sales in order to operate, which—good news—means snacks are always available.

In recent years, while Richmond has gotten national attention for its emerging food and drink scene (Saison, Grandstaff & Stein, and Heritage may satisfy your early evening cravings, and don't pass up the chance to visit the Jasper, Cobra Cabana, or GWARbar—a local metal bar created by the band GWAR, offering nachos all day and night), there are gems to be found around the state. Alexandria's Captain Gregory's, a hidden speakeasy inside Sugar Shack Donuts, provides wildly creative cocktails with small bites and hand-rolled donuts. The cocktail menu sees a monthly rotation of house concoctions, homemade vermouth, bitters, and fernet, in addition to Tiki Thursdays and Experimental Sundays, when bartenders test out new recipes for anyone attending the bar. B Side in Fairfax features drinks named after B sides on albums (well played on the Guess Who's "No Sugar Tonight") and plays records through the night. Virginia Beach's Repeal Bourbon & Burger not only celebrates its name with a wide variety of delectable burgers and spirits, it offers a terrific choose-your-own-adventure menu layout for Old Fashioneds and Manhattans, giving you the option to select varying whiskeys, vermouth, bitters, and garnishes to make the magic.

Charlottesville, home to the University of Virginia, has a healthy number of cocktail dens for a smaller city. Micah LeMon, author of *The Imbible*, is also the bar manager of Alley Light, a terrific restaurant in the Downtown Mall area specializing in French cuisine and a fine selection of creative cocktails overseen by LeMon and his bar team; the McClure brothers opened Lost Saint, a Prohibition-style speakeasy, which fits only thirty people at a time, with an extensive cocktail list; and the Fitzroy, on Main Street, does a bang-up job of modernizing classic recipes while providing house-made tonic and the ever-popular Fitz Spritz, made with Aperol, grapefruit juice, Cocchi Americano, and sparkling brut.

"Virginia is for Lovers," a phrase now commonly associated with the state, was created in 1969 as a travel advertisement to run in *Modern Bride* by the Virginia State Travel Service. It was the 1960s, baby. Free love! Beach love. Mountain love. All kinds. Like America, it was right there, waiting for you to reach out and grab it.

The Bamboo Cafe is a Richmond classic. The staff never really changes, the prices rarely ever have, and they make a killer Irish coffee that no one seems to know about. Some people think "dive bar" has a negative connotation and would argue that Bamboo doesn't deserve to be called such names, but in my mind a dive bar attitude can exist in a place that feels homey and warm, that also might just happen to serve the best chicken wings in town.

—Brandon Peck, beverage director, the Jasper (Richmond)

VIRGINIA SPIRIT
A. SMITH BOWMAN DISTILLERY WHISKEY
Fredericksburg

American whiskey originated on the James River in 1620, so it should come as no surprise that people settled in parts of Virginia in hopes of growing families and starting new traditions to carry on the family's legacies. A. Smith Bowman purchased farmland in 1927 and opened its distillery in 1935, after Prohibition. Between 1934 and into the 1950s, Bowman was the only legal whiskey distillery in the Commonwealth of Virginia. In 1988 the distillery moved from its original location to its current spot in Fredericksburg, where it continues to produce award-winning bourbons, limited-edition whiskeys, vodka, gin, rum, and a must-try experimental series, such as espresso bourbon and rye-based gin.

VIRGINIA'S OLDEST BAR
THE TAVERN
Abingdon, 1779

Yep. It's just called "the Tavern." Over the years it's been a bank, a bakery, a general store, a cabinet shop, a barber shop, a private house, a post office (first one on the western side of the Blue Ridge Mountains, thank you very much), an antique shop, and even a hospital for wounded Civil War soldiers. But now, it's just a tavern—and not just any tavern, it's *the* Tavern, as owner Max Hermann says, and it belongs to you.

VIRGINIA BUCKET LIST BAR
COBRA CABANA
Richmond

I was lucky enough to visit the Cobra when it was a wee little youth in the Richmond bar and nightlife scene, having opened in late 2018. Upon entering, a small Santa Claus statue wearing sunglasses and a Megadeth T-shirt waved to me from the window, one TV was screening *Better off Dead* and the other was showing *Big Top Pee-Wee*, and the bar counter had over thirteen thousand pennies strategically placed to resemble snakeskin. The Cobra's "Snake Juice" menu is a playful cocktail mix of Bloody Marys, Piña Coladas, and Margaritas, all constructed with precise care and effortless heavy metal charm, but if you really wanna rip the sleeves off of that T-shirt holding you back from stage diving, go for an "antivenom" shooter.

VIRGINIA COCKTAIL BAR
THE JASPER
Richmond

The Jasper has been producing thought-provoking cocktails since opening its doors in January 2018. Beyond paying homage to the regional influences of yesteryear, such as the house Quoit Club Punch, they razzle-dazzle with modern bar sorcery by serving Zombies—a legendary rum and fruit-based tiki cocktail—on draft. "Full pours, honest prices," is the Jasper's motto. I would add "Inventive cocktails, Italian sub sandwiches, and great people" to that as well.

STATE FACT
About 60 percent of all Internet traffic flows through the northern part of Virginia. Think about it: all those GIFs you've been sending over the years, somehow living in miles of wires throughout Loudoun County (which actually sounds like a cocktail name . . .).

BAR SNACK
In Virginia, you are allowed to be twenty-one years old the day before your twenty-first birthday. Heads up to my nephew Joe Bartels.

Sadly, this spot was torn down, but Fatty B's in Fredericksburg was one of my favorite bars ever. It was basically a glorified shack with a rickety porch attached. There was a purple Lincoln limousine parked out front with a fat cigar painted on the side. You sat on the porch, drinking Coors Light by the bucket, sipping Margaritas from a jug, and trying not to breathe too deeply for fear of falling into the murky Rappahannock River.

—Emily Morton, bar director, Deli/126 (Burlington, VT)

QUOIT CLUB PUNCH
The Jasper, Richmond

Just outside of Charlottesville, Virginia, down a windy road and up a gravel driveway, sits the distillery that produces all of the brandy for Laird's apple brandy, all of it made from Virginia apples. The facility is one of the most rustic buildings I have ever seen, and the juice that flows from the still in North Garden recalls a time when our country was young. It's so cool to be able to drink something that has been made since the 1700s.

—Brandon Peck, beverage director, the Jasper (Richmond)

The Jasper is a modern-day homage to the great city of Richmond, the people who have lived there, and freedom and equality for everyone: The laid-back, cocktail-focused, fun-loving Carytown bar was aptly named after legendary local barman Jasper Crouch, and the bar occasionally serves up one his most famous creations. Buchanan Springs Quoit Club was a place in Richmond where one gathered to throw quoits (basically iron donuts—funny the name and game didn't stick) around posts, have some barbecue with cayenne, and sip on a cocktail created by Crouch, a freed slave who used lemons, sugar, Cognac, Jamaican rum, and Madeira—a fortified, sweet, acidic wine from an island in Portugal (named Madeira) offering flavors of stewed fruit, caramel, and roasted nuts. This recipe is based on David Wondrich's assessment of the original recipe. To make this punch, you must first prepare the oleo-saccharum, made by coating lemon peels in sugar and allowing them to sit for at least four hours, which draws the oils from the peels.

Serves about 18 (6 ounces per serving)

One 750 ml bottle Appleton Estate Signature rum

One 750 ml bottle rainwater Madeira wine

One 750 ml bottle brandy (Jasper uses Korbel)

2 cups oleo-saccharum (recipe follows)

2 cups fresh lemon juice (should be roughly the amount of juice that will come from the lemons you peel for the oleo-saccharum, but you may need to juice more)

Garnish: lemon wheels

Pour the liquors and lemon juice into the oleo container to get all the sugar into the punch. Stir until the sugar is incorporated, then strain out the lemon peels and discard them. Refrigerate the punch for up to 3 days or serve immediately. To serve, pour the punch into a large punch bowl. Add a large chunk of ice to chill the punch, and continue to add smaller ice chunks to achieve your desired dilution. Ladle into chilled glasses and garnish the glasses with the lemons.

Oleo-Saccharum

Makes 2 cups

Peels of 12 lemons   2 cups sugar

In a quart container, combine the lemon peels and sugar, layering the peels and sugar so that the peels are evenly dispersed in the sugar. Lightly press the top of the sugar once the container is full, to help start the process of leaching the oils from the peels. Leave the oleo *unrefrigerated* for at least 4 hours, but preferably overnight for maximum oil extraction.

LITTLE SECRETS
Sophia Kim, Saison, Richmond

*In Warrenton,
Virginia, for
sixteen years
our mayor was
a man by the
name of George
B. Fitch, the man
who co-founded
the Jamaican
Bobsled Team.
That's right, our
mayor was the
man played by
John Candy in
Cool Runnings.
How awesome
is that? I spent
most of my
early twenties
frequenting
Richmond's
Ipanema Cafe
and being hired
there felt like a
dream come true.
It was there that
I developed a love
for spirits and
learned how to
bartend, and peo-
ple like Saison's
Chris Elford (now
in Seattle at No
Anchor and Navy
Strength) and
Anna Wingfield
at New York's
Mother's Ruin
helped inspire me
to be a better
bartender.*

—Brandon Peck,
beverage director,
the Jasper
(Richmond)

Saison is located on a corner space in the historic Jackson Ward neighborhood, known for its African American heritage and the iconic Jefferson Hotel (famous for at one time having alligators in its lobby pool, naturally). The bar specializes in a wide variety of house-made seasonal cocktails and small plates, such as roasted Virginia peanuts. The cozy little bar can get lively on any given night, as many bar and restaurant industry colleagues enjoy spending time here when they're not working, and especially when Sophia Kim is mixing drinks. "She rules," said my Richmond tour guide. And she does. And so does this drink, which she served me the night I visited, and is the drink my tour guide orders every time he visits Saison and Sophia is bartending. Doesn't "toasted coconut fat-washed Plantation 3 Stars rum" sound awesome? It could be the opening band for a Tame Impala concert, or the title of the next Flaming Lips album. I wanna hear it in my mouth!

1 ounce Averna amaro

1 ounce El Dorado 5-Year rum

1 ounce toasted coconut fat–washed Plantation 3 Stars rum (recipe follows)

Stir the ingredients with ice in a mixing glass until chilled; strain into a chilled cocktail glass and serve neat or over fresh ice in an old fashioned glass.

Toasted Coconut Fat–Washed Plantation 3 Stars Rum

Makes about 30 ounces

½ cup unsweetened shredded coconut

½ cup unrefined coconut oil

One 750 ml bottle Plantation 3 Stars rum

Toast the coconut flakes until golden brown. Combine the coconut, coconut oil, and rum in a nonreactive container. Let sit at room temperature overnight, then freeze for 4 hours. Strain while ice cold through cheesecloth and discard the solids. Store in a bottle or the nonreactive container for up to 6 months. It does not need to be refrigerated.

BAR SNACK

Fat-washing became a more familiar craft cocktail technique after Don Lee created the Benton's Old Fashioned at PDT in 2007 New York, for which he added 1 ounce bacon fat to 1 bottle of bourbon, let it sit at room temperature for 4 hours, placed it in the freezer for 12 hours, then separated the solid fat and rebottled the liquid bourbon. Lee credits New York bar pioneer Eben Freeman for the inspiration, as Freeman was fat-washing brown butter and rum at Chef Wylie Dufresne's acclaimed restaurant WD-50, after being inspired by pastry chef Sam Mason's recipe-testing using a traditional perfumer's technique, which is a good reminder: Inspiration can be found anywhere. If you are working at a bar connected to a restaurant, there is no better source of cocktail inventiveness than what is being stored, tested, and produced in your nearby kitchen. Make friends with your kitchen.

The term moonshine originated in Great Britain and was a reference to doing something illegal and uncouth at night. In ye olden days, jars were marked "XXX," which meant the product was distilled three times and properly strong, and most likely contributed to the many nicknames attributed to moonshine over the years: White Lightning, Mountain Dew, Popskull, Happy Sally, Homebrew, Hooch, Snail Venom, and, naturally, 'Shine.

West Virginia

NOT MANY PEOPLE know a lot about West Virginia, but really, the state's identity bridges connections to many neighboring states. How's this for history: The Mountain State is the southernmost northern state; Mother's Day was first recognized in West Virginia at a church in Grafton on May 10, 1908; in 1949, residents of Mole Hill changed their town's name to Mountain (get it?); and the first state sales tax went into effect here in July 1921. History abounds!

The Golden Delicious apple was created in Clay County. The first brick street laid in the world went down on Summers Street in Charleston on October 23, 1870. West Virginia also holds the record for the most towns named after cities in other countries: Athens, Berlin, Cairo, Calcutta, Geneva, Shanghai, and so on. And due to the healthy number of Italian Americans working in the coal mines of Clarksburg back in the day, the pepperoni roll is a source of state pride after all these years.

The West Virginia state motto is "Mountaineers are always free." If only that were true for the famous pepperoni rolls, too, we would all probably be singing a little John Denver as a little "free" karaoke. Mr. Denver is responsible for the state's famous song "Take Me Home, Country Roads," a celebratory sing-along.

West Virginia is nearly 75 percent forest, so there are plenty of places to hide and cook up a nice little batch of moonshine, if you're picking up what I'm putting down. People attend West Virginia University college football Saturday tailgates with their own legit 'shine, and provide small samples of their homemade hooch to anyone seeking a sip of otherworldly potables, some good, some god-awful, but all of it original and untaxed by our eagle-eyed US government. "On football Saturdays," says Tin 202's Josh Graham, "the entire city of Morgantown is out and in full force." West Virginia locals take pride in having a little moonshine tucked away whenever someone is looking to toast an occasion, and the rule of thumb is: You know where to get it simply by playing it cool.

WEST VIRGINIA'S OLDEST BAR
NORTH END TAVERN
Parkersburg, 1899

More pub and brewery than cocktail haunt, the North End Tavern & Brewery has been making people happy long enough to be considered a destination spot for its famous burger, known as the "N.E.T." burger, and its friendly, casual atmosphere. The brewery has been around since 1997, and its house classic is Roedy's Red amber ale, named after the owner.

WEST VIRGINIA BEVERAGE
MOONSHINE

Moonshine is made from a combination of field corn, sugar, yeast, and soft creek water (bonus points if it's from the foothills of one of the many mountains surrounding Summersville). Basically, it's unaged whiskey. The strongest proof is "white lightnin'," which typically registers as 170 proof and higher. Mountaineers make a wide variety of flavors, such as apple pie, coffee, peach, black cherry, blueberry, Cinnamon Toast Crunch, and many more, but no matter the flavor, it needs to be served in a Mason jar, a tradition that must remain unbroken, like the dribble on your chin after sipping.

TIN 202
Morgantown

Every American bar needs a personable, hardworking, and knowledge-able bartender, and it helps if every bartender knows how to make a proper Old Fashioned, Manhattan, and Gin Martini. My personal favorite cocktail to make is a Vieux Carre.

—Josh Graham, Tin 202 (Morgantown)

What is wrong with a cocktail menu featuring all Matthew McConaughey catchphrases from *Dazed and Confused*? This is a trick question. The answer is an emphatic nothing. Tin 202 is located on the aptly named Pleasant Street and serves Morgantown from the space of a former pharmacy and soda fountain, continuing the longstanding tradition of community-focused small business. It has been widely recognized for its charms, including being named Best Bar in West Virginia by *Southern Living*.

SMOOTH AMBLER
Maxwelton

Opened in Greenbrier County in 2009, Smooth Ambler bills itself as "Appalachian Whiskey" and specializes in quality whiskey aged in well-selected barrels. One of the signature spirits is Contradiction, a blended bourbon with four different grains and combined with young wheated bourbon and mature rye bourbon, which is a highly unusual pairing. But my favorite might be Old Scout, a seven-year bourbon with a higher rye profile, lovely cinnamon and gingerbread notes on the nose, with a round, caramel-rich, pleasant peanut-y finish. Smooth—and definitely capable of making one amble after a few sips.

BAR SNACK
Moonshiners doctored their automobile engines to get a little faster during the days of Prohibition, which led to friendly (and unfriendly) little competitions with other moonshiners and Johnny Law, and that behavior eventually led to the creation of the National Association for Stock Car Auto Racing, or NASCAR.

GREENBRIER RESORT
White Sulphur Springs

Visiting the Greenbrier is very much taking a turn-back-the-clock experience. Operating since 1778, Greenbrier offers multiple professional golf courses, a casino, designer boutiques, countless banquette rooms, and a spa, and that's just in the lobby! But seriously, the unique cocktail history of the Greenbrier actually points to the Mint Julep having been created in the famous Old White Tavern, which would later become the Greenbrier, in the early 1800s. The resort was a summer travel destination for southern gentry, and the lobby bar was *the* place to see and be seen—and have a very refreshing drink, as it were.

This is going to sound very "West Virginian," but at my annual family reunion, after all the kids go to sleep in their tents, all the adults will stand in a big circle and pass around jars of moonshine. Just talking and catching up with everyone. It is a family tradition I always look forward to.

—Tyler Davidson, bar director, General Lewis Inn (Lewisburg)

THE INDUSTRY STANDARD
Josh Graham, Tin 202, Morgantown

In Morgantown, there is the best dive bar around. Gene's is the oldest bar in the city and it is my Cheers. Everyone knows most everybody else and it is a very welcoming place with cheap beer and amazing hot dogs. There is also a separate pool room downstairs if you want to get away from the noise and just shoot a few games.

—Josh Graham, Tin 202 (Morgantown)

Josh Graham entered the Industry Standard in a cocktail competition through the Beehive Bitters Co. on Instagram and won with this lively libation. It is featured on Tin 202's menu as well. "Easy to make, simple ingredients, and super tasty," Josh says. Feel free to give this a little dash of Beehive's spiced orange bitters and see where that improvisational dance move takes you.

1½ ounces Pikesville rye

¾ ounce Aperol

½ ounce honey syrup
(recipe follows)

½ ounce fresh lemon juice

Garnish: fresh rosemary sprig

Shake the ingredients with ice until chilled; fine strain into a chilled coupe glass. Express the rosemary sprig by slapping it over your hand a few times to release more of its scent and then use it to garnish the drink.

Honey Syrup

Makes 1 cup

½ cup honey

½ cup water

Combine the ingredients in a nonreactive container and store in the refrigerator for up to 10 days.

CHIMNEY SWEEP
Tyler Davidson, General Lewis Inn, Lewisburg

The General Lewis Inn is a historic space on a hilltop just outside of the village of Lewisburg. Tyler, the head bartender, creates impressive drinks by using homemade tinctures, bitters, and infusions. The house Mint Juleps are made with the mint growing in the back of the hotel and incorporate local honey from hives kept nearby, and the bar itself was repurposed from the original front desk. One taste of a frosty Julep in the summer, and of this smoky, warming concoction in the winter, and you'll want to stay at the General Lewis Inn year-round.

1 ounce Casamigos mezcal

¾ ounce Courvoisier Cognac

½ ounce Aperol

½ ounce sweet vermouth
(Tyler's is homemade, but you can use your favorite)

1 teaspoon maraschino liqueur

2 dashes grapefruit bitters
(again, homemade, but you can use a commercial version)

Garnishes: smoking cedar stick (3 to 4 inches) and orange peel

Fernet-Branca amaro atomizer (optional; you can add 1 or 2 drops on top of the drink if an atomizer is unavailable)

Stir the mezcal, Cognac, Aperol, vermouth, maraschino liqueur, and bitters with ice until chilled; strain into a chilled coupe glass. Light the cedar stick on fire just before serving and then blow out the flame so it smokes. Serve on the side of the cocktail, on a fire-resistant surface, and garnish the drink with the orange peel. Atomize (or add 1 or 2 drops) Fernet-Branca over the cocktail.

Kentucky

Hunter S. Thompson, who was born in Louisville, described the Kentucky Derby in memorable terms, saying: "It's a fantastic scene—thousands of people fainting, crying, copulating, trampling each other and fighting with broken whiskey bottles." While some might object to this assessment, we can all agree that booze is certainly a prominent figure at the races. Some 120,000 Mint Juleps are purchased at the Derby every year.

WHEN I WAS younger, I was mesmerized by Fort Knox, and how they could store all that gold in the ground. So, to me, as a kid, Kentucky was Egypt. It took me a while to get there, but I was always fascinated by the Bourbon and Bluegrass State. If you ever drive through the beautiful countryside, with its rolling hills and lush pastures, you might understand why it would be happy just being its own balloon.

Kentucky is known for Louisville Sluggers, Muhammad Ali, the Kentucky Derby, Colonel Harland Sanders (aka "the Colonel" of Kentucky Fried Chicken fame), Kaelin's restaurant in Louisville, which in 1934 served America's first cheeseburger, the bluegrass festival in Lexington every June, and one of my all-time favorite nonconformists, Hunter S. Thompson, who was born and raised in Louisville.

There are many little nuggets of Kentucky worth visiting—and the distilleries alone could keep you occupied for endless moons. Longstanding distilleries such as Jim Beam, Buffalo Trace, Wild Turkey, Maker's Mark, Woodford Reserve, and Heaven Hill are great places to start, and then you can check out some recently renovated institutions, notably Whiskey Row in downtown Louisville,

Kentucky, oh, Kentucky, How I love your classic shades, Where flit the fairy figures, Of the star-eyed Southern maids; Where the butter- flies are joying 'Mid the blossoms newly born; Where the corn is full of kernels And The Colonels Full Of Corn!

—Will Lampton, in *Irvin S. Cobb's Recipe Book*, 1934

featuring such notables as Michter's, Copper & Kings, Angel's Envy, and Rabbit Hole, which opened for production and tours in 2018, and features the Overlook tasting room developed with Proprietors LLC (which owns Death & Co., one of the most influential bars in modern-day New York craft cocktail history). After visiting all those distilleries in close proximity, you'll probably want to unwind with a cocktail, right?

Which is a great segue to celebrate the Old Fashioned cocktail—allegedly named by someone at the esteemed Pendennis Club in Louisville. Though there's no proof, beyond their boast, and the brief mention in the Old Waldorf Days cocktail book (1931) by Albert Stevens Crockett. The Old Fashioned, originally called a Whiskey Cocktail, was a cocktail of spirit, sugar, water, and bitters, and was first created with simplicity; then bartenders started tinkering with the original recipe, to which stubborn drinkers would reply, "Make me the drink in the old fashioned style," establishing one of the first widely known cocktails as an obvious classic. The Old Fashioned has endured ups and downs throughout our United States cocktail history and become one of the most beloved and oft-ordered drinks today. Thanks, Kentucky!

KENTUCKY BUCKET LIST BAR
THIRD STREET DIVE
Louisville

It's one thing to have the local bar-tenders recommend another place to grab a drink when you visit their town, but everyone in Louisville seems to agree on one thing: when in doubt, Third Street Dive it out. And when I began hearing from about a half block away a live music intro to Aerosmith's "Sweet Emotions" by a hard-rocking cover band who were playing to a bar of fifteen people as though it were a sold-out arena rock show, I knew they were right. Inside, locals gathered to toast the silver Kentucky moon, sip on affordable drinks, and high-five a stranger or two.

KENTUCKY SPIRIT
BOURBON
Everywhere in the State

Elijah Pepper started a still in Lexington in around 1780, but Evan Williams wins the award for signing on the dotted line, starting his bour-bon distillery the old-fashioned way, by officially registering whiskey in Kentucky circa 1783. The term *bour bon whiskey* did not appear until 1821, so speculation of Elijah Craig's status as the inaugural bourbon has been long debated. As the nineteenth cen-tury cantered along, "bourbon" only grew with its (*ahem*) age. Bourbon was declared "America's Native Spirit" in a 1964 act of Congress, and the first bourbon festival was held in Bardstown in 1992.

IMPORTANT KENTUCKY INFO:

- *Approximately 95 percent of all bourbon is distilled in the state of Kentucky.*
- *Approximately thirty-two oak staves are used to build a tradi-tional whiskey barrel.*
- *A traditional whiskey barrel can hold up to approximately fifty-three gallons.*
- *An estimated 60 to 70 percent of whiskey's flavor comes from the wooden barrel.*

BAR SNACK
In 1953, Marjorie Samuels and her husband purchased a little distillery in Loretto, Kentucky. Marjorie emphasized the notion of "craft" as it pertained to distilling, how the approach to making bourbon should be celebrated. So she had an idea: Make a signature red-wax label for each bottle, and call it "Maker's Mark."

KENTUCKY'S OLDEST BAR
THE OLD TALBOTT TAVERN
Bardstown, 1779

If people visited where I grew up (Henderson, Kentucky), they would encounter the elderberry wine made from wild elderberries that grow along the train tracks in my hometown. It's made by a retired teacher and former coworker of my mother's. He gives my folks a few bottles every year and it's delicious and super unique.

—Brooks Reitz (born in Henderson), owner, Jack Rudy Cocktail Co. (Charleston, SC)

Not many other still-existing taverns in America can claim they have bullet holes courtesy of Jesse James, so welcome to the Talbott, the oldest western stagecoach stop in America and "America's Oldest Bourbon Bar." Apparently there are more than a few ghosts running amok on the grounds, as Talbott has received top honors as one of the most haunted places in America, so make sure you say hi to Abraham Lincoln, Stephen Foster, and the lady dressed all in white. It operates as a bed-and-breakfast and restaurant, which is known for its burgoo, a spicy multi-meat stew with an empty-the-fridge mentality. Grab the ladle and get ready for the Derby. Just ask the kitchen to hold the extra side of ghost.

KENTUCKY COCKTAIL BAR
PROOF ON MAIN
Louisville

Located inside the 21c Museum Hotel, Proof on Main has been charming locals and travelers with its modern art and architecture, expansive bourbon list, and delectable cocktails for some time now. The bartenders pay their respects by incorporating local bourbon in some of their cocktails, along with products from terrific new distilleries, such as Copper & Kings, and create wonderful spins on classics, like the Soñada con Puerto Rico, a Negroni riff made with Castle & Key gin, toasted coconut, sweet vermouth, salt, and papaya that won the 2018 Negroni Week Kickoff Cocktail Competition. Rare for a hotel bar, this one makes you want to stay inside and ignore the rest of the city for a while.

STATE FACT

Long ago, the East Coast dominated the distilling trade, until heavy taxation in the 1790s pushed out many farmers and distillers, who decided to ply their trade in the frontier territories, such as Kentucky, Ohio, Indiana, and Tennessee. This terroir, along with the bountiful supply of corn, was ideal for whiskey production, and when other states wanted product, shipping was handled by boats up and down the nearby rivers. Some of these shipments took months to arrive at their destinations, and as a result, the receivers found something remarkable: The whiskey sitting in the barrels had changed flavor profile due to maturation during the time spent in the oak barrels. Though the French had been aging Cognac in charred barrels since the fifteenth century, and the Scottish and Irish started aging whiskey in the 1800s at a time when Cognac was in short supply, the practice of aging local whiskey and making it American bourbon was developed by Americans.

BAR SNACK

In the 1790s, a Kentucky farmer (by way of Germany) named Johannes "Jacob" Beam started making bourbon in Kentucky, only the bourbon was named Old Tub until Prohibition ended, when then master distiller James Beauregard Beam (great-grandson of Johannes) resuscitated the distillery and changed the Old Tub name to Jim Beam. They have maintained the same proportions of corn, rye, and barley in their mash bill ever since they started making bourbon, and today, Kentucky's Jim Beam Bourbon is the bestselling bourbon in the world.

MINT JULEP

Brian Bartels

Sugar, mint, and liquor may seem feeble foundations for a civilization—but on such concoctions a young republic was nursed. Sip a few, and taste history.

—Paul Clarke, The Cocktail Chronicles

Virginia, Washington, DC, and West Virginia have all claimed the invention of the Mint Julep, but Kentucky has made this unforgettable classic its own pride and joy for decades, thanks to the Kentucky Derby, which declared the Mint Julep its official cocktail in 1938. Though everyone associates bourbon with Mint Juleps, the originals were made with Cognac and peach brandy. An outbreak of phylloxera (tiny microscopic bugs that attack the roots of grapes) in the 1880s decimated so many grapevines that Europe lost approximately 90 percent of its grapes. This gave bourbon a welcome opportunity to step in, making drinkers during hot American summers very happy indeed.

8 to 10 fresh mint leaves

½ ounce simple syrup
(1:1 sugar to water)

2 ounces bourbon

Garnish: mint sprig

Muddle the mint and simple syrup in the bottom of a chilled silver Julep cup or highball glass. Fill with crushed ice and add the bourbon. Swirl with a bar spoon until the outside of the glass frosts. Top with a little more ice and garnish with the mint. You're off to the races.

PENDENNIS CLUB

Brian Bartels

Louisville's Pendennis Club, where the Old Fashioned was allegedly first called the "Old Fashioned," has been open since 1881, and was named after a fictional character in a William Makepeace Thackeray novel. As Toby Cecchini writes in *Saveur*, "Curiously enough, the Pendennis Club itself doesn't seem to know exactly where, how, when, or who first concocted the drink. While I still hope to someday snoop the club's attic for the solid historical skinny on this drink's birth, for now I happily content myself with the nightly fortuity of shaking and savoring a Pendennis in blissful ignorance." The Pendennis Club wields enough complexity that it might be hard to guess its secret ingredient—an ounce of apricot brandy can be overbearing if wrongly used in a cocktail, but the Pendennis Club bridges the gap between gin and citrus by allowing the apricot more of a starring role, and the payoff is full of promise.

2 ounces gin

1 ounce apricot brandy
(Giffard and Luxardo apricot are dandy)

¾ ounce fresh lime juice

4 dashes Peychaud's bitters

Garnish: brandied cherry

Shake the ingredients with ice until chilled; strain into a chilled coupe glass and garnish with the cherry.

BAR SNACK

The Seelbach Hotel is now famous for its Seelbach Cocktail, but not in the way one would expect. The bartender Adam Seger invented the cocktail in 1995 but claimed it was from the famed Louisville hotel circa 1917. Verity aside, it is now a classic. Sometimes truth doesn't make a noise.

Tennessee

The first hour I was in Tennessee, someone offered me a drink, a meal, and a ride to the airport whenever I wanted to leave. The great city of Knoxville went above and beyond with showing me all its magical properties, many of which start first thing in the morning at their engaging farmers' market, Nourish Knoxville. Memphis and Nashville did not disappoint, either, and demonstrated the same kind of hospitality. Imagine having a cocktail party with Nashville natives Dolly Parton and Elvis Presley. Who's making the drinks? Which one starts the karaoke party? Which one grabs the bottle of tequila first? No lie: every time I eat a bologna sandwich from Robert's Western World, I make the same face as Elvis.

FOOD IS IMPORTANT in Tennessee. My first official day in the Volunteer State took place at the Knoxville farmers' market, hosted by Nourish Knoxville and featuring more than one hundred farmers from the surrounding community. I had a Bloody Mary for breakfast, made with Beauregard Dixie black pepper vodka, and was served a large biscuit for my bread course, a very filling intro before I received my food, and when the fried chicken arrived, it came with a heap of white gravy on top of four more biscuits! And then I didn't eat anything else for the next two days.

Knoxville cocktails have become more elevated in the past few years, with the Public House and Sapphire cocktail bar starting the trend, followed by the speakeasy Peter Kern Library and PostModern Spirits, which served me one of my favorite White Negronis in recent memory, using all their own house spirits for the recipe. PostModern opened in downtown Knoxville in 2017, next to a brewery and across the street from the famed JFG coffee plant in Old City. PostModern makes its own gin, amaro, vodka, and elderflower, chamomile, and cacao liqueurs. Co-owner Stanton Webster is true blue Tennessee soul, with a smile and an aura of feel-good vibes. When I was there one Saturday night, it was glam rock night, so you know they can throw a party.

Memphis—the birthplace of rock and roll—lays claim to Elvis and Graceland, Ida B. Wells, Aretha Franklin, Three 6 Mafia, Booker T. & the M.G.'s, and Stax Records, which helped bring soul, funk, and rhythm and blues to this great nation. Come for the music history and stay for the wonderful array of new cocktail spots, like perennial favorite Alchemy; balance James Beard Award–nominated cuisine with dynamite cocktails at sister spots Catherine & Mary's and the Gray Canary, with both menus featuring drinks from next-door Old

I am always supremely entertained by secret shot menus that a bar staff will make for themselves. You know, it's that time of night: The last customers are paying their bills, a barfly or two are still hanging on to half a glass of wine, the kitchen starts breaking down, glasses still need to be polished, but the night is essentially over and you've all managed to survive. Everyone on staff finds a moment to collect over a shot. You take a shot together and then you're done, and then go on and finish your shift like normal. I love that. It's a whole language built inside the tradition of shift drinks.

—Morgan McKinney, Dodici at Bari (Memphis)

Dominick Distillery, the first Memphis distillery to legally produce whiskey since Prohibition; drop in to the Blind Bear for an excellent meal-in-itself Bloody Mary; and you're in luck if you make it to Dodici at Bari when Morgan McKinney is working the bar—she has a black belt in keeping it real!

Nashville, home of the Grand Ole Opry, the Country Music Hall of Fame, and the Ryman Auditorium (the "Mother Church of Country Music"), is worth checking out over a long weekend. Grab yourself some turnip greens with potlikker (the liquid used in boiling the greens—not actual alcohol). Pinewood Social balances fun cocktails with bowling; Attaboy opened its second location in Nashville (the original is in New York, page 28, where Milk & Honey used to be) and it became a popular destination overnight, with no phone, no website, and no menus—just trust the bartender to make you something magical; Robert's Western World is a must-visit for fans of live music, fried bologna sandwiches, and Boilermakers; Old Glory's cathedral-like space will make you think you've died and gone to cocktail heaven; Bar Sovereign is the quintessential spot for low-key vibes with attentive bartenders; and the Geist Bar is an interior designer's dream, with the cocktails elevating the architecture.

Meeting someone in Tennessee is not unlike making an immediate connection with your new best friend: They might offer you food or a drink, or a ride across town in the first five minutes of knowing them. That level of community shines from every person you meet the way the afternoon sun paints Bob Ross happiness across the buildings, hills, and YOU'RE THE ONLY TEN I SEE T-shirts, one of which, yes, I do now proudly own, though I regret not picking up a Dolly Parton tank top when I was in town.

TENNESSEE'S OLDEST BAR
SPRINGWATER SUPPER CLUB
Nashville, 1896

The Springwater has endured many a day and night of lively Tennessee times—and many names, in fact, as it was originally called the Tennessee Centennial and International Exposition, but that just doesn't seem to be a name that would fly in the twenty-first century. People now congregate there to have a cold drink while listening to some live music in the outdoor courtyard bar.

TENNESSEE COCKTAIL BAR
SAPPHIRE FINE FOOD + FANCY DRINKS
Knoxville

Owner Aaron Thompson and his talented bar team have been wowing the good people of downtown Knoxville for more than a decade now, and the Sapphire space itself is a hallowed location to behold. Check out its website, which features a rotating specialty cocktail recipe for the home bartender. Then check out the brick-and-mortar bar, which is located in an old jewelry store on the main street, right around the corner from the wonderful farmers' market. The staff approaches the integrity of cocktails and service as well as any program I have come across. Knoxville is lucky to have such dedicated professionals ready to serve the masses.

STATE FACT
Though commonly associated with origins in Pennsylvania and Maryland, rye whiskey had a hero in Tennessee, as the frontiersman Evan Shelby became one of the first distillers in America to produce a rye-based (more than 51 percent of the mash bill must contain rye) spirit in 1771 in Sapling Grove, Tennessee.

TENNESSEE BUCKET LIST BAR
EARNESTINE & HAZEL'S
Memphis

Whenever you're done writin' your little article or whatever it is, get your little fanny back to E&H and have a soul burger and play "Green Onions" by Booker T. & the M.G.'s. It'll save your life.

—Woman from Earnestine & Hazel's (Memphis)

E&H's was originally built as a church in the late nineteenth century, then became a dry goods store during Prohibition, and the building's owner eventually handed the space over to two cousins, Earnestine and Hazel, who ran the beauty salon upstairs, then turned the downstairs into a jazz café. Due to its proximity to Stax Records, they had plenty of musicians (James Brown, Ray Charles, and other gifted rabblerousers) swing by, and eventually transformed the second floor into a brothel. And the ghosts? Yes, there very much are ghosts to be seen and felt in this hallowed space. One of them is dancing the boogaloo in a corner. One of them is eating E&H's famous soul burger, eyes closed, with a cigarette in the other hand. One of them is singing out "Mustang Sally" as though they're the only person ever born to belt the words. And they've all got soul.

TENNESSEE BEVERAGE
FRUIT TEA

Also referred to as Fruit Punch or Tea Punch, Fruit Tea started gaining traction in Franklin, Tennessee in 1974, when local legend Daisy King started adding pineapple juice to her iced tea recipe. Shortly after putting it on the menu, Daisy was getting visits from not only the locals, but people all over the state.

BAR SNACK
Sour mash is simply the wet solids from a previously used batch of mash bill (in Jack Daniel's case, the mash bill is corn, rye, and malted barley) that are added to the new mash bill. Many if not all straight bourbons use this same process today, though smaller distilleries often don't. Sour mash lends a sweeter, deeper flavor to the final product.

TENNESSEE COCKTAIL BAR
THE PATTERSON HOUSE
Nashville

The Patterson House is known to be the first cocktail bar in Tennessee's new cocktail movement, opening on Tax Day 2009. They were popular then, and they most definitely are still popular. Not only are the staff friendly and accommodating, they enjoy being there, as evidenced by the dance moves they improvise while building well-crafted cocktails behind the bar. Staff camaraderie is as balanced as the cocktails they produce, which adds to the comfort of the well-designed space, modeled after pre-Prohibition cocktail dens, with literature on the shelves, vintage chandeliers, and civilized house rules: "No play fighting, no talk about play fighting, no name dropping, and no starfucking." Huzzah.

TENNESSEE SPIRIT
JACK DANIEL'S
Lynchburg

Founded in 1875 in Lynchburg, Tennessee, and famously produced in a dry county, Jack Daniel's whiskey needs no introduction, as it is one of the highest-selling spirits in the United States, and has obtained brand sustainability through endless audiences of Jack and Coke fans, Frank Sinatra fans, and anyone who has ever searched for a taste of what the kids call "rock and roll." It has been around since long before we were here, and it most likely will be here long after we are gone. Jack Daniel's: You are sweet. You are sour (mash). You have been looking at me from the shelves of every bar I have entered and worked and passed by since I have been paying attention. Like Ryan Seacrest, there is simply no avoiding you.

LYNCHBURG LEMONADE
Brian Bartels

The Lynchburg Lemonade was named after Jack Daniel's Distillery, located in Lynchburg, Tennessee, sacred ground for Tennessee whiskey purists. The sweet-and-sour combo agitates the barrel-aged layers used in Jack Daniel's caramel, maple, vanilla-y roundness. It's lip-smacking—and just tart enough to respect its integrity, and dangerous enough you don't know if it's okay to drink it so fast on a hot day, as it's a thirst-quencher on par with iced tea.

2 ounces Jack Daniel's whiskey

1 ounce fresh lemon juice

½ ounce simple syrup (1:1 sugar to water)

3 ounces Seltzer

Garnish: lemon wheel

Shake the ingredients with ice until chilled; strain over fresh ice in a chilled highball glass. Top with seltzer and stir. Garnish with the lemon.

THE WORLD, REVERSED
Morgan McKinney, Dodici at Bari, Memphis

This smoky, minty-fresh recipe was first published in *Imbibe* magazine in 2018. Morgan is the kind of hometown hero bartender we should all be lucky to have in our cities. She works hard, creates great cocktails, and she holds a black belt in Krav Maga, so you know she means business—especially when she answered my email questions typing with a broken finger! #boss. This recipe asks for five drops of Angostura bitters. I didn't ask Morgan if that was a reference to the five-point palm exploding heart technique from *Kill Bill*, because I did not want to upset her. I wanted to live to finish this book.

1 ounce brandy (Bertoux works well)

¾ ounce Branca Menta amaro

½ ounce Sfumato amaro (a smoky amaro, and one to have in your home cabinet)

¾ ounce fresh lemon juice

¼ ounce simple syrup (1:1 sugar to water)

3 dashes orange bitters

1 pinch ground cinnamon

¾ ounce egg white

Garnish: 5 drops Angostura bitters (optional)

Combine the ingredients in tin shakers without ice and seal tightly (liquid inside the shakers will pressurize and expand when shaken without ice). Vigorously dry shake for approximately 15 seconds. Add ice and shake until chilled; fine strain into a chilled coupe glass. If you have a dropper bottle, garnish with the bitters.

BAR SNACK

A "Batman" shot is a drop shot: A pint glass is filled halfway with Sailor Jerry spiced rum and Coca-Cola and then is served with a shot glass filled with equal parts Bailey's and vanilla vodka. The shot is then dropped into the pint and chugged. "It is truly vile," says Morgan McKinney, "but a Memphis staple in some of the local industry bars. It's ordered by pressing your hands together in a prayer position and nodding to the bartender."

The North Carolina license plates read "First in Flight," in honor of the Wright Brothers, and that cardinal flying up at the top of the page just so happens to be the North Carolina state bird, which reminds me of a little-known fact: Any time someone sees a cardinal, they go, "Hey, look at that cardinal!" And almost every time it's as though the cardinal hears them and flies away. Or maybe that's just me.

North Carolina

North Carolina is known for barbecue, University of North Carolina basketball (including but not limited to Michael Jordan), having both mountains and beach, and NASCAR.

—Sara Camp Milam, co-author, *The Southern Foodways Alliance Guide to Cocktails* (born and raised in Raleigh)

IN 1903, THE Wright brothers took flight from Kill Devil Hill near Kitty Hawk, and though kill-devil is a nickname for rum, the record shows rum had no part in the first flight. North Carolina started mini-golf, Krispy Kreme donuts, Pepsi, and Michael Jordan, and though the state didn't invent furniture, High Point is the furniture capital of the world.

The restaurants of North Carolina are happily taking the cocktail baton and running away with some wonderful cocktail programs to accompany outstanding southern dishes. James Beard Award–winning chef-author-restaurateur Ashley Christensen has been serving quality food to the good people of Raleigh for years, and her beverage menus are equally impressive. She even runs a celebrated cocktail bar, the Fox Liquor Bar, underneath her acclaimed fried chicken restaurant, Beasley's Chicken + Honey. The windows at all of her spots share the same message: "Don't Forget Kindness." Ashley is a steadfast activist for equality in her restaurants and deserves a heap of praise for her efforts to maintain respect and integrity within the workplace and, yes, a little more kindness makes all the difference.

The great news about North Carolina's cocktail scene is that the options in every town seem to only be getting better. Charlotte's Dot Dot Dot, the Punch Room, and the Cellar at Duckworth's are some standouts in a crowd of many worthwhile options. In addition to celebrated cocktail menus, Sidebar in Cary has live jazz; Hello, Sailor in Cornelius has an outdoor deck overlooking pristine Lake Norman for quality summertime tiki vibes; Winston-Salem's Fair Witness Fancy Drinks serves creative libations to accompany its science-fiction inspirations (it took its name from a character type in *Stranger in a Strange Land*); Asheville alone has Copper Crown, the Times at S&W, and the Waterbird scattered throughout its typically beer-focused college town; and Raleigh brings it all home with the Haymaker, Brewery Bhavana (scary-delicious cocktails for a brewery), and Bittersweet, featuring a menu of house cocktails and a separate coffee cocktail menu, as it's a coffee shop by day before turning the switch to spirits at night.

Kudos to University of North Carolina grad Seán McKeithan, who penned an essay in 2012 titled "Every Ounce a Man's Whiskey?," reflecting on the long tradition of marketing whiskey as a symbol of heterosexual white southern masculinity, when Seán was a young gay southern man seeking to break down the stereotypes. Additionally, the essay "Bourbon and Gender" by Sara Camp Milam in *The Southern Foodways Alliance Guide to Cocktails* is worth a read. To quote Milam: "Life is too short to order a drink you don't love because you're trying to be manly, womanly, cool, or 'Southern,' whatever that means to you."

Life is too short.

BAR SNACK

Tippling house is another word for *speakeasy*, and there are other monikers for this type of establishment: *blind pig*, *blind tiger*, *speak softly shop*, and *roadhouse* among them. And yes, I, too, have seen the movie *Road House* more than ten times.

NORTH CAROLINA
COCKTAIL BAR

THE CRUNKLETON
Chapel Hill

The Crunkleton is the one American bar I tell everyone to visit, and it is also my bucket list bar of choice.

—Sara Camp Milam, co-author, *The Southern Foodways Alliance Guide to Cocktails* (born and raised in Raleigh)

If bartenders could be folk musicians, Gary Crunkleton is North Carolina's Woody Guthrie. Chances are, if you are in a North Carolina cocktail bar, and the bartender is wearing a bowtie, and the cocktails are well balanced and delicious, and everyone is having a wonderful time, you are in the Crunkleton. Gary Crunkleton opened his seminal cocktail bar on Franklin Street in Chapel Hill in 2006. Slinging well-made cocktails from classic and modern recipes, along with a hearty collection of spirits, the Crunkleton steals time from anyone lucky enough to sit at the bar.

NORTH CAROLINA'S OLDEST BAR
THE TAVERN IN OLD SALEM
Old Salem, 1784

The Tavern opened as an annex to the original 1784 Salem Tavern, and has managed to stay cooking as a restaurant ever since, offering food inspired by the Moravian families inhabiting Salem in the early 1800s. There's beer cheese soup, rustic gingerbread, and the famous chicken pot pie delivered to tables by servers in nineteenth-century outfits and enough hearth, candlelight, and charm to briefly convince you it could be 1816 all over again.

NORTH CAROLINA BEVERAGE
CHEERWINE

"Soft drinks" have been around for a long time—and have even been popping up on mocktail menus (aka cocktail menus sans alcohol) the past few years, but Cheerwine and its cherry-red glory has been cheering up North Carolina people since 1917, owned by the same family in Salisbury. The cherry-flavored regional folk soda was actually conceived in a former whiskey distillery.

The "wine" describes its deep burgundy hue, though people confused it for alcoholic wine for years. So back in the day, when kids would order it at restaurants, some servers would inform them, "Sorry, we don't serve alcohol to minors." Thankfully, that all got sorted out.

NORTH CAROLINA
BUCKET LIST BAR
SLIM'S
Raleigh

Apart from having a name associated with old cowpokes, Slim's gets the best out of life with its live music (which is mostly punk, and mostly cacophonous), Mind Erasers (a quick and questionably delicious cocktail of vodka, Kahlúa, club soda, and furious reckoning), and Slim's Rules, written on a chalkboard facing the bar, which pretty much sum up the room:

SLIM'S RULES
Drink
Don't be a dick
No music requests
Tip or DIE

NORTH CAROLINA SPIRIT
FAIR GAME
BEVERAGE COMPANY
Pittsboro

Apple brandy was prevalent in the early days of North Carolina home distilling, with farmers in the Appalachian Mountains experimenting with distilling the apples they grew. Fair Game produces an apple brandy that uses North Carolina cider distilled in copper pots and aged in oak bourbon barrels. They also produce a terrific Tobago pepper vodka for your next Bloody Mary party, and if you can snag a bottle of the limited-edition Carolina Agricole rum—a rarity in the United States—please invite me to that party. I'll bring the pretzels.

CHERRY BOUNCE
Brian Bartels

I'm often amazed at the brilliant creations filling Instagram, but for me, I enjoy the classics, and I'm still learning about the dynamic flavors they offer when made correctly.

—Gary Crunkleton, owner of the Crunkleton (Chapel Hill), in *Imbibe* magazine (2019)

The Cherry Bounce goes all the way back to 1769, before Raleigh was even a city, and George Washington. This drink really proves how brandy and cherries benefit from a little sugar. North Carolina tavern owner Isaac Hunter served Cherry Bounces to thirsty locals in the late 1700s, and the North Carolina Assembly was so moved by Hunter's tavern (and possibly his recipe for the drink) that they decided the North Carolina state capital must be within ten miles. So though North Carolina did not invent the Cherry Bounce, the state claims it as one of the most influential cocktails in its history. The most popular recipe for a modern North Carolina Cherry Bounce is made with vodka, which is exactly why I am making this one with bourbon.

1½ ounces bourbon

½ ounce Cherry Heering
(or cherry juice, to lower
the ABV)

½ ounce fresh lemon juice

½ ounce simple syrup
(1:1 sugar to water)

2 dashes Angostura bitters

Shake the ingredients with ice until chilled; strain into a chilled rocks glass with fresh ice.

PARADISE PUNCH
Cynthia Turner, Imperial Life, Asheville

This punchy little paradise-sipper was featured in Gaz Regan's "101 Best Cocktails of 2013," in which Gaz stated, "Did I like it? I loved it!" Batavia arrack and falernum are uncommon spirits most bars in America don't carry, but they should, as they add wonderful dimensions to many cocktail variations. They can be used like spices in food.

1 ounce Ransom Old Tom Gin

¾ ounce Batavia Arrack

½ ounce The Bitter Truth
Velvet Falernum

½ ounce Cherry Heering

¾ ounce fresh orange juice

½ ounce fresh lime juice

Splash of club soda

Garnishes: grated nutmeg and
lime wheel

Shake the ingredients with ice until chilled; strain over fresh ice in a chilled highball glass and then top with the club soda. Stir briefly and then garnish with the nutmeg and lime.

BAR SNACK

A pony is not only a small horse, it is also a smaller measure of alcohol. Essentially, it is a liquid ounce, or thereabouts. Let's keep it simple. One pony = 1 ounce. A pony was often associated with having a smaller amount to drink so one could function in society. One theory places its origin in horseracing, where attendees would grab a small ("pony") drink between races. It arrived in bar circles near the end of the nineteenth century, and was associated with sherry, port, and small wine offerings, and try as we might to get rid of the measure forever, like your favorite comfortable T-shirt with the holes all over it, it endures. We have a few pony glasses behind our bar at Fedora in New York, and though I seem to say aloud, like a nagging mother, "We should probably throw those things out," they are still there.

The famous pineapple fountain in Charleston's Waterfront Park is a symbol of unflinching hospitality, and has been there since 1990. Since it gets plenty hot during Lowcountry summers, kids are encouraged to wade in the pool to keep cool, and wouldn't you know it, adults are too. Well played, Holy City!

South Carolina

MANY AMERICANS WOULD be surprised to know that, in 1973, South Carolina passed a law restricting bars and restaurants to serving liquor in 1½-ounce mini-bottles, and that this lasted until 2005. Instead of freely pouring from larger bottles, bartenders had to pour from tiny airplane bottles. The idea behind the practice was twofold: It aided taxation of alcohol and maintained a standardization of the amount of alcohol served in each drink. South Carolina bars are now welcome to have full bottles of spirits on their back shelves, which generated a huge sigh of relief from bartenders, who no longer had to open one million tiny bottles during each shift.

Charleston makes a good argument for being a terrific cocktail destination of late. Innovative bars have sprouted in the Holy City over the past few years, and they work overtime to serve libations when visitors flood the town during the popular food and wine festival every March—and throughout the year. The Gin Joint is not only a catchy old-time name, it also features a wonderful array of juniper-based spirits from all over the world. If you love impressive selections of bourbon and delicious cocktails, check out the Bar next to the famed restaurant Husk, which features a Charleston punch cocktail from 1792.

Punches were very common in the 1700s throughout the South but especially in Charleston, where the St. Cecilia—an exclusive ladies' club—filled punch bowls with rum, fruit, and Champagne, while always taking time to stop and hear the music. (Cecilia is the patron saint of music. I'm not sure if Simon and Garfunkel named their famous song after her, but I can attest that nearly every time I attend a karaoke bar, someone performing believes they invented that song, and are performing for 30,000 people, bless their hearts.) During concerts, the exclusive club held dances with very strict rules: no cutting in, no smoking on the dance floor, and no drinking except for punch, so, yes, there was drinking, but not, you know, *drinking*.

Though the spirit historically associated with South Carolina is Madeira wine, which was regularly consumed during the colonial period, the locals of Charleston trended into doing shots of Grand Marnier ("GrandMa's") at the turn of the century, although Fireball is gaining prominence these days (as it is in a lot of other towns across America).

As a fan of iced tea, cold beverages, lemons, and, well, alcohol, I have to tell you not to knock South Carolina's Firefly Sweet Tea vodka until you have tried the magical elixir. There's a reason it's one of the most popular spirits in the country. My family drinks it when we have reunions, which is a great way to fake out the grandparents and make them believe you're pacing yourself.

The first mixed drink I had was E + J Brandy mixed with Dr Pepper. I had it at a friend's house when his parents weren't home. I loved it, and it was my first official "drink of choice" before I could legally drink. My first real cocktail in a bar was a Gin and Tonic at Rosebud in Lexington, Kentucky.

—Brooks Reitz,
Jack Rudy Co.
(Charleston)

SOUTH CAROLINA SPIRIT
HIGH WIRE DISTILLING CO.
Charleston

Located in downtown Charleston and operating since 2013, High Wire produces small-batch spirits often sourced from local ingredients and artisanal grains. Its limited-edition Jimmy Red whiskey was produced with Jimmy Red corn seed, a moonshiner's corn that was nearing extinction until High Wire helped resuscitate the grain. High Wire sources black tea, yaupon holly (think yerba mate), and tangerine for its proprietary Southern amaro, but the distillery's flagship is Hat Trick gin, which rests in a barrel for six months before bottling.

SOUTH CAROLINA'S OLDEST BAR
McCRADY'S TAVERN
Charleston, 1778

There are not many old institutions with James Beard Award–winning pedigrees, but until he left the organization chef-owner Sean Brock not only revitalized this near-extinct city landmark (George Washington once dined there), he built it into one of South Carolina's best restaurants. One of the oldest bars in the country, McCrady's holds its own for best cocktails as well. The drinks program balances house originals with classic cocktails, and often incorporates the products of local distillers in the recipes.

SOUTH CAROLINA BUCKET LIST BAR
THE GRIFFON
Charleston

The Griffon is a timeless, lived-in bar that does indeed serve spirits—which are tucked behind the endless stickers and dollar bills festooning the walls—but the showcase at Griffon is beer, beer, beer. There's a dartboard in the corner, but don't ignore the possibility of rich conversation with the regulars, or the stories hanging from the walls.

SOUTH CAROLINA BEVERAGE
JACK RUDY TONIC

I was tempted to give the nod to the Charleston Tea Plantation, as iced tea is surely South Carolina's go-to beverage, but since we're talking cocktails, Jack Rudy has set a new bar. Jack Rudy produces small batches of bitters, tonic syrups, Bloody Mary mix, and grenadine syrups with artisanal renown. Jack Rudy's bourbon cocktail cherries are addictive and always get me in trouble. Their tonic is noncarbonated (so make sure you grab some seltzer or dust off that SodaStream when you're whipping up homemade Gin and Tonics) and built from lemongrass, cane sugar, orange peel, and quinine. Named after affable owner Brooks Reitz's great-grandfather, Jack Rudy has been operating since 2014.

SOUTH CAROLINA COCKTAIL BAR
THE LIVING ROOM BAR AT THE DEWBERRY HOTEL
Charleston

Unfortunately, most hotel bars often have a lifelessness to them, as though they expect you to show up and order a drink and not be wowed, but rather just charmed by the accessible location. The Living Room Bar elevates the hotel bar experience. There is thoughtfulness to the design of the space: midcentury architecture, crystal stemware, and house plants to accompany a surprisingly decorated Cognac selection in a city so drenched in bourbon, and if those don't float your schooner, set sail for the Dewberry Daiquiri, made with Plantation pineapple rum, a welcome scallywag on any cocktail adventure. Add in the hospitality of the charming, easygoing staff, and you've got a place worth being a regular, even if you're not staying the night.

SCREAMING VIKING
FIG, Charleston

FIG is one of the more tenured legendary restaurants and bars in Charleston's burgeoning cocktail scene. Legend has it this drink was inspired by an episode of the famous bar-focused '80s sitcom *Cheers* in which Norm invents a cocktail (called "the Screaming Viking") to save Woody his bartending job.

2 cucumber slices

6 fresh mint leaves

1½ ounces gin (Beefeater, Tanqueray, or J. Rieger are always nice)

4 ounces chilled tonic water (preferably Fever-Tree)

Garnish: 1 cucumber slice (be creative with the shape—it's okay, we're all judging you)

In a chilled highball glass, muddle the piece of cucumber with the mint leaves. Fill the glass with ice, add the gin, and top with the tonic water. Stir gently and then add the cucumber to garnish.

DEAD MONKS SOCIETY
Kevin King, McCrady's, Charleston

This is the only drink that has stayed on the menu since McCrady's opened as its current concept in 2016. This cocktail honors the Bénédictine monks who are responsible for the eponymous herbal liqueur. Madeira holds a special place in South Carolina and our nation's history: It was used to toast the Declaration of Independence, and George Washington ate a lavish meal and drank many a Madeira at the original McCrady's.

1¼ ounces Rittenhouse rye

¾ ounce Broadbent Verdelho Madeira wine

Light ¼ ounce Bénédictine

Light ¼ ounce Ramazzotti amaro

2 dashes Regan's orange bitters

Garnish: orange peel

Stir the ingredients with ice until chilled; strain into a chilled cocktail glass and serve up. Express the oils of the orange peel around the rim and then place it in the glass.

STATE FACT

Before being known as the Palmetto State, South Carolina was known as the Iodine State. If you've ever been to Marion, legend has it that anyone who drinks from Catfish Creek becomes enchanted by the area and wishes to remain there. Forever. Oooohh. . . .

In the bars and restaurants throughout Georgia, everyone seems to know everyone, which automatically makes me feel more relaxed. And that's something I noticed about Georgians: They. Always. Seem. Comfortable. And that's important. Especially when I can't decide between a Ticonderoga Cup cocktail at the Ticonderoga Club (shout out to their skeleton mascots, the "Bone Soldiers," in this image) or a Watchman's Daiquiri at Watchman's seafood restaurant next door, both terrific cocktail destinations located inside the fetching Krog Street Market.

Georgia

GEORGIA IS "HOME of Coca-Cola, peaches, and hip-hop," as hometown Atlanta bartender and my former colleague Brad Goocher says. Georgia produces more peaches, peanuts, and pecans than anywhere else in the United States (check out the Forest Park farmers' market), and is the site of the founding of NASCAR, and hosts the Masters golf tournament at Augusta National every year, where more Bloody Marys are served than at a Wisconsin family reunion (and that's a lot).

A Savannah militia put punch on the map in the 1850s with the Chatham Artillery Punch cocktail, blending Cognac, rum, and brandy with a healthy dose of Champagne, which is a lethal weapon for anyone believing they can be a universal soldier after having two or more of these wild puppies.

Athens Seabear Oyster Bar is known for its Dirty Dawg Old Fashioned, which is a Bourbon Old Fashioned with a splash of Coke instead of sugar. The Old Pal in Athens does a great job listing people's names and the drink someone bought for them when they visited. And the Expat, owned by Jerry Slater, co-author of the excellent *Southern Foodways Alliance Guide to Cocktails*, has a balanced cocktail menu to accommodate seasonally inspired, cocktail-friendly food.

Atlanta has developed its own cocktail game over the past few years. Beverage director Miles Macquarrie has made Kimball House and Watchman's two must-visits, the Bookhouse Pub makes everyone a believer with its tiki taco Tuesdays, and don't miss Holeman & Finch Public House, a sophisticated bar with zero pretension. Holeman & Finch celebrates "good food, drinks and people," and their food and beverage menu—reflecting images of past restaurant, bar, and entertainment generations—clearly embraces the sentiment. There are too many fine cocktail programs to list in this book, but Atlanta can proudly claim the award for best airport cocktail bar in the country: One Flew South, located in Atlanta's Hartsfield-Jackson. You might say the cocktail program there is first class. "The staff at One Flew South greet a huge chunk of their guests by name," says the author and bartender Misty Kalkofen. "Which is extremely rare to find in an airport bar."

Plenty to see and do in Atlanta, and if one is at Manuel's Tavern in the Poncey-Highland neighborhood, and surrounded by good friends, it's perfectly acceptable to conjure "Hope that we feel this, feel this way forever" lyrics by Atlanta's very own OutKast.

BAR SNACK
"Shots shots shots . . .": Where did this catchy phrase originate? There has to be a song, right? Yes. It just so happens that when people ring out the words "Shots shots, shots shots shots, shots shots!" they are referencing the LMFAO song "Shots," featuring Atlanta's Lil Jon, who often tweets "Ohhhhhh yeah" and #mic #drop. The first shot I ever learned to make was a Kamikaze. When I make it today it's called a "Snaquiri" (a shot portion of a Daiquiri). Don't do a Snaquiri shot alone, and don't sit near anyone who is doing one alone.

Me: *What was your first American cocktail?* Murray: *Jack and Coke.* Me: *What is your favorite cocktail to make?* Murray: *Jack and Coke.* Me: *What is your least favorite cocktail to make?* Murray: *Jack and Coke.*

—From an interview with legendary Seattle bartender Murray Stenson, November 2018

Coca-Cola. Delicious! Refreshing! Exhilarating! Invigorating! The new and popular soda fountain drink containing the properties of the wonderful Coca plant and the famous Cola nut.

—*Atlanta Journal*, May 29, 1886

GEORGIA BEVERAGE
COCA-COLA

What's a cocktail book without Coca-Cola? What's a Jack and Coke without Coke? (Probably a Jack and Pepsi.) Arguably one of the most celebrated beverages in our lifetime, Coca-Cola has no shortage of American connections: From the gigantic sign in Times Square to the billboards and signs in little towns across America, from being in Beatles lyrics ("Come Together") to having Elvis promote the beverage on his final 1977 tour, from "I'd like to buy the world a Coke" to "Mean" Joe Greene tossing a bottle of Coke to a young fan, you simply can't beat the real thing. Dr. John Pemberton invented the syrupy wildfire we call Coca-Cola in 1886; it was named by Pemberton's bookkeeper and first sold at an Atlanta soda fountain in a pharmacy.

GEORGIA BUCKET LIST BAR
KIMBALL HOUSE
Decatur

Named after a historic Atlanta hotel, Kimball House (located in a former train depot) is an exquisite place. It has a gorgeous pine bar (fashioned from the building's original floorboards) where you'll want to sit and drink for some time, and the apron-clad bartenders are knowledgeable and courteous, and known to make a gorgeous Ramos Gin Fizz. Just consider ordering another drink to sip while you wait, since the Ramos takes a healthy bit of time to create. There's mixing, shaking, chilling, and setting involved. As Savannah's Big Boi would say, "Life moves fast. You gotta document the good times." Amen B.B.

GEORGIA SPIRIT
RICHLAND RUM
Brunswick

Rum is beginning to make an impact in Georgia, with domestic sugarcane playing a big part. Richland has been operating the only single-estate, single-barrel rum distillery in the United States since 2009, and began bottling in 2012. Pretty remarkable results for water, sugarcane, and yeast.

GEORGIA'S OLDEST BAR
THE PIRATES' HOUSE
Savannah, 1753

No, there won't be any Jack Sparrows bartending here, but there will be a building looking as weathered as your favorite Disney pirate. Originally opened to be a botanical garden modeled after the Chelsea Physic Garden in London, the Pirates' House mutinied against those efforts in around 1754. The fifteen-room restaurant has early pages of Robert Louis Stevenson's *Treasure Island* hanging on the walls, and the cocktails served there today take inspiration from the salty seas and pirate legends of books, films, and stories, which reminds me: Also, did you hear about the new pirate movie? It's rated RRRRRRR...

GEORGIA COCKTAIL BAR
TICONDEROGA CLUB
Atlanta

Ticonderoga Club has been flying under the radar for too long, and deserves more national recognition. Its signature cocktail, the bar's namesake, features rum, Cognac, sherry, and pineapple, served over crushed ice in a copper Julep cup, a wild forest of mint canvassing the exterior. Co-owners Paul Calvert and Greg Best started an Avengers-style team of bartending in Atlanta when they opened this place in 2014, and balance the world of cocktails and food as well as anyone in the United States.

UPPERCUT

Miles Macquarrie, Kimball House, Decatur

Miles manages to provide a proper nod to home state icon Coca-Cola by using it as the syrup portion of this recipe (published originally on *Tasting Table*). Bourbon and spiced rum are a nice Batman and Robin for cocktail crime-fighting.

1½ ounces bourbon

¾ ounce spiced rum (such as Scarlet Ibis)

½ ounce Punt e Mes vermouth

½ ounce Coca-Cola reduction (recipe follows)

4 dashes Regan's orange bitters

Garnish: orange peel

Shake the ingredients with ice until chilled; strain over fresh ice in a chilled rocks glass and garnish with the orange.

Coca-Cola Reduction

Makes about 1½ cups

One 12-ounce can Coca-Cola

1 tablespoon sugar

½ teaspoon fresh lemon juice

In a small saucepan over medium-high heat, bring the Coca-Cola to a boil. Cook to reduce the liquid to ¾ cup, 5 to 7 minutes. Whisk in the sugar, stirring constantly, until it dissolves. Remove from the heat and add the lemon juice. Let cool and store in an airtight container in the refrigerator for up to 2 weeks.

GEORGIA ROAD

Hunt Revell, Seabear, Athens

Georgia Road is basically a four-part sour honoring the Peach State. Richland Georgia Rum is a single-estate sugarcane product from the southwestern part of the state, and Atlanta Spirit Works is a new distillery with connections to Athens (where Seabear is located).

¾ ounce Richland rum

¾ ounce Atlanta Spirit Works Armour & Oak apple brandy (or Laird's)

¾ ounce equal parts St. George Spiced Pear and Hamilton Pimento Dram

¾ ounce fresh lime juice

1 teaspoon salted turbinado syrup (recipe follows)

Garnish: star anise

Shake the ingredients with ice until chilled; fine strain into a chilled coupe glass and garnish with the star anise.

Salted Turbinado Syrup

Makes about 2 cups

1 cup water

1 cup turbinado cane sugar

2 teaspoons kosher salt

In a small saucepan over medium-high heat, stir the ingredients until the sugar and salt dissolve and bring to a boil. Remove from the heat and let cool. Store in an airtight container in the refrigerator for up to 10 days.

Bootlegging was rampant throughout South Florida during Prohibition.
William McCoy was one of the most legendary figures responsible for the
secretive trade, who famously acquired whiskey and rum from all over the
world, which was a reputation-building effort when most local spirits during
Prohibition were not known for their quality (see "bathtub gin"). Though he
was a non-drinker, McCoy's name spread far and wide enough for trading
noble product and fair business practices, and to this day that authenticity earned his product with a reputation of being "the real McCoy." Also,
it's a little-known fact, but alligators love rum so much they bathe in it.

Florida

SOUTH FLORIDA IS the only place in the world where alligators and crocodiles coexist in the wild, and one cannot think of Miami without thinking of sandy beaches, sprawling resorts, Little Havana, Crockett and Tubbs, mangoes, flamingos, fast boats, art deco, all-night clubs, Burger King (first spot opened in Jacksonville in 1954), and orchids, which is probably why the explorer Ponce de León called it "La Florida," or "the flowery place."

Fort Lauderdale paved the ground for a midcentury tiki boom. The aftermath of World War II and the dawn of television led to an era that valued the ability to escape, and what better place to find solace than a tiki bar, like the acclaimed Mai-Kai, showering people along Florida's Gold Coast (the coastal line connecting Miami, Fort Lauderdale, and West Palm Beach) with Polynesian razzle-dazzle?

Orlando sees more tourists for its amusement parks than any other city in America. And Orlando's Universal Studios has gone and done the unthinkable for any *Simpsons* fan: In 2015, it opened a replica of Moe's Bar, where visitors can order a Flaming Moe, a Duff Beer, or a Krusty Burger.

Take an extended weekend if you hope to see all the great bars in Miami, as there is something waiting for everyone. Lost Boy not only provides a fun atmosphere for bar games—the cocktails make you happy to waste an evening inside its walls; the Anderson piano bar is ideal for anyone looking to sing along while sipping on a Martini; and Mac's Club Deuce, a historic dive in South Beach, has a happy hour that starts when it opens every morning at 8 A.M. (yes, 8 A.M.).

Bob's Your Uncle, a popular neighborhood bar near Miami Beach, is the second outpost of the popular original in New York. Their slogan is pretty inviting: "We Treat You Like Family (when you don't want to be around your own)." The cocktail menu is unfussy, featuring a nice selection of Moscow Mule variations. Photos of famous Bobs (Hope, Newhart, Marley, Dylan, De Niro, Uecker, et al.) line the wall, making you feel like, well, if you can't stay home, and you can't seem to connect with a stranger in the bar, then rest easy, because there is a wall of Bobs here to keep you company.

The Rum Runner is a great pit stop if one is traveling through the Florida Keys to the most famous key, Key West, and one Ernest Hemingway, who claimed residence there in the 1930s for days of writing, fishing, and sailing, and nights hanging at Sloppy Joe's, an iconic dive bar that opened on December 5, 1933, the day Prohibition was repealed. Hemingway gets mentioned in pretty much every cocktail book that's ever been published, so it goes without saying that he enjoyed cocktails while he spent time on earth, which might have been one of the reasons he claimed, "Every day on earth is a good day." Amen, Papa.

The first time I visited the Broken Shaker in Miami I was transfixed by the energy it totally imprinted on me. Not the normal sort of bar I seek out but the bar feels like vacation and is so different than anywhere else. I appreciate the diversity of experience it offers.

—Tobin Ludwig, co-owner, Hella Cocktail Co. (Long Island City, NY)

FLORIDA SPIRIT

ST. AUGUSTINE DISTILLERY
St. Augustine

This project was one built from passion, perseverance, and the long-overlooked fact that there were few distilleries in Florida. Open since 2014, St. Augustine makes small-batch spirits focusing on whiskey, rum, gin, and vodka using 100 percent Florida-farmed sugarcane, working with farmers on a regular basis to source local ingredients like citrus and corn. The distillery is located in the historic Ice Plant building, Florida's first commercial block ice company, and the space has been restored to provide food and drink connected to the distillery at the Ice Plant Bar, a beautiful composite of vintage aesthetics capable of transporting you back to turn-of-the-century motifs.

FLORIDA'S OLDEST BAR

THE PALACE SALOON
Fernandina Beach, 1903

Let's face it: You have not heard of Fernandina Beach. That's okay. I had not heard of Fernandina Beach. But I was delighted to find out that this little town on Amelia Island has a local tavern affectionately nicknamed "The Palace." Legend has it that it was the last American tavern to close during Prohibition. The bar is chock-full of its original design elements—pressed-tin ceiling tiles, Italian marble, mahogany bar, and inlaid mosaic floors, and was co-designed by Adolphus Busch, founder of Anheuser-Busch. It also holds the honor of being the first hard liquor bar to serve Coca-Cola in 1905, which helped catapult the Cuba Libre ("Free Cuba") cocktail into prominence throughout Florida and the southern states.

FLORIDA BUCKET LIST BAR

THE FLORA-BAMA LOUNGE AND PACKAGE
Perdido Key

The Flora-Bama Lounge and Package—located right on the state highway connecting Florida and Alabama—is anything but a lounge, as it's enormous, and has seen it all: hurricanes, shirtless dads, offbeat dancers, an oil spill, and countless mullet-tossing contests. There's even a Sunday church service right on the beach bar, which makes sense, as their signature cocktail, the Bushwhacker (rum, coffee-flavored liqueur, and ice cream) usually makes people pray to God the next morning. To quote my brother Dave: "The Flora-Bama is *everything*. It's a sweat-filled *mess*. You *gotta* go!"

BAR SNACK
During Prohibition, "Spanish Marie" Waite became one of the most influential rum runners the country has ever seen, known for being "a fickle and dangerous person, with morals as free as the four winds," as she was depicted in Malcolm Willoughby's *Rum War at Sea*. She ran a very successful operation between Havana and Key West until she was caught one night in Miami in 1928, and briefly released to see her children, only she never came back, and was never heard from again, and if that's not inspiration for a movie, call me Keyser Söze.

This is important: A twist is not a garnish. It is a functional ingredient. Not a garnish.

—Dave Arnold, author, *Liquid Intelligence*; co-owner, Existing Conditions (Manhattan, NY)

I learned a lot about drinks from Willy Shine, I learned a lot about professionalism from Julio Cabrera, and I've learned a lot about hospitality from Julio Bermejo, but the bartender I look up to most is the bartender that is completely comfortable working at the exact bar that they should be working at. You don't have to have great drink knowledge, or be well known, there are thousands of great bartenders out there that we'll never read about, that can make you feel at home when you walk into their bars.

—John Lermayer, from a 2018 interview with the *Huffington Post*

FLORIDA BEVERAGE
GATORADE

Gatorade was developed in 1965 at the University of Florida, whose mascot is the Gator. When Michael Jordan (pun intended) jumped in as a spokesperson in the early 1990s, Gatorade's popularity and its attention-grabbing electrolytes skyrocketed. It is now the official sports drink of just about every professional team in existence, and if you ever win a big game, turn around, Coach, because someone is about to dump an entire cooler of it on your head.

FLORIDA COCKTAIL BAR
SWEET LIBERTY
Miami

Miami is nothing if not a haven for refreshing cocktails, and Sweet Liberty provides them in steady succession. The bar, founded by the late John Lermayer, proved its worth by receiving recognition as one of the top fifty bars in the world in 2018. Its most popular cocktail is the Piña Colada, because, in my opinion, everyone deserves a Piña Colada, whether they've been behaving or not. Sweet Liberty's is made by combining two different strains of rum, pineapple juice, and coconut cream, plus they add Jamaican coffee beans and a Pedro Ximénez sherry float.

FLORIDA COCKTAIL BAR
THE BROKEN SHAKER
Miami

Most people in southern Florida go for the usual: dance clubs, jet skis, and Instagramming yourself on the beach in January. But when the Broken Shaker opened in 2012, Miami became a premier destination for handcrafted cocktails. A welcome respite from the dizzying Miami club scene, the Broken Shaker has received best-of awards from just about everyone: *Esquire*, Tales of the Cocktail, the James Beard Foundation, and *The Daily Meal*, which named it the number-one bar in America in 2018.

STATE FACT
The first US Navy station started in Pensacola in 1914.

I tell everyone to visit Mai-Kai in Fort Lauderdale. It is the last of the grand tiki palaces of old—a huge restaurant with a floor show, gardens with bridges and waterfalls, and a gorgeous romantic nautical bar with fake rain on the windows.

—Rebecca Cate, author and co-owner, Smuggler's Cove (San Francisco, CA)

BAR SNACK
Though a Rum and Coke and Cuba Libre are both essentially rum plus Coke, a classic Cuba Libre requires a squeeze of lime for authenticity.

The quintessential 1940s cocktail was the Cuba Libre—rum and Coca-Cola— a harmless invention that was helped along by the Andrews Sisters song of the same name. The tune came from Trinidad, where some fifty thousand American servicemen were stationed at a naval base.

—William Grimes, in *Straight Up or On the Rocks*

MOJITO
Brian Bartels

The Mojito originated in Havana, and was introduced to Florida in the 1960s when the Cuban community started arriving in South Florida; the drink sky-rocketed to popularity when Pierce Brosnan's James Bond handed one to Halle Berry in *Die Another Day*. There are many different variations on this classic, and some will tell you it can be made only with Cuban rum, but the truth is you can feel free to experiment with young and aged rums (and besides, Cuban rum is not so easy to find in the States). Everyone deserves to be an explorer.

8 to 10 fresh mint leaves

¾ ounce simple syrup
  (1:1 sugar to water)

2 ounces white rum

¾ ounce fresh lime juice

1 ounce club soda

Garnish: fresh mint sprig

In a chilled pint glass, muddle the mint and simple syrup for 10 to 15 seconds, then add the rum and lime juice and top with ice (ideally crushed ice) and the club soda. Garnish with the mint sprig.

GINGER SPICE
John Lermayer and Chris Hopkins, Sweet Liberty, Miami

Sweet Liberty is well known in Miami cocktail circles, and a big reason behind that was John Lermayer, who we unfortunately lost too soon. Everyone loved John, who was a bon vivant of the finest degree, a decorated global brand ambas-sador, and a bartender's bartender, who looked after his guests and staff with unflinching kindness. John's legacy offers us an important reminder, as posted on the back bar of Sweet Liberty: "Pursue happiness." The recipe for one of this bar's most popular drinks was first published in *PUNCH*.

1-inch cube of peeled ginger

1½ ounces rum (preferably
  Caña Brava)

½ ounce The Bitter Truth
  golden falernum (another
  velvet falernum would be
  okay)

¼ ounce yellow Chartreuse

1 ounce fresh lime juice

½ ounce orgeat

Garnish: ginger slice and lime
  wheel

Muddle the ginger in a mixing tin. Add the remaining ingredients and shake with ice until chilled. Fine strain into a tiki mug and top with crushed ice. Garnish with the ginger slice and lime.

Dry counties, bourbon drinkers,
and liquor and package stores. Bars
in Birmingham are taking modern
day civic pride to new levels. When
I walked into my first bar, the bartender introduced himself and made
me feel right at home. It was later
in the afternoon. The sun was just
beginning to fade and the city felt a
little quiet, but all that changed when
the bartender asked, "What brings
you in tonight?"Alabama celebrates
the yellowhammer bird (not only the
state bird, but also a cocktail) and
black panthers (not only a formidable
wildcat, but responsible for inspiring
the Legendary Sex Panther cocktail
at Birmingham's Atomic Lounge).

Alabama

THOUGH PROHIBITION HAD a major impact on Alabama (the state went bone dry in 1915, five years before Prohibition began, and 386 illegal stills were seized to begin that dry spell, which made plenty of thirsty Alabama whiskey drinkers mighty upset), it's refreshing to know there were people looking to celebrate life a little by throwing parties in nearby caves while the Eighteenth Amendment was in effect. The Bangor Cave Club, for example, served the Heart of Dixie in a speakeasy tucked away in the Bangor Cave, where gambling, dancing, and, yep, even the devil's milk itself—alcohol—were being served. Alabama legalized alcohol in 1937, but many counties remain dry to this day.

It might surprise you to learn that Alabama—not Louisiana—introduced the Western world to Mardi Gras, as Mobile holds an annual celebration even older than the one in New Orleans. During the celebration, revelers drink on the streets, thanks to liberal open container laws, and toss Moon Pies, along with the more expected beads. And speaking of pies, black bottom pies—creamy, chocolaty custard pies with a little bit of rum and a chocolate cookie crust—are a local delicacy you should definitely sample, after having some catfish, boiled peanuts, and fried green tomatoes.

Drinking doesn't happen just in Mobile during Mardi Gras, of course. Many of the Birmingham locals love dropping by Lou's Pub & Package Store, for instance. Part bar, part package store (aka liquor store), Lou's has been around since 1987, and serves a balance of cheap, cold bottled beer next to elevated, well-balanced cocktails made with fresh ingredients. It's a no-fuss atmosphere and one that celebrates locals, regulars, and the almighty spirit of Louis Zaden himself, who passed away in 2008, leaving such an impact on the neighborhood they held a block party to mourn his passing, featuring complimentary beer donated by Budweiser. Come by Sunday or Wednesday, when notable barkeep Angel Negrin features Church Night, a brazen nod to the Holy Spirit. I was tempted to buy the "LOU'SER" T-shirt, but felt that it could be worn only by a true regular.

One cannot leave Birmingham without stopping by LeNell's Beverage Boutique. LeNell Smothers hosts regular craft spirits tastings and features obscure, hard-to-find liquors at her tiny shop, along with celebrating female winemakers and winemakers of color. LeNell is a roll-up-the-sleeves, take-no-nonsense kind of person; she doesn't answer emails, drives a car with a "Bourbon" license plate, and balances the rowdy with the classy as well as anyone I have ever seen. "Better drinkin' for better livin'" is the motto for LBB.

While Birmingham has developed into a worthwhile destination for all things food, drink, and art, throughout the city there are important reminders of its history of civil rights struggle. The Birmingham Pledge, which was introduced in 1998, says, in part: "I believe that every thought and every act of racial prejudice is harmful; if it is my thought or act, then it is harmful to me as well as to others. Therefore, from this day forward I will strive daily to eliminate racial prejudice from my thoughts and actions."

These iconic cocktails that are so simple—they have no author. Everybody's the author. It's why I believe the name Martini was probably associated with Martini vermouth, which was the most widespread vermouth in its heyday. Somebody put it with gin and that's the end of the story. The idea that one person came up with it at a bar is ridiculous. It's Occam's Razor—the simplest explanation is usually the truest.

—Robert Simonson, author, *The Martini, A Proper Drink, The Old Fashioned,* and *3-Ingredient Cocktails* (Brooklyn, NY)

ALABAMA SPIRIT
CLYDE MAY'S CONECUH RIDGE WHISKEY
Kentucky

Clyde May served in the army's 77th Infantry in World War II and received a Purple Heart and a Bronze Star. His legacy of making illegal whiskey continued for the next few decades, until he died in 1990. His son Kenny took over the business after that, and Clyde May's Conecuh Ridge whiskey was subsequently named Alabama's state spirit in 2004; however, distilling spirits in Alabama was illegal until 2013, so Clyde May's sources its Bourbon from Kentucky, bottles it in Florida, and sells it throughout the US. What a country.

ALABAMA'S OLDEST BAR
THE PEERLESS SALOON
Anniston, 1899

The Peerless opened in 1899 and still boasts the impressive mahogany bar constructed for the World's Fair in 1904. Robert E. "Daddy" Garner, the original owner, served his own whiskey from bottles crafted in his glass company. Called "Old Wildcat," the whiskey was served in "scant" bottles, which were approximately seven ounces, or slightly less than half a pint, or what we commonly use as juice glasses today. Come on down for a fried green tomato shrimp stacker, which makes me feel like there's a Bloody Mary already in my hands. Where's yours?

ALABAMA BEVERAGE
COKE AND PEANUTS

Dropping a handful of peanuts into a perfectly chilled bottle of Coca-Cola may sound wild, but the pairing of sweet Coke with salty peanuts is believed to have started in the 1920s with farmers and manual laborers who didn't want to wash their hands to eat a full meal but also needed a little snack while they were working. Soda and peanuts are always available in filling stations, so it's a popular road-trip combination. That's the best way to "Roll Tide!"

ALABAMA COCKTAIL BAR
THE COLLINS BAR
Birmingham

No, they do not have a cocktail menu at this wonderful little emporium, and no, it's not very pretentious to sit and have a drink, and if I'm in Birmingham, no, that seat next to me is not taken. And yes: The wallpaper behind the bar's liquor bottles is the periodic table of elements, and yes, the elements are replaced with Birmingham themes (Civil Rights is Cv, owner Andrew Collins is Ac, and there in the middle is Me, for the late Marty Eagle, local bar owner and advocate of live music), and yes, you want to take a photo for Instagram, and yes, you'll probably need to charge your phone at one of the many available chargers at the bar, and yes, probably have some chicken and waffles to pass the time, and no, I won't be mad if you want to eat them all by yourself. You know you're in the right place when the bartender says, "My name is William, but my friends call me 'Wild Bill.'"

ALABAMA BUCKET LIST BAR
THE ATOMIC LOUNGE
Birmingham

The Atomic is a space built for the history of Birmingham and its wonderful people (big props to the Angela Davis room, named after the local social activist and female superhero). They have costumes to wear—literally: costumes like a full banana outfit, a shark, or Cookie Monster (everyone who wears this one gets a cookie). Everything about this place is inviting and comfortable, and it shows in the people dropping by and the mega-talented staff working the room. Hell, even the door guy opened the door for me when I entered! There are not many bars like the Atomic. Alabama is lucky to have it, and America is as well.

ALABAMA SLAMMER
Brian Bartels

Though the Yellowhammer (a vodka and rum variation with pineapple juice) has been making more of a modern impact at University of Alabama football pregames, Alabama has long been associated with the Alabama Slammer. ("Slammer" is a reference to the shot serving: You take a shot and "slam" it, or drink it down quickly.) I made my fair share of these shaken masterpieces during what I call my "Saved by the Bell: College Years"—but in Wisconsin, and most bars, this was more often served as a shot and not an actual cocktail. It's no surprise this little devil caught on alongside the sweet, syrupy drinks of the 1970s and is a staple of college life, and it would probably have disappeared for good if it weren't for Tom Cruise calling it out in *Cocktail*. (See? Tom Cruise still finds a way to influence us all.) So here we are. Southern Comfort, originally called "Cuffs and Buttons" and created by a New Orleans bartender in 1874, is a must here.

Serves 5 (shots)

1 ounce Southern Comfort

1 ounce Luxardo amaretto liqueur

1 ounce Hayman's sloe gin

3 ounces fresh orange juice

5 dashes grenadine

Shake the Southern Comfort, amaretto, gin, and orange juice with ice until chilled; strain into five shot glasses. Dash the top of each with grenadine. Bottoms up!

THE LEGENDARY SEX PANTHER
Atomic Lounge, Birmingham

The Atomic is famous for many things, such as its mural of the 1967 Beatles album *Sgt. Pepper's Lonely Hearts Club Band* behind the bar—except with Birmingham locals as the band and club members—but the cocktail everyone talks about is the Legendary Sex Panther. The Legendary Sex Panther is named after a cologne in Will Ferrell's movie *Anchorman*. "It may or may not be made with bits of real panther. Sixty percent of the time it works every time." Every order gets served with a sex panther temporary tattoo. Not only is the Atomic a popular cocktail destination, the Sex Panther is easily the most popular cocktail on the menu, often Instagrammed alongside the tattoo.

1½ ounces Old Grand-Dad bourbon

½ ounce Cynar amaro

¼ ounce Hoodoo chicory liqueur

¼ ounce Demerara simple syrup (1:1 Demerara sugar to water)

1 dash Angostura bitters

Garnish: flamed orange peel (or plain orange peel, if you don't have matches)

Temporary (or permanent) Sex Panther tattoo (optional)

Stir the ingredients with ice until chilled; strain and serve over (ideally) one large ice cube in a chilled rocks glass and garnish with the orange. To flame an orange peel, hold the orange-colored side of the peel approximately 3 to 4 inches (7 to 10 cm) from the glass, with a lit wooden match between the peel and the drink, and squeeze a couple of times. Serve with the tattoo on the side, if you'd like.

The rain was steadily falling when I made my way across Mississippi state borders, but it did little to curb my enthusiasm to experience the Delta Blues history, Abe's Bar-B-Q, and meeting some of the most accommodating bartenders in the country. (Though I sadly did not get a chance to see any catfish playing blues music on a fence). In Oxford, I stopped by William Faulkner's grave to pay my respects to the literary lion. Empty whiskey bottles and flowers were scattered everywhere, and I was reminded of his famous quote: "Don't bother just to be better than your contemporaries or predecessors. Try to be better than yourself."

Mississippi

LOTS OF LEGENDARY products claim Mississippi as their birthplace, such as pecans, cotton, catfish, sweet potatoes, towboats, and Pine-Sol, invented in Jackson in 1929. Blues music originated in Mississippi. Robert Johnson sold his soul to the devil at a Mississippi crossroads in the 1930s in order to become the greatest guitarist of all time. Bootleggers and blues-influenced music runneth deep in the history of Mississippi. Mississippi was the last state to repeal Prohibition, finally turning a corner in 1966 after outlawing hooch in 1907, so Mississippians have a lot of catching up to do with the rest of the country.

Juke joints—post-emancipation southern establishments featuring music and dancing, and clandestinely serving alcohol—were kickin', hootin', and hollerin' from the stages to the dance floors in the 1940s, some of them staying open all day long to keep the party in full sweat swing (homemade moonshine was popular, but even after Prohibition ended, blacks were still not being admitted to many licensed bars). The most popular joints were situated around the Delta, most of the music was ragtime or blues, and the dancing that took place was unapologetically American. The blues took shape in these hallowed places, and they are sadly disappearing.

Mississippi was formerly known for its Milk Punch cocktail, enjoyed on riverboats and often used as a hangover cure, but its popularity eventually faded everywhere except New Orleans, which is not a surprise, as the drink is essentially the South's version of a Long Island Iced Tea, a boozy cocktail packed with a mind-bending 4 ounces of Cognac, rum, and bourbon waiting to derail your plans for not only the rest of the night but a good portion of your following morning. "Professor" Jerry Thomas, the first American celebrity bartender, was responsible for putting the Mississippi Milk Punch on the map in 1862, publishing the first recipe in his seminal *The Bar-Tender's Guide, or How to Mix Drinks*, and the spirits and cocktail historian David Wondrich captured its historic American essence best in *Esquire* when he wrote about the drink in 2007: "Consider the origins of its ingredients: French cognac, American bourbon, Jamaican (and therefore British) rum, Mediterranean (and therefore Spanish) lemons, and sugar. It's Mississippi history in a glass—de Soto, Louis XIV, Bull Connor, and all."

Feel free to expand your cocktail survey throughout the state of Mississippi, as many towns feature wonderful cocktail menus, such as Hattiesburg's Branch Cocktail Bar (which has an extensive menu) and Mahogany Bar ("each cocktail is crafted individually with loving, often calloused hands").

Starkville is the location not only of Mississippi State College, but also the Guest Room, where co-owner Brian Kelley and his talented team of bartenders have been making residents very happy over the years. One of their famous cocktails is the Slaughter Tobacco Company, a Four Roses bourbon–based cocktail with tobacco syrup, citrus, honey, and hickory sumac bitters, named after Ray Slaughter, a local Starkville legend and one of the first regulars at the Guest Room. His family owned the town Chevrolet dealership for many decades, and you still see plenty of old Chevys with "Slaughter Chevrolet Company" branded on the bumper.

Oxford alone has a surprisingly large number of bars worth visiting for a town of only 24,000 people. City Grocery is a can't-miss for a cold beverage and its legendary status as a literary haunt; the Blind Pig is where everyone in the industry hangs their hat after a long bar shift (so you know it's worth paying a visit); and it's never wrong to angle toward the elevated cocktail programs at Saint Leo and the Saint Leo Lounge, co-directed by the talented, praiseworthy, and always cool-under-pressure Joseph Stinchcomb.

MISSISSIPPI COCKTAIL BAR
SNACKBAR
Oxford

Snackbar is a busy place with lots of comfortable, casual energy going on, and the bar is a feel-good destination for classic cocktails, creative house-made originals, and award-winning food. I managed to speak with everyone in proximity, which is an interesting social dynamic. An older man started talking to me as though we had been speaking for some time, and he said we as men need to be more careful with our hips. "My doctor said this to me," he said. "And we just happen to have a proclivity to need hip replacements more than women. And that's good to know." They featured a female musician menu when I visited, with a great quote from Dolly Parton: "God tells us not to judge anyone, no matter what anyone's sexual preferences are or if they're black, brown, or purple." Love you, Dolly!

MISSISSIPPI SPIRIT
CATHEAD VODKA
Jackson

Downtown Jackson has been lucky enough to host Cathead since 2010. Cathead Distillery got its name from the area's close relationship to blues (as anyone from the Mississippi Delta who is a blues musician is called a "cat head"), and the distillery provides support to the local music scene on a regular basis. The honeysuckle and pecan-flavored vodkas are top choices for people's boogie shoes at the nearby juke joints, but don't skate on the Hoodoo chicory liqueur or aged gins.

MISSISSIPPI'S OLDEST BAR
KING'S TAVERN
Natchez, 1789

Richard King acquired this historic building in 1789 and turned it into a tavern, an inn, and the town's post office. Stories surrounding the bar include one of a ghost being spotted in the tavern, allegedly the mistress of Mr. King (no relation to Stephen . . . or is there . . . ?). It was a private residence from 1823 to 1973, but was taken over by the native queen of Natchez, Chef Regina Charboneau, and King's now offers wood-fired flatbread pizzas, farm-to-table food, craft cocktails, mixology classes, and complimentary hauntings.

BUCKET LIST BAR
THE APOTHECARY AT BRENT'S DRUGS
Jackson

The Apothecary, located in the back of Brent's Drugs, was the first craft cocktail bar to open in Jackson, in 2013. They name their cocktails after memorable figures in and around Mississippi's bygone era of soda fountain lore (a nod to Prohibition-era bartenders who stayed in the United States instead of traveling overseas to bartend, some of them working in soda fountains, serving nonalcoholic beverages), featuring drinks such as the Doc Noble, named after an actual Brent's Drugs pharmacist employed there in the 1960s. Take a seat at the bar, take a photo or two of the back bar—which is home to a series of vintage wooden drawers used during their early soda fountain days—and sip your barrel-aged Negroni amid the unfussy refinement.

BLOOD ON THE LEAVES
Joseph Stinchcomb, Saint Leo, Oxford

Come take a journey on the Mississippi Blues Trail to visit some of the greatest juke joints in the world. You might never be the same.

—Brian Kelley, owner, the Guest Room (Starkville)

In February 2018, Joe Stinchcomb, a black bartender, made waves in the local community for putting out a cocktail menu honoring African Americans affected by racial oppression, including famous black bartenders like John Dabney, who was born a slave in 1824 and made Mint Juleps for privileged white people in Virginia before earning enough money to negotiate his freedom, and Tom Bullock, a famous St. Louis bartender and author of *The Ideal Bartender*, the first cocktail book published by a black author, in 1917. When a black bartender is being whistled at, or finger-snapped, or called with "Ay, boy," there is still a problem. I visited Oxford the same weekend a rally was going to take place in defense of the Confederate flag. These issues are unfortunately still with us. They need to be addressed. Joe, thank you for raising awareness.

1 ounce Pusser's rum	¾ ounce orgeat
1 ounce Cruzan Black Strap rum	¾ ounce fresh lime juice
¼ ounce Campari	2 dashes Bittermens 'Elemakule Tiki bitters
1 ounce blood orange juice	Garnish: fresh mint sprig

Combine ingredients with ice in a shaker and shake until chilled. Strain and serve over ice in a chilled highball glass.

THE PILOT
Ivy McLellan, Snackbar, Oxford

Living in the South and being so close to Tennessee, I would say whiskey is our go-to state spirit. We don't have many distilleries making whiskey in Mississippi but we sure love to drink it.

—Joseph Stinchcomb, head bartender, Saint Leo (Oxford)

Ivy McLellan is a true gentleman bartender and has been representing the wonderful Snackbar for a few years now. He moves through the busy space with hospitality and finesse, and conjures some very delicious cocktails in the process. One of the best is the Pilot, a terrific summer cocktail honoring Mississippi by using local favorite Bristow gin—though when I asked Ivy what the state's cocktail should be, his droll answer was: "Light domestic beer and humidity."

1¾ ounces Bristow gin	1 ounce watermelon juice
½ ounce Luxardo maraschino liqueur	¼ ounce fresh lime juice
	Garnish: 3 fresh basil leaves

Shake the ingredients with ice until chilled; fine strain into a chilled Collins glass with fresh ice. Garnish with the basil.

....

What does every American bar need? Heavy hands, good personalities, and a copy of this book.

—Ivy McLellan, Snackbar (Oxford)

The truth is, the modern-day bartender is only getting more dapper, as evidenced by many craft cocktail bars across the country, and this razorback is making it look easy. Razorbacks are not only adept at keeping the peace inside their bars, but they roll Bloody Marys without spillage with the best of them, and manage to style and profile like no other. Is that tailored shirt J.Crew?

Arkansas

When I was very young, my dad used to take me to a bar called Hugo's here in Fayetteville. One of those times he ordered a Black and Tan. That was definitely one of the first drinks I tried. When I got older, my family and I traveled to watch my stepsister in some games. We'd end up at a place called "the kitchen," huddled around an actual kitchen of the place while friends and family piled in and cooked turtle soup and gumbo. They were playing Irish folk songs and passing around a bottle of Red Breast 12 year. I will always remember that: music, dance, cooking, and drinking. Toasting to every sip and every song. If that's not a tradition, it should be.

—Charlie Rausch, bartender, the Vault (Fayetteville)

THE ONE AND only Natural State is full of apple blossoms, spinach, championship duck calling, mockingbirds, pine trees, fiddles, diamonds, hot springs, and the first Walmart ever opened, in Rogers. Arkansas was the French interpretation of the Sioux word *acansa,* meaning "downstream place."

Prohibition did a number on Arkansas, but that didn't stop an ambitious real estate developer from opening Wonderland Cave, near the Ozark Mountains. Bella Vista already had a reputation for being a resort town, but the developer wanted a nightclub that was more international, serving exotic food and illegal liquor to hundreds of attendees at tables and booths surrounding a dance floor—inside an actual cave. Nineteen-thirties Arkansas owned the theme: See no evil, hear no evil. But certainly get your groove on.

Today, there's no need to hide away the best cocktail venues. Fayetteville boasts a wide variety of cocktail-focused destinations, such as the Vault, an elevated cocktail bar in a former bank worth every penny for its cocktail creativity, Cannibal and Craft (named after a Caribbean beach bar and featuring fresh-ingredient cocktails and live music), and Nomads, an eclectic art-filled bar and restaurant in a converted gas station.

Little Rock, the capital of Arkansas, also has a nice diversity of cocktail options. South on Main and Big Orange are great starts, and make sure not to miss Atlas Bar, offering a mix of house originals and a list specializing in Highball cocktails from all over the world.

I walked into Little Rock's Midtown Billiards on a Thursday night, expecting a quieter evening and maybe the chance to chat up some locals shooting a friendly game of pool. But I walked into a Bottle Toss tournament. Bottle Toss might sound like an elaborate game, but it's really simple: (1) Take a garbage can and place it in an area where the only thing that can break are beer bottles. (2) Pick another area where you can throw a bottle from a healthy distance. (3) Make sure there are plenty of empty bottles. (4) Have a woman with cigarettes in her vocal cords hold a microphone and shame you while you try throwing an empty bottle from a distance into the garbage. (5) If the bottle goes in and doesn't break, you get a beer. (6) If it breaks you're disqualified. (7) If you're wearing an Old Navy shirt, you get hazed even more.

It was actually a lot of fun to watch.

BAR SNACK

Hope, Arkansas, is not only famous for being Bill Clinton's birthplace, it is the watermelon capital of the world, holding an annual watermelon festival, and an image on the town's municipal logo—though in college, Clinton was likely less interested in fruit than in Snakebite cocktails (equal parts lager beer and cider).

ROCK TOWN DISTILLERY
Little Rock

Americans are a funny lot. They drink whiskey to keep warm; then they put some ice in to make it cool. They put sugar in to make it sweet; and then they put a slice of lemon in it to make it sour. Then they say, "Here's to you," and drink it themselves.

—India's ambassador to the United States, B. N. Chakravarty

It took a little while, but the first distillery in Arkansas opened in the Land of Opportunity in 2010, offering tasty bourbons, single-barrel reserves, a healthy mélange of flavored fruit vodkas and liqueurs, and hickory-smoked whiskey. The company practices local sourcing by only using grains grown within 125 miles of the distillery, its single-barrel bourbon was voted the 2015 US Whisky of the Year by Jim Murray's *Whisky Bible*, and they have a nice spacious tasting room, featuring whiskey flights, specialty cocktails, and a healthy collection of vinyl records.

THE OHIO CLUB
Hot Springs, 1905

Just staring at the beautiful mahogany back bar (hand-carved in the 1800s) can make you feel like you're stepping back in time. The Ohio Club opened as a nightclub and casino around the turn of the twentieth century, and Prohibition thwarted its popularity only for a moment, as the owners turned some of the space into a cigar shop while operating a speakeasy in another part of the space, attracting local "tourists" such as Al Capone and Bugsy Siegel. Even though anti-gambling laws went into effect in 1913, the Ohio Club kept up its gambling game defiantly through 1967, because that's what outlaws do. As the bar's website reflects: It's "the best night in town."

MAXINE'S TAP ROOM
Fayetteville

Maxine's has been a Fayetteville institution for over six decades, known for its business-savvy, take-no-guff matriarch Maxine Miller, who opened the bar at twenty-four years old in 1950 after borrowing money from her parents. Maxine unfortunately passed away in 2006, but the new owners brought some modern-day cocktail prowess to the vintage décor and added a beautiful copper bar. There's even a Maxine cocktail, made with gin, blood orange juice, and rosemary syrup, though Maxine preferred Dr Pepper and coffee with salt. Speaking of salt, many memories linger over the years, but none more touching than the spirit of the old days, when sweetheart Maxine would deliver her farewell message for last call by microphone: "You have ten minutes to drink up and get the hell out."

109 AND CO.
Little Rock

When you sit at the 109 bar, there are a series of elevated wooden coasters with little bots of charred wood aligning the bar top. Each cocktail on the 109 menu gives the drinker the option of smoked wood for the glass—applewood, whiskey barrel oak, hickory, mesquite, or alder. A signature cocktail is the El Verano ("summer"), which, the menu says, "will be the best Margarita you will ever try." And it tasted like the sun shining on my face!

BAR SNACK
The Little Rock Nine changed history in 1957 by walking into an all-white high school after *Brown v. Board of Education* deemed segregation unconstitutional, a major victory for civil rights, influencing the world enough that Paul McCartney was inspired to write "Blackbird" in honor of desegregation.

STATE FACT
Johnny Cash was born in Kingsland, and wrote the song "Five Feet High and Rising" after the 1937 flood in Dyess Colony evacuated everyone in town.

EVERYONE'S IRISH TONIGHT
Charlie Rausch, the Vault, Fayetteville

Art's Place in Fayetteville is great. Cheap booze, cheap food, pool tables, old MGD signs, jukebox, sports, free peanuts. Honestly a damn good burger as well.

—Charlie Rausch, bartender, the Vault (Fayetteville)

This is a take on Irish Coffee, and the name pays homage to *The Boondock Saints*, a cult favorite movie of many bartenders I have known over the years, and "Catch you on the flip side" is one of the many quotes you can entertain from the movie. The drink is intended to be a simple riff on the classic, but low ABV. It's a fine tipple on your way to Tipperary or wherever else the wind be takin' ye.

1 ounce Tullamore D.E.W. blended Irish whiskey (for the soft vanilla and black currant notes)

¾ ounce cold brew coffee (store-bought, or see page 39 for homemade concentrate recipe)

½ ounce simple syrup (1:1 sugar to water)

4 dashes Bittercube Corazón bitters (a nice balance of cocoa nibs, cinnamon, and chile)

1 pinch of salt (to wake everything up)

2 ounces heavy cream

Sambuca in an atomizer (optional)

Stir the whiskey, cold brew, syrup, bitters, and salt with ice until chilled; strain into a chilled coupe glass. Shake the cream in a sealed shaker without ice for a good 30 seconds to thicken it. Very slowly top the drink with the cream so it rests on the top.

If desired, spray Sambuca three times over the drink, and if you're really adventurous, light a wooden match and hold it between the cocktail and the Sambuca, then point the Sambuca atomizer toward the cocktail and over the flame, which will spray the top of the cocktail with flickering flames, leaving a delicate aroma of burned sugar and anise on top.

WINTER IS COMING
Christian Huisman, Rock Town Distillery, Little Rock

I popped in Rock Town on a Thursday in February and asked Christian, the bartender, to make me something from the Rock Town catalogue. He wheeled out this remarkable cocktail, a spice-forward celebration of bourbon, bitters, and all things *Game of Thrones*. It was exactly what I needed. Added to that sorcery: "This is the second cocktail I have ever created," Christian told me. Born and raised in Little Rock. Hometown hero. Bar steward. Slayer of White Walkers.

2 ounces Rock Town Single Barrel bourbon

½ ounce Campari

¼ ounce St. Elizabeth allspice dram

2 dashes Angostura bitters

Garnish: lemon peel

Stir the ingredients with ice until chilled; strain into a chilled cocktail glass and serve up. Garnish with the lemon.

Long associated as the birthplace of American jazz, the Pelican State also boasts a strong culinary and beverage heartbeat. Ask any horn player on Frenchman Street, any person attending a crawfish boil, and anyone walking around with a Pimm's Cup "go cup" and they'll tell you the same. Though it originated in early nineteenth-century London, New Orleans deserves all the credit for putting the Pimm's Cup on an American cocktail map, as it started making NOLA waves in the 1940s at Napoleon House in the French Quarter. It's low-alcohol, photogenic, and one can even "play jazz" with some of the ingredients and garnishes. It's the ideal drink for hot summer weather, backyard barbecues, post-golf outings, and watching the kids run around the pool while mama pelican fixes another round.

Louisiana

FROM THE MUSIC in the streets to the people you are lucky to meet, New Orleans holds a special place in my heart. It is the first city I have ever visited where I was plotting my return as I was boarding my flight out of town.

New Orleans cocktail history is not only on par with that of many other cities associated with creating new cocktails, you could make the argument that the city is the Mecca of Cocktails, as chances are you have enjoyed five or six of its famous recipes all over the world. These days, New Orleans holds cocktail court sessions with Tales of the Cocktail, the annual conference for bartenders, bar owners, liquor brands, and all learned fans of libations, held every July. The city is a "living history exhibit" as the southern writer John T. Edge calls it, and still has longstanding bars making some of the most unforgettable Sazeracs (first served at the Sazerac House in the 1890s), Ramos Gin Fizzes (first made in 1888 by Henry Charles "Carl" Ramos at Pat Moran's Imperial Cabinet, but still alive and kicking today at the Roosevelt Room), Hurricanes (from Pat O'Brien's in 1942), Brandy Milk Punches (popularized in the 1940s at the venerable classic Brennan's), Vieux Carrés (originated at the carousel bar at Hotel Monteleone in 1934), Grasshoppers (from Tujague's—pronounced "two jacks"—since 1919), French 75s (originally from Europe, but adopted by the venerable Chris Hannah during his time behind the stick at Arnaud's French 75 Bar on Bienville Street, where they are made with Cognac instead of gin), Brandy Crustas (from Jewel of the South circa the 1950s), and the Napoleon House's Pimm's Cups (originating in London but claimed by New Orleans in the 1940s). Pretty much any bartender off Bourbon Street is equipped to build these classic cocktails, but there are some standouts.

There are bartenders in NOLA who gain acclaim for enduring, and Chris McMillan is an ideal example. *Imbibe* included McMillan as one of the top twenty-five most influential bar people of the twentieth century. He is not only an accomplished bartender with extensive knowledge of classic cocktails, he is a cofounder of the Museum of the American Cocktail, headquartered in New Orleans. McMillan's bar, Revel, is a wonderful place to visit when you wish to see consummate bar professionals at work.

So many great historic and modern cocktail bars are waiting for you in New Orleans: the well-designed and cocktail renaissance–inspiring Cure, Old Absinthe House, Beachbum Berry's Latitude 29, Pat O'Brien's, SoBou, Bar Tonique, Jewel of the South (recently reopened with notable NOLA libations guru Chris Hannah and rum savant Nick Detrich at the helm, who are also responsible for the Cuban-inspired Manolito), and Barrel Proof, to name a few. A stop at the Bourbon O Bar in the Bourbon Orleans Hotel shows how the well-documented history of New Orleans and its drinking traditions can come alive in accomplished hands, like those of bar director Cheryl Charming. New school and old school. Like a well-seasoned gumbo, just waiting for you to grab a spoon and dig in.

There's no question that New Orleans, founded by Jean-Baptiste Le Moyne de Bienville in 1718, is the heartbeat of Louisiana. We should all bow to the beauty of New Orleans, the people who have lived, loved, and endured in its magnificent streets. Its culture knows no equal.

LOUISIANA SPIRIT

LEGENDRE OJEN

New Orleans

With a program that pays homage to the melting pot of cultures that defines the historic port culture of New Orleans, Cane & Table is unlike any other cocktail bar in the country. The minimalist décor (they literally just stripped the bar down to its original bones in many instances) makes it feel like you're stepping into a bar that would have existed there on Decatur during colonial times, and the drinks—a mixture of pre-tiki and modern recipes with ingredients plucked from historic trade routes—are always balanced and memorable. To me, it's perfect in every way.

—Emma Janzen, author of Mezcal

Originally made in Ojen, Spain, ojen ("oh-hen") made its way to New Orleans in the mid-1800s and eventually became the de rigueur spirit for Mardi Gras, when people would sip it for good luck. It is a popular New Orleans anise-flavored liquor no one outside the city has ever heard of—and it nearly went extinct in 2009, until it was brought back in 2016 by the venerable Sazerac Company. The true Ojen cocktail hasn't changed in more than a hundred years, and is remarkably simple and equally delicious: a shot of ojen, a few drops of Peychaud's bitters, and some club soda over ice.

LOUISIANA'S
OLDEST BAR

LAFITTE'S BLACKSMITH SHOP

New Orleans, 1770s

My first memories of New Orleans were the graveyards we drove through to get downtown, and one of my first bar memories was visiting Lafitte's, the oldest continuously operating bar in America, and how there were magical spirits inside its candlelit domain—along with ghost tours taking place in and around the bar while people drank Lafitte's famous cocktail, the Obituary, a Martini spin made with gin and equal parts dry vermouth and absinthe. Its subtitle is "the highbrow of all lowbrow drinks."

LOUISIANA COCKTAIL BAR

ARNAUD'S FRENCH 75 BAR

New Orleans

Grab a Martini, Gin and Tonic, or the unforgettable French 75 cocktail that's the bar's namesake and embrace how much this place feels like drinking in a time capsule. To drink at Arnaud's is to absorb a small fraction of New Orleans history, steeped in tradition.

LOUISIANA
BUCKET LIST BAR

ERIN ROSE

New Orleans

Whenever I am lucky enough to visit Erin Rose, the world immediately begins to relax, as it's got the quintessential neighborhood bar *feeling*—a truly amazing accomplishment, given its proximity to Bourbon Street. A frozen Irish Coffee from Erin Rose is a don't-miss experience of visiting New Orleans and strolling down Bourbon Street in the French Quarter, as it's not the place just everyone knows and goes, but rather, that special local spot warranting a pit stop to escape the madness of Bourbon Street, and life in general. My mouth is watering for that frozen Irish Coffee as I type these words. Damn it.

LOUISIANA BEVERAGE

PEYCHAUD'S BITTERS

Apothecary Antoine Amédée Peychaud's was the first commercially produced bitters in America. Peychaud operated a pharmacy on Royal Street in the French Quarter and made the bitters in small quantities for New Orleans customers until manufacturing and selling nationally in 1840. Second to Angostura, it is the most common bitters on any bar throughout America, and it most certainly is on every bar in New Orleans, as having Peychaud's nearby is a necessity when making a Sazerac cocktail.

BAR SNACK

It's a sub-masochistic treat to order a Ramos Gin Fizz at the Sazerac Room in New Orleans Roosevelt Hotel. One catches the small pain in the corner of the bartender's eye as they politely nod in preparation for making the labor-intensive cocktail, much like the house staff in Jordan Peele's *Get Out*.

SAZERAC
Brian Bartels

What's a unique American drinking tradition? On Christmas Day in New Orleans, bartenders and bar regulars all meet in Jackson Square to drink mulled wine. Everyone brings a bottle of something to add to the mix, which Chris Hannah presides over.

—Brad Goocher, bar manager, Cane & Table (New Orleans)

The Sazerac is the official cocktail of New Orleans and goes down as one of the most important cocktails of all time. *Sazerac* sounds like it could be the next competitor to Amazon—it seems to be a reference to a high priestess, or a medieval golden amulet capable of eradicating whole villages, or someone with more money than God. In reality, it's simply a delicious fucking cocktail. Last time I was in New Orleans, I ended up at the famous live music venue Tipitina's, and the bartender offered us shots with our beers, and they said they would be happy to make Sazerac shots, and I said, "I love you." Though the original gets mistaken for having Cognac or brandy, rye started the revolution in the 1890s. To see a good New Orleans bartender make one is to witness a little Vegas flair of showmanship, as they first roll the tumbler glass with absinthe by tossing the glass into the air, which we all appreciate, even if it looks like they might easily drop the glass. Still, I can't help but be mesmerized by the theatrics. The Sazerac might go down in history as one of the most inconsistently made cocktails ever created, as I feel every bartender makes their own version, and has anywhere from two to fourteen dashes of Peychaud's, but at least we can all sip on a little history together.

1 teaspoon absinthe

2½ ounces rye whiskey

¼ ounce simple syrup
  (1:1 sugar to water)

5 dashes Peychaud's bitters

Garnish: lemon twist

Roll the absinthe around a chilled Old Fashioned glass to coat the inside of the glass. Shake the remaining ingredients with ice until chilled; strain into the absinthe-rinsed glass and serve up, garnished with the lemon.

VIEUX CARRÉ
Brian Bartels

The Vieux Carré is a legendary New Orleans cocktail that people have either never heard of before or mispronounce. But it doesn't matter. What matters is that the drink was created in the 1930s by Hotel Monteleone head bartender Walter Bergeron at the very special carousel bar, which slowly rotates as customers sit and sip away the day. This is a true French cocktail, celebrating the influence of France in Louisiana's heritage, hence its name: Vieux Carré ("voo-kray") means "French Quarter," which is where the Hotel Monteleone is located in New Orleans. It's boozy, yes, but oh so refreshing when served with the proper amount of ice.

1 ounce Cognac

1 ounce rye whiskey

1 ounce sweet vermouth

¼ ounce Bénédictine

2 dashes Angostura bitters

2 dashes Peychaud's bitters

Garnish: lemon peel

Stir the ingredients with ice until chilled; strain into a chilled rocks glass with fresh ice and garnish with the lemon.

Local Prices. Local Chaos. Local Love.

—Erin Rose's slogan (New Orleans)

Oklahoma was the number one oil
production state in America from
1907 to 1930, and still remains one
of the higher states in production
today. Oilmen have enjoyed a fine
cocktail since the beginning of time,
especially when they can lean on a
sturdy oil well barstool. Favorite
Oklahoma cities with cool names:
Corn, IXL, Cookietown, Slapout,
Moon, Bushyhead, Straight, and Gay.

Oklahoma

I'm from Tulsa, Oklahoma. I was raised here and threatened to leave many times, but I love this town. I don't think there are many drinking traditions that would surprise visitors in Tulsa, but most people coming through town are surprised by the breadth of great drinking culture here. It started with craft beer, but we now boast cocktail and wine programs that would be relevant in the cities known for theirs.

—Aaron Post, owner, Valkyrie (Tulsa)

LOTS OF WONDERFUL inventors hail from Oklahoma: Sylvan Goldman invented the first shopping cart (originally called a "folding basket carrier"), the "YIELD" sign was first designed and tested in Tulsa, the world's first parking meter was installed in Oklahoma City in 1935, the first tornado warning was issued in Oklahoma in 1948, and voicemail was created by a Tulsa man in 1970 and patented in the 1980s. But credit Bob Dunn from Braggs in the 1930s for first recording something that most of us enjoy when the lights go down: the electric guitar.

"Tulsa was an oil boom town and suffered the ups and downs associated with that industry," says Aaron Post, owner of Tulsa's go-to cocktail bar Valkyrie. "Downtown Tulsa is home to a great assortment of deco and gothic architecture, Cain's Ballroom (famous for originally being a garage in the 1920s before becoming a dance academy, nearly abandoned, then resurrected in its current iteration as a music venue), and is the birthplace of Western Swing, providing live music and dance for people at Cain's and outdoor venues through the 1930s and 1940s."

It took a little while for Oklahoma to catch up to all modern-day tipplers, as the state whose motto is "Labor Conquers All Things" didn't repeal Prohibition until 1959, and liquor drinks were not (legally) available until 1985. In particular, Oklahoma City, nicknamed "the Big Friendly," has been getting friendlier and friendlier with its cocktail programs the past few years. Bars are stepping up their game and putting in basketball-like triple-doubles on a nightly basis (I don't know what that basketball reference means exactly either, but it's safe to say that Oklahoma City cocktails are firing on all cylinders, so everyone wins!). Bar Arbolada is a bright new beacon for people to pop into and enjoy the vibes, and Ponyboy—inspired by the lead character in Tulsa-born S. E. Hinton's *The Outsiders*—is simply waiting for you to soda pop in and say hello. Hinton wrote *The Outsiders* while still in high school. She used her initials as a recommendation from her publisher, so male book reviewers wouldn't dismiss the male-heavy novel as inauthentic coming from a female voice. *The Outsiders* still sells over 500,000 copies each year. Drop the mic.

BAR SNACK

The University of Oklahoma's mascot is the Sooner, but many are unfamiliar with the term. Oklahoma hosted a land rush, taking place on April 22, 1889, when nearly two million acres of Native American land would suddenly become available to white settlers, because, hey, that was fair, right? On that day, when the clock struck a designated time, settlers rushed in and claimed land marked in specific areas. "Sooners," on the other hand, grabbed the land markers before the competition had officially started; so essentially, sooners were cheaters, albeit clever ones.

OKLAHOMA SPIRIT
OKLAHOMA DISTILLING CO.
aka Cocktails and Tacos

If memory serves me, my first cocktail was a 7 and 7 from a bar I should not have been at on account of my age. The first cocktail I had was a Pimm's Cup from a Tulsa bar called the Continental Club. I worked there for a stint, but it closed after a few years, being ahead of its time, and operating in a market with little to no craft cocktail culture. The Continental, however, set the stage for the great drinking culture that exists here now.

—Aaron Post, owner, Valkyrie (Tulsa)

One of the best distilleries in Oklahoma happens to be one of the youngest, started only in 2017 by master distiller Hunter Stone Gambill. ODC's first spirit was Indian Grass vodka, named after the state grass of Oklahoma and using Ice Age water from the Great Salt Plains in western Oklahoma. Each bottle features one hand-picked blade of Oklahoma prairie grass. The distillery not only features Oklahoma-inspired spirits and a variety of cocktails, it rocks a legitimate taco game, which we all know makes the wheels on the bus go round and round. Check out their merch table:

+ T-shirt: $18
+ Hats: $15
+ Pins: $5
+ Taco Recipe: $10,000

OKLAHOMA'S OLDEST BAR
EISCHEN'S BAR
Okarche, 1896

Eischen's has an awning outside reading "Oldest In Oklahoma," so you know it's legit. It's survived some hellish moments in its longstanding history: closed during Prohibition in the 1920s, fire in 1993, and losing James Harden to the Rockets, Kevin Durant to the Golden State Warriors, and then, sadly, Russell Westbrook to the Rockets. The bar is famous throughout the state for its whole fried chicken.

BAR SNACK
In Topeka, it is illegal to sing the alphabet on the streets at night.

STATE FACT
Oklahoma State Bird: the scissor-tailed flycatcher, of course!

OKLAHOMA BUCKET LIST BAR
THE SOUNDPONY
Tulsa

"We are a bar! We are a bike team! We are an athletic club! We are fashion! Who are we? SOUNDPONY!!!" That is the introduction to the Soundpony if you check its website, but really, there is nothing that compares to seeing the Soundpony in person. Located next to the historic Cain's Ballroom, the Soundpony has been serving a full bar, craft beer, views of the Tulsa skyline, live music, stage diving, dancing, and unflinching passion for bicycling and alternative transportation since the mid-2000s. Locals bow to it, out-of-towners revel in it, and all the full-size horses are jealous of how much fun it has on a regular basis.

OKLAHOMA'S COCKTAIL BAR
VALKYRIE
Tulsa

Valkyrie's motto is "Playfully serving serious drinks," which is an ideal environment when one wants to be elevated by the potential cocktails living on its back bar shelf while being served by engaged professionals who might riff on the cocktails from the extensive menu—and it is nothing if not extensive. If you follow Valkyrie on Instagram, you will know the staff like to have fun, drink, and playfully humiliate their barbacks before promoting them. All necessary rites of passage before we grow as human beings.

My first cocktail I ever had was a Long Island Iced Tea at T.G.I. Friday's in Oklahoma. I was underage and had a fake ID.

—Joseph Stinchcomb (born in Oklahoma), head bartender, Saint Leo (Oxford, MS)

LUNCHBOX

Edna's, Oklahoma City

As the story goes, Edna Scott will get on the bar and dance if you play "Great Balls of Fire." The Lunchbox allegedly grew out of Edna's insistence on not putting anything to waste. Regardless, the drink became popular, to say the least: Edna's has sold nearly two million Lunchboxes since the early 1990s. Does there need to be more of a reason to go there than that? If so, please put this book down and go wash your mouth out with soap.

1 ounce amaretto

2 ounces orange juice

8 ounces Coors Light

Pour the ingredients into a chilled beer mug. (It's very important that the glass is chilled.)

HADRIAN'S WALL

Tanner Scarborough, Valkyrie, Tulsa

Hadrian's Wall was built more than two thousand years ago as a way for the Roman Empire to control movement in Scotland and the United Kingdom. The cocktail itself has an impressive foundation in Scotland, too, as Ardbeg is peaty, smoky Scotch at its finest. The coffee concentrate, coupled with cinnamon spice, is a nice pop to the system. Owner Aaron Post says, "It's one of the more rad drinks we've done."

1½ ounces Ardbeg Ten Years Old Islay Scotch

1½ ounces Cynar amaro

½ ounce cold brew (store-bought, or see page 39 for homemade concentrate recipe)

½ ounce cinnamon syrup (recipe follows)

4 dashes Bitter Truth spiced chocolate bitters

3 drops vanilla extract

Stir the ingredients with ice until chilled; strain into a chilled cocktail glass and serve up.

Cinnamon Syrup

Makes approximately 4 cups

4 cinnamon sticks at 3 inches each

2 cups water

2 cups sugar

Bring the cinnamon sticks and water to a boil in a medium saucepan. Add sugar and stir until it dissolves completely. Reduce heat and allow to simmer for 10 minutes. Remove pan from heat and allow the ingredients to cool and steep for 1 hour. Strain out cinnamon and store in the refrigerator for up to 2 weeks.

BAR SNACK

If you think miracles don't happen, you haven't heard the story of the Ponca City Tornado, where a tornado elevated a couple off the ground in their house, lifting off the roof and the walls, yet keeping the floor where the couple were standing intact, eventually settling them back down to the ground unharmed.

It's easy to be a lone star in the Lone Star State, which spreads as big and wide as any state I have ever attempted to drive across, leaving one to feel awful lonely on a long trip. But wherever this lonesome cowboy wrangled this behemoth of a Margarita, the stars at night are big and bright—especially if he finishes the drink.

Texas

CHUCK NORRIS FACT: Chuck Norris (a Texan) is the fastest reader on the planet. He's already finished this book and made most of the cocktail recipes. His favorite was the Black Squirrel Old Fashioned (page 31).

On July 20, 1969, *Houston* was the first word spoken on the moon. Texas can certainly feel like another planet on occasion, but nope, it's still Earth. Especially in Earth, Texas (population: 1,109), the only city named after our planet. Lots of chaparral, cactus, and mesquite cover the huge expanse that is Texas, a state of more than 267,000 square miles, so big that El Paso, located on the far western side of the skillet, is closer to California than it is to Dallas.

These days, spirits in Texas are receiving a new mezcalitude. Mezcal bars like Ruins (Dallas), the Pastry War (Houston), Downstairs at the Esquire (San Antonio), and upstairs at Whisler's (Austin) are working hard to impress on people the merits of good mezcal—of which there are many. Tongue-Cut Sparrow's Alex Negranza singlehandedly guided my brother through a mezcal tasting when he stated that he had a rough time accepting its smoky, somewhat esoteric flavors.

Icehouses were typical places to get a drink back in the hot Texas days of yesteryear, but while just a few of the classics remain, Houston is fortunate to be home to most of them, such as the West Alabama Ice House, the D&T Drive Inn, and the Moon Tower Inn, all serving "cold ass beer and no bullshit." Why am I mentioning icehouses in a cocktail book? Spend any time with a craft cocktail bartender, and you will recognize a threshold. Crafting cocktails can be labor intensive and mentally exhausting, and a cold beer helps alleviate the stress levels, aiding in restoring simplicity. Most bartenders *love* a Boilermaker at the end of their shift, or on their days off. It's uncomplicated and refreshing. "I love the West Alabama Ice House," says author and bartender Jacob Grier. "There's not much better on a Houston night than a plate of tacos from the truck next door and a cold bottle of Shiner Bock." Beer and cocktails have a symbiotic relationship, and I wouldn't be surprised if we started to see a few more icehouses opening in the future.

Just as Houston (aka Space City) has come a long, long way in a galaxy of icehouses into the modern-day cocktailia solar system, there are some truly great bars throughout Texas, so make sure to spend some time when you visit. Austin is the cool aunt or uncle you want to hang with whenever your parents are away. It's got live music, hip bars, great food, South by Southwest, Austin City Limits, and Donn's Depot, where old-timers are still showing the young kids how to dance. Don't hesitate to jump into Barton Springs if you need to cool off on a summer day, and at night, cool off in the Roosevelt Room, a cocktail bar making everything pretty—and pretty damn delicious.

After visiting Austin, Dallas, Houston, and San Antonio, I have come to realize a few certainties: Austin lets its freak flag fly, high-speed scooters are not going away anytime soon, grackles are the strangest-sounding bird I have ever heard, and bartenders are superheroes, as evidenced by the Houston bartending community's efforts to help the city after Hurricane Harvey.

TEXAS SPIRIT
TITO'S HANDMADE VODKA
Austin

Donn's Depot is one of the only places in Austin where you can find old cowboys dancing alongside young hipsters—everyone is welcome. And there's always dancing; I'm not much of a dive bar dancer myself, but with owner Donn there usually playing piano and people of all ages enjoying themselves over cheap beer, it's really hard to not have a blast just sitting and people-watching.

—Emma Janzen, author of Mezcal

Bert "Tito" Beveridge (yes, that is his last name, and yes, it has been pointed out to me that my last name is *Bart*els) started the award-winning vodka company in 1997, distilling vodka from a one-man micro-distillery shack, single-handedly raising the money and sources for opening Texas's first legal distillery, hand-bottling his batches and slapping Elmer's glue on the labels, and hoofing it around Texas in an effort to build a following. It took more than eight years, but the hard work, sleepless nights, and steadfast perseverance paid off. Tito's has now captured an audience of millions in the years since its inception, producing upward of sixty million bottles of vodka per year and still growing.

TEXAS BUCKET LIST BAR
DONN'S DEPOT
Austin

Operating out of Austin since Donn started kicking up dust in 1972, the Depot has long been an Austin local favorite. You know you're in a sacred place when you find all the industry folks hanging out at a bar during their time off. Sitting at a table while sipping a shot and a beer watching the old-timer band playing hit after hit and seeing older couples cutting a rug with shiny new dancing shoes and showing the kids how it's done is an experience not to be missed.

TEXAS'S OLDEST BAR
SCHOLZ GARTEN
Austin, 1866

Operating as one of the oldest beer halls in America, Scholz has been hookin' horns with the locals, University of Texas students, and passersby with a proud German heritage menu featuring bratwurst, schnitzel, and obatzda, a Bavarian cheese dip served with smoky paprika and bread. Scholz gets a healthy number of its customers for the German beer selections, but what should not be overlooked is the terrific German spirit menu. On top of some speedy delivery draft cocktails, Scholz has a nice medley of German liqueurs, brandies, and bitters to sample, a rarity among German beer hall menus. That's swell enough to make a punk rocker polka.

The Mexican Martini is a unique Texas cocktail, which is essentially a Dirty Margarita, made dirty with the addition of olive brine, and was rumored to have been created here in Austin in the late 80s.

—Justin Lavenue, owner, The Roosevelt Room (Austin)

STATE FACT
"Don't Mess with Texas" started in the 1980s as a "Don't Litter" campaign to combat the common behavior of motorists tossing their empty beer cans out their windows while driving, and eventually caught up to replace anti-litter sentiment with a source of pride for being from Texas.

TEXAS BEVERAGE
RANCH WATER

When I think about cocktails in Texas, the Margarita always pops to mind first because it's ubiquitous throughout the state—from your average Tex-Mex restaurants to upscale cocktail bars, everyone has a Margarita on the menu. And most places always ask the classic question: "frozen or on the rocks," because the icy-cold, blended counterpart is just as important as the one that's shaken and served over ice. Nothing says Texas to me more than the frozen Margarita.

—Emma Janzen, author of Mezcal

The Ranch Water cocktail is a spritz-y Margarita variation. Most bartenders make it by combining tequila and lime juice before topping off the drink with Topo Chico, a sparkling mineral water that some say is required for the drink to be authentic. Though the drink has been around West Texas for decades, the Gage Hotel, a historic hotel in Marathon, Texas, finally put it on its menu at the White Buffalo Bar in 2010 after serving it for years, and articles in *PUNCH* and the *New York Times* followed, proclaiming it to be Texas's unofficial state cocktail. If it's between May and September, when it's arguably hotter than the surface of the sun in West Texas, there's only one thing to do—keep 'em coming.

TEXAS COCKTAIL BAR
ANVIL BAR & REFUGE
Houston

Bobby Huegel co-founded the most talked-about bar in the South in 2009. Most people simply refer to it as Anvil, and to experience the bar is to submit to cocktail history and majesty at the same time, as Anvil boasts a rotating list of one hundred classic cocktails on its epic menu, along with a smaller selection of house originals, which you could argue should all be considered modern-day classics. Each staff member is engaged and friendly. At the end of each night, the least experienced bartender requests to taste an unfamiliar spirit, and all the closers sit and sip and reflect on its legacy. It's also meant to foster a sense of community, as everyone closes together. "No one should ever have a shift drink alone," says Huegel. Preach on, good sir.

. . . .

Anyway, whacking a surly bartender ain't much of a crime.

—Larry McMurtry (born in Archer City), in *Lonesome Dove*

TEXAS BEVERAGE
FROZEN MARGARITA

The Margarita is the most Instagrammed cocktail in the world for good reason: It's refreshing, delicious simplicity in a glass. On a warm, sunny day, is there anything more fucking delicious than a Margarita? Anything? Cold and tangy. Sweet and sour. A little bit nice, a little bit naughty. Did you just break up with your girlfriend? Here's a Margarita. Flight delayed? That's okay, because a Margarita is always on time. Is it your day off? Here's a Margarita! Have you been staring at a computer all day? Margaritas are known to help ease one's eyes. Are your sinuses bothering you? Have a Margarita.

Joy of Mixology author Gary "Gaz" Regan said it best when he stated the Margarita has as many histories as rabbits have bunnies, but there is one origin for the frozen Margarita: Dallas, Texas. In 1971, Mariano Martinez, owner of a Tex-Mex restaurant, concocted a pitcher of frozen Margaritas made in a soft-serve ice cream machine, and the slushy goodness was picked up by every backyard barbecue, chain restaurant, and college kegger looking to impress. Houston even has a slew of drive-thru locations where one can acquire a frozen Margarita on a hot Texas day without stepping out of the car, but be warned: Drinking and driving is still illegal.

TEXAS BEVERAGE #2
DR PEPPER
AND PEANUTS

Following the Southern tradition of Coke and peanuts, where one takes a bottle of Coke and puts a handful of salty peanuts inside the glass, we now give you the Texas-born soda Dr (there is no period after the "Dr") Pepper and peanuts, a novelty adored in the state where Steve Martin, that wild and crazy guy, was born in 1945.

PLINY'S TONIC

Bobby Huegel, Anvil Bar & Refuge, Houston

The Pliny's has been a standard at Anvil Bar & Refuge since the bar opened in 2009, and is featured on the Anvil classics list, located between the seasonal selections and "The 100 List," which includes some of the most commonly ordered cocktails from the past two centuries. New bartenders at Anvil are responsible for learning all of these recipes. The list is a way to elevate the quality of its staff, a remarkable training technique, which should be lauded and copied by more bar programs across the country. This recipe hails from Paul Clarke's wonderful book *The Cocktail Chronicles*.

- 2 ounces gin (Citadelle recommended)
- 1 ounce fresh lime juice
- ½ ounce rich simple syrup (2:1 sugar to water)
- 2 fresh mint leaves
- ¼-inch-thick cucumber wheel (about the size of the pickle in your Whataburger burger)
- 2 drops Bittermens Hellfire habanero shrub bitters
- Garnish: fresh mint leaf

Combine the ingredients and shake until chilled; fine strain into a chilled coupe glass and serve up, garnished with the fresh mint leaf.

CIGAR BOX

Justin Lavenue, Roosevelt Room, Austin

Justin was kind enough to share this recipe after I had the pleasure of experiencing it at his wonderful bar in downtown Austin. I am a sucker for anything smoky on a cocktail menu, and when a drink features mezcal, lapsang souchong tea, and tobacco essence, it is a no-brainer for me to order. And the presentation is worth the price of admission: the drink arrives on a square glass ashtray with a smoking cinnamon stick riding sidecar. Every sip was a win. The tobacco essence is a bit labor intensive for the home bartender, so try using a smoky bitters instead.

- 2 ounces Del Maguey Vida Single Village Mezcal
- ¼ ounce Lapsang Souchong Syrup (recipe follows)
- 3 dashes Scrappy's Lavender Bitters
- 3 dashes Crude "Pooter" Bitters Smoke & Salt, Mister Bitters Honeyed Apricot and Smoked Hickory, Cocktail Punk Smoked Orange Bitters, or other smoky bitters
- Garnish: 1 cinnamon stick

Combine all ingredients in a chilled rocks glass with plenty of ice and stir until chilled. Burn one end of the cinnamon stick until it starts to smoke and set it next to (but not inside) the drink on a proper ashtray or plate to serve.

Lapsang Souchong Syrup

Makes 2 cups

- 1 cup of loose lapsang souchong tea
- 4 cups water
- 1 cup Sugar

Steep the tea in the simmering water for 10 minutes, stirring intermittently. Strain off the tea using a fine strainer. Measure the volume of the liquid, then add an equal volume of sugar (1:1 ratio). Stir well to dissolve all the sugar, then bottle. Keep refrigerated between uses for up to 2 weeks.

LUX PRINCESS
Sarah Crowl-Keck, Coltivare, Houston

This recipe comes from the January 2019 *Imbibe* issue featuring temperance drinks, which have grown in popularity in the past few years. Coltivare's cocktail menu wields a lovely balance of seasonal offerings, homespun classics, and an equal number of zero-proof cocktails. We are all seeking a little more balance in our day-to-day lives, and these nonalcoholic drinks are terrific alternatives to feeling we have to burn the candle at both ends on a regular basis. The "soft cocktail" movement provides a lighter, equally tasteful, more refreshing buoyancy to alcohol's weightier, sometimes derailing alternative. Look on the bright side: You get to keep your wits about you!

3 ounces coconut water

1 ounce fresh lime juice

½ ounce orgeat

½ ounce cherry syrup (recipe follows)

3 dashes salt tincture (recipe follows)

Handful of fresh mint leaves

1 ounce sparkling water

Garnish: fresh mint sprig, Luxardo maraschino cherries, and powdered sugar (if you have it)

Shake all the ingredients except the sparkling water with ice until chilled; strain into a chilled glass with (preferably) crushed ice and top with the sparkling water. Garnish with the mint sprig, a few cherries, and a sprinkling of powdered sugar, if you plan on using.

Cherry Syrup

Makes approximately 3 cups

3 cups cherries, stems removed

1 cup sugar

1 cup water

2 tablespoons lemon juice

Combine cherries, water, and sugar in a large saucepan over medium heat. Cover and cook until bubbling. Uncover and stir frequently until cherries grow very soft (about 20–25 minutes). Take off heat and strain cherries into a bowl, pushing down on cherries to extract more juice. Add lemon juice to the syrup and stir. Store in an airtight container and refrigerate for up to 10 days.

Salt Tincture

Makes approximately 2¾ ounces

20 grams Diamond Crystal kosher salt

⅓ cup water

Combine the salt and water and shake until the salt is dissolved.

. . . .

In terms of unique drinking traditions, it would be where you slam your glass down after cheersing, then drink. I guess I didn't really notice this one until I moved to Texas.

—Travis Hernandez, bartender, Half Step (Austin)

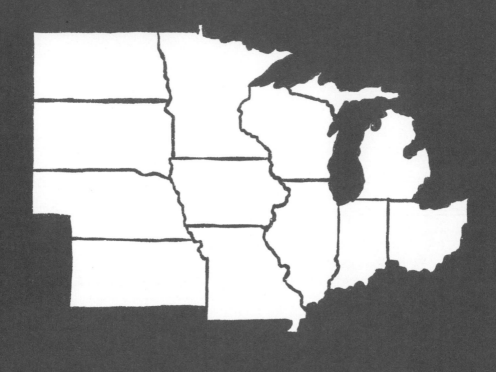

Does every American bar need to have a cocktail menu? Absolutely not. However, being upfront with a guest as to what they can expect from your bar is important. If you are a beer and shot kind of spot, maybe your menu is just a list of beers and straight spirits with prices. If you are a neighborhood spot with a rotating cast of part-time bartenders, you keep a short list of things that everyone knows how to make. Giving a guest something to order from makes them more comfortable—it gives them a map. No one likes to feel lost, just give 'em a map!

—Kevin Denton (from Atchison), senior advocacy manager, Pernod-Ricard (Manhattan, NY)

The Midwest

Ohio *Michigan*
Indiana *Illinois*
Wisconsin *Minnesota*
Iowa **Missouri**
Kansas Nebraska
South Dakota *North Dakota*

Ohio

According to NASA (National Aeronautics and Space Administration—I'm curious how many people would miss that Jeopardy answer), twenty-five of their astronauts are Ohio natives, having made nearly eighty space flights, and three of those flights were visits to the moon. John Glenn (Cambridge, OH) was the first American to orbit the Earth in 1962, and Neil Armstrong (Wapokoneta, OH) was the first man to ever set foot on the moon. Space Martinis. Radical.

Pinball was introduced in 1931, and was almost immediately labeled a menace to society, a time-waster and corrupter of youth. Considered gambling, pinball was banned until the mid-1970s in most American big cities. Naturally, it became a symbol of youth and rebellion, right along with rock and roll.

—From a sign inside Cleveland's Rock and Roll Hall of Fame

THE TERM *ROCK* and roll was first coined by a Cleveland DJ, and the Rock and Roll Hall of Fame carries the torch of that musical legacy for everyone. Added to that: LeBron James, Drew Carey, and Mr. Martini himself, Dean Martin, an illustrious group who all hail from the Rock and Roll State.

The Splificator, a drink that one never sees on modern menus and sounds like a villain in the Marvel superhero universe, was also born in Ohio and is attributed to bartender Chris Lawlor of the Burnet House, in Cincinnati, who published a recipe for his cocktail of whiskey, ice, and "Apollinaris Water" (German club soda) in 1895. It is still made today, but simply called a Highball. Manhattan bartender Patrick Gavin Duffy gets all the glory, claiming he invented the cocktail in the 1890s, mixing whiskey (which today can be any spirit) with ice and soda water and, in certain circles, ginger ale. However, while Ohio narrowly missed being able to claim a significant contribution to cocktail history, its drink-related future seems bright, Highballs or not.

It's hard to talk about Ohio without mentioning bourbon aficionado and bartender Molly Wellmann, who practically put craft cocktails squarely on her back and made Cincinnati a must-visit cocktail destination. Molly is an admired and respected co-owner of Japp's since 1879 in Over-the-Rhine and Myrtle's Punch House in East Walnut Hills, both neighborhoods in Cincinnati. Molly received the Nightclub and Bar Award of Best Bartender-Owner of the Year in 2019. She is, as author, cocktail historian, and soul guru David Wondrich puts it, "the bar queen of Cincinnati."

Cincinnati has plenty of other terrific cocktail destinations as well, including the Lackman, Sundry and Vice, Longfellow, and Low Spark, which features a cocktail called Nicolas Cage, made with Jack Daniel's rye whiskey, Luxardo amaro, and aromatic bitters, guaranteed to make you feel as wild as your favorite Nicolas Cage movie. But don't miss the Overlook Lodge, a bar based on the hotel bar in *The Shining*, featuring a "Here's Johnny!" surprise shot of the bartender's choice.

Cleveland is another cocktail center, and while it may have put rock and roll on the map back in the 1950s, today its bar scene is what attracts people from near and far. The Vault is located in the basement of a former bank, and serves live music. Quintana's Barber & Dream Spa doesn't sound like a craft cocktail speakeasy built above a barbershop, inside a regular-looking house, owned and operated by a wife and husband, and producing some of the finest cocktails in Cleveland, but it is. And if you're looking to be truly transported, the exotic Porco Lounge and Tiki Room, located in a nondescript building in the Tremont neighborhood, beckons thee, inviting you to swing by and escape for a spell. Bartenders wear Hawaiian shirts, the music is lush exotica, and the vibe is perpetual oasis island getaway. The wait to enter may be a little while, but it's worth it, as the room is never crowded. After you've ordered one of their well-balanced tiki tipplers, take pleasure in being at the birthplace of the World's Largest Daiquiri, a record claimed here in 2016. The ninety-five-gallon barrel they used to serve the colossal cocktail proudly hangs in the main bar, surrounded by patrons wearing a glow on their faces as they sip a little bit of heaven and forget about the world for a while.

Not just limiting itself to massive Daiquiris, Ohio boasts another impressive booze-related world record. The World's Longest Bar (at 405 feet, 10 inches in length) is located at the Beer Barrel Saloon on Lake Erie's South Bass Island, just east of Toledo. Affectionately called "the Barrel" by its regulars and locals, the bar holds 160 barstools and 56 beer taps, and can accommodate 1,200 sitting imbibers, operating with more than twenty bartenders on a busy summer night. I can only imagine what it takes to clean that place at the end of a shift.

OHIO SPIRIT
WATERSHED DISTILLERY
Columbus

Watershed began distilling in Columbus in 2010, and was only the second Ohio distillery to open since Prohibition, and the first to make bourbon. The company focuses on not only making consistent quality-driven spirits, such as an apple cider–based vodka, bourbon-barrel aged gin, and nocino liqueur, made with 100 percent Ohio walnuts. Watershed excels in its passion for sustainability and incorporating eco-friendly thoughtfulness to its carbon footprint.

OHIO'S OLDEST BAR
YE OLDE TRAIL TAVERN
Yellow Springs, 1827

After you enter under one of the most beautiful outdoor bar signs in the country, German influence abounds throughout this historic spot—walls are decorated with many a stein and feature countless signs written in German. The tavern has long been an ideal pit stop for people traveling between Cincinnati and Columbus, and has recently been renovated by new owners.

OHIO BUCKET LIST BAR
LBM
Lakewood

What was the first cocktail I ever had? Frozen Brandy Alexander at Kelleys Island in Ohio.

—Brian Nixon (born and raised in Ohio), owner and bartender, Truxton Inn and McClellan's Retreat (Washington, DC)

Billed as "your friendly neighborhood Viking cocktail bar," this cozy little hangout in the Cleveland suburbs just wants to have fun, celebrate dragons, wolves, and deer, and leave all the pretensions at home. It was opened by a collective of bar and restaurant industry friends and veterans who built out the space on their own steam. And yes, if you are wondering, the seasonal menu features Viking-themed cocktail names, such as Sower of Oblivion, Set upon a Pyre, and the Gust of a Thousand Winds, a grappa-based drink with pisco, verjus blanc (sour, acidic grape juice), and honey, as well as a category for shots, titled "Rage." They borrow a page from the acclaimed sustainability team of Trash Tiki by recycling their citrus products and collecting weekly compost. This alone earns them the privilege of playing heavy metal, because there's nothing more badass than sustainability.

OHIO COCKTAIL BAR
VELVET TANGO ROOM
Cleveland

The Velvet Tango Room has been serving an encyclopedic list of cocktails since 1996 in a Prohibition-era speakeasy space, which probably explains the bullet holes in the ceiling. Menu categories reflect classic cocktails, bold spirits, sours, "The Four Ladies" (an ode to sophisticated feminine cocktails inspired by the Pink Lady cocktail, a 1930s classic made with gin, applejack, lemon grenadine, and egg white), fizzes and flips, and "unclassifiables." The bartenders' consistency in making well-crafted classic cocktails preceded the cocktail revival movement, so you might say they were setting trends before the trends arrived. Super bonuses: live jazz every night, intoxicating paintings of women, and everyone who works there is a sweetheart. As the menu reads from the opening, "We've been waiting for you . . ."

STATE FACT
Ohio's flag is the only non-rectangular state flag in the United States.

BAR SNACK
Besides alcohol, many taverns, saloons, and establishments of yesteryear would provide free lunches to entice new patrons. In places like Ohio, where there was less local traffic, the saloon environment could be competitive, so owners had to get creative, and within that creativity, a free lunch could keep people hanging around and spending money. Historian Madelon Powers found saloon-goers seeking transformative "joys of intoxication and euphoria" when entering said establishments. Attendees bubbled through the room with unhinged playfulness, operating under a multiplicity of drunk synonyms: woozy, tipsy, sloshed, soused, pickled, bamboozled, flushed, fuzzied, tiddly, half seas over, skunked, crocked, juiced, and canned.

Porco Lounge is an American bar I tell everyone to go visit. Those guys do it all right: décor, drinks, and friendly bartenders. It's one of my favorite bars in the US. And it's only two hours from Pittsburgh.

—Sean Enright, owner, Spork (Pittsburgh, PA)

MAÑANA DAIQUIRI
Herb Smith

I know. It seems odd to associate a Daiquiri with Ohio. Blame David Embury. He first published this cocktail in his everyone-must-read *The Fine Art of Mixing Drinks* in 1948. David acquired this original recipe from Herb Smith, one of the best bartenders Embury had seen since Prohibition repeal, of the Spanish Room at the Deshler-Wallick Hotel in Columbus. Though the classic Daiquiri originated in late-1890s Cuba and started making the rounds in 1930s Washington, DC, the original recipe (rum, lime, and sugar) was adjusted in this Ohio spinoff, influencing Embury's legendary scrupulous palate enough to convince him it needed to be documented in his book. If you don't like the sweeter angles this version provides, add a dash or two of bitters.

1½ ounces white rum (Bacardi, El Dorado 3-Year, and Banks 5 Island rums all work well)

¾ ounce apricot brandy

½ ounce grenadine (I prefer homemade, but Giffard makes a good one)

½ ounce fresh lemon juice

Shake the ingredients with ice until chilled; strain into a chilled coupe glass and serve up.

BLOOD EAGLE
Eric Ho, LBM, Cleveland

LBM is famous for its cocktail names, such as "Flannel Is the Color of My People," but most of its names evoke the spirit of the Vikings. Co-owner Eric Ho is a trained aerospace engineer who is still building rockets, only now they're called cocktails. Blood Eagle has been on LBM's menu forever, and for good reason: one sip and the spirit will take hold of you—but hopefully not in the true Viking spirit of a Blood Eagle ritual, an uncomfortable method of execution in which one's ribs, lungs, and intestines are pulled out through a hole cut in the back, forming the shape of wings. Hey, kids, who's hungry?

1½ ounces roasted beet–infused Beefeater gin (recipe follows)

¾ ounce Averna amaro

½ ounce Campari

2 dashes Angostura bitters

1 dash Peychaud's bitters

Garnish: orange peel

Combine the ingredients in a mixing glass filled with ice. Stir and strain over fresh ice in a chilled Old Fashioned glass. Express an orange peel over the edge of the glass and place in the drink to garnish.

Roasted Beet–Infused Beefeater Gin

Makes about 1 bottle (750 ml)

2 medium whole red beets

One 750 ml bottle Beefeater gin

Preheat the oven to 350°F. Wrap the beets in aluminum foil and roast for 3 hours. Let cool completely. Using a kitchen towel, rub the skin off the beets. Cut the beets into small pieces and put them in a nonreactive container. Add the gin. Set aside at room temperature to infuse for 24 hours. Strain through a fine-mesh sieve and transfer back to the bottle; cover and store at room temperature for up to 6 months.

There are good people all over this land. Alex Lauer took me on a tour of
Detroit when I did not know a Motown soul (though Detroit's Aretha Franklin
still lives on as one of my favorite singers and water skiers of all time),
and helped me find some magnificent parts of the Motor City, which has a
cocktail culture only growing greater by the day. And being in Ann Arbor
was long overdue, and made easier by dear friends who took me to the Last
Word bar, where I did in fact have a Last Word cocktail (born in Michigan).
With modern distilleries like Two James, Michigan is making day and night
moves (and yes, that is a Bob Seger reference. What can I say. Turn the
page. And yes, that is another Bob Seger reference. I'm still the same.)

Michigan

I worked in Ann Arbor at a restaurant called the Kerrytown Bistro, which is no longer around, and I kept a bottle of Gordon's gin behind the bar (I was able to buy a bottle of Gordon's and keep it behind the bar, amazingly), and after every shift, I would pour myself a gin Gimlet as my shift drink. I liked gin Gimlets at that time because they were sweet, tart, delicious, and refreshing. I have since grown beyond the Rose's lime juice stage of Gimlets, as they are far better with fresh lime juice.

—James Lauer, GM/Partner, Fairfax, bar Sardine, and The Jones (Manhattan, NY), raised in Detroit, champion of hugs and high fives

FIRST OFF, LET'S give it up for the highest recycling refunds in the country at ten cents a can! Though the Wolverine State no longer has wolverines, Detroit residents were the first to acquire telephone numbers in America in 1879, the first to feature air-conditioning in cars (1939), and they created Vernors ginger ale in 1866. Battle Creek was the home of Kellogg's cereal—responsible for everyone's favorite childhood cereal flavors—not to mention Eggo waffles, Pop-Tarts, Pringles, and my brother Gabriel Stulman's favorite, Cheez-It snack crackers (circa 1906). They introduced the world to McClure's Pickles, a welcome accompaniment to any Bloody Mary.

If you're in the Upper Peninsula hanging with "Da Yoopers," make sure to visit the Yukon Inn's weeklong hot dog eating contest, Catmando's in Escanaba, and the Michihistrigan Bar in Gould City, boasting the "World's Best Guest Bartender," a charming fellow named Warhoop, who can balance several bottled beers on top of each other and deliver them to customers.

With Canada so close, rum-running was a big industry in Detroit during Prohibition (second only to the automotive industry in 1929). There were between 16,000 and 25,000 speakeasies operating in the Detroit area in 1928, according to the *Detroit News*. Michigan became the first state to ratify the amendment repealing Prohibition. I'm not saying that was a "Ray of Light" (hi, Madonna, born in Michigan), but I'm not *not* saying it, of course.

Detroit has been stepping up its cocktail bar exposure over the past few years. Evening Bar is a cozy little nook tucked inside the Shinola Hotel, Lady of the House not only serves delectable dishes from chef-owner Kate Williams, but their house Gin and Tonic with pickle brine is a pro-tip must-have, and Standby has cocktails and artwork worth its weight in Motown classics. Their amaro-based Grasshopper was minty, chocolatey, fluffy, and made me want to listen to Jackie Wilson records all night long.

My favorite story involves visiting Lafayette Coney Island, a legendary chili-dog institution in downtown Detroit. We grabbed a seat at the counter, ordered our coneys, and as I was taking photos of the iconic space and looking like a bona fide tourist, a random diner at the end noticed this and discreetly bought our coneys for us. I couldn't help but smile and cherish the kindness, noshing on my chili dog after a night of Motor City cocktails as I stared at a Nike poster reading "Detroit Never Stops."

MICHIGAN SPIRIT
TWO JAMES SPIRITS
Detroit

Two James is located in Corktown, Detroit's oldest neighborhood, and has revitalized the city's spirits since 2013, when it became the first distillery to open in Motown since Prohibition. The Two James Spirits assembly is one of the most varied and accomplished I have come across in the United States, and the creativity of its labels and packaging make the bottles practically jump off the shelves. Drop by the circular bar offering a selection of house spirits accompanying a rotating list of local artists work on the walls. My kind of place.

MICHIGAN BEVERAGE
VERNORS GINGER ALE

Vernors originated in Detroit in 1866 and became America's first soda pop. James Vernor, Michigan's first licensed pharmacist, was working on beverage recipes when he was pulled away to the Civil War, and when he returned four years later the liquid he had preserving in an oak barrel had a gingery flavor to it. Vernors also serves its soda in little baby cans, which are adorable, which is why, to this day, if you say the word *Vernors* to a Michigander, their eyes light up.

MICHIGAN'S OLDEST BAR
OLD TAVERN INN
Niles, 1835

Located in the southwest corner of the state and operating as a longstanding pit stop between Chicago and Detroit, the Old Tavern has been serving locals and travelers with hearty hot ham sandwiches and goulash for some time now, as evidenced by the road sign featuring a stagecoach and horses. Get in there already and play a game of Keno!

MICHIGAN BUCKET LIST BAR
CAFE D'MONGO'S SPEAKEASY
Detroit

Cafe d'Mongo's has been operating as a best-kept secret in downtown Detroit for more than a decade, though it gives off the impression it's been around for a hundred years, and the history spilling off the walls is an important reminder of Detroit's story through its recent revitalization surrounding the civic heartbeat of the Motor City. Expect some live music, chatting with friendly strangers, and straightforward drinks. Let the rest of the day be complicated. Don't forget to order one of the classic grilled cheeses before you leave.

MICHIGAN COCKTAIL BAR
THE SUGAR HOUSE
Detroit

The Sugar House gets plenty of recognition as the first new Detroit bar of the twenty-first-century cocktail revival, producing some of Detroit's most talented bartenders. In 2011, it established itself as a must-visit cocktail destination in Detroit's Corktown neighborhood, subsequently arriving on *Esquire*'s "Best Bars in America" list in 2018, and it's showing no signs of slowing down. The staff there does classics, they do originals, and they do themed menus, like "The Field Guide of Michigan," which featured flora and fauna cocktails. Is there anything the Sugar can't do?

THE LAST WORD
Brian Bartels

Life is filled with firsts and lasts. Created at the Detroit Athletic Club in 1915 but captured in Ted Saucier's *Bottoms Up!* (1951), the Last Word is truly balanced simplicity with commendable herbal dexterity. Today it is a source of pride for a bartender to find a creative way to riff on the classic recipe, as over the past decade a multitude of versions have cropped up on craft cocktail menus across the country, largely thanks to legendary Seattle bartender Murray Stenson, who discovered the recipe while reading *Bottoms Up!* and started serving it to his guests at the famed Zig Zag Café. My recipe sticks to the original formula while adding a couple dashes of orange bitters for a little more texture.

¾ ounce gin

¾ ounce green Chartreuse

¾ ounce Luxardo maraschino liqueur

¾ ounce fresh lime juice

2 dashes orange bitters

Shake the ingredients with ice until chilled; strain into a chilled cocktail glass and serve up.

THE HUMMER
Brian Bartels

In 1968, Jerome Adams, a dishwasher turned bartender at Detroit's Bayview Yacht Club, combined Kahlúa, white rum, ice cream, and a few ice cubes in a blender, and the rest, as they say in Michigan, is Hummer history. After finishing a regatta, racing teams toast with the drink, which became a staple of the sailing set. Now found in southern Michigan all the way north up to Mackinac Island, the drink is so popular throughout the state that you can find it served in plastic cups at backyard barbecues, via slushie machines in dive bars, or in elegant stemware at fancy restaurants. One person has claimed to enjoy them with shrimp cocktail and calamari, to which I answer, "No." Adams, now in his seventies, still bartends five nights a week at the yacht club, and when asked about the history of naming the beverage, he said, "When I served someone their second round, they sipped it and said, 'You know, after two of these, it kind of makes you want to hum.'" Fine by me. Just don't forget to serve it with a Michigan cherry on top and then high five a stranger.

1½ ounces Bacardi rum

1½ ounces Kahlúa (or another coffee liqueur)

2 scoops vanilla ice cream

½ cup ice cubes

Garnish: fresh cherry

Combine the ingredients in a blender and blend until the ice is broken down; serve in a chilled rocks glass, garnished with the cherry.

....

Growing up, as soon as Christmas dinner was cleared, the blender was brought out and Hummers were made for all of the adults. To this day, my dad always has vanilla ice cream in the freezer, and Bacardi and Kahlúa in the liquor cabinet.

—Julie Haase, general manager, the Sugar House (Detroit)

The first Indy 500 was held in 1911 and the winner came in at seventy-four miles per hour. The 1913 winner, Jules Goux, actually chugged Champagne at every pitstop before claiming the prize (drinking was understandably outlawed the following year). Since 1956, the winner chugs a bottle of milk in Victory Lane. That's quite all right, but just make sure you save some for the Tom & Jerrys (rum, brandy, eggs, spices, and milk!) we'll be drinking later on.

Indiana

INDIANA ADOPTED THE nickname of "the Hoosier State" more than 150 years ago, inspired by a poem titled "The Hoosier's Nest," written in 1833 by Richmond's John Finley. The etymology of *hoosier* remains a mystery, sparking countless theories, some of which are: Is it a roughneck from Upland South? Or derived from Old English to mean "high" and "hill?" Or is it slang for saying "Who's here?" when some pioneers came a-knocking on the frontier's front door? As Albert Einstein has famously said, "The most beautiful experience we can have in the mysterious."

There's plenty to see in the "Crossroads of America," which is an apt motto for a state that has more major highways intersecting it than in any other, but be mindful when driving or walking anywhere in the state: Indiana people do not cross the street if there's a "Don't Walk" sign, even if there's no traffic.

Cocktail bars are sprouting up throughout the state. College town Bloomington has worthwhile destinations like C3 (Crafted Cocktails + Cuisine), the Atlas Ballroom for good old-fashioned bar fun and games (yes, that is Skee-Ball over in the corner), and FARMbloomington, which always offers a cocktail menu reflecting classics on one side and a theme on the other, such as cocktails inspired by the movie *The Sandlot*, with the obligatory "You're Killing Me, Smalls!," made with Plymouth gin, green apple pucker, Midori (a melon liqueur rarely seen on menus), fresh lemon juice, and carbonated coconut water (also rarely seen).

Indianapolis has plenty of cocktail bars waiting to distract you. Libertine Liquor Bar is a sublevel oasis worth its weight in elevated cocktails and playful inventions, unafraid to infuse vodka with pink Starburst, for example; Thunderbird balances whimsical, well-balanced disco-dancing cocktails and southern-inspired food with the best of 'em; the Dorman Street Saloon, running since 1908, holds the longstanding trophy for best laid-back neighborhood cocktail bar that doesn't try too hard to be a cocktail bar, and accomplishes the task marvelously, with a knockout jukebox to boot; and the Brass Ring is an industry hangout for everyone to visit after they've worked a shift at their own spots. The house shot is Sambuca.

Though he was not born there, it just so happens there is a Santa Claus, Indiana, which receives its fair share of letters and requests during Christmastime.

I keep coming back to this bar in Indianapolis called The Brass Ring. It's where the industry people go when they're done working their shifts at other bars and restaurants in town. Brass Ring plays old black-and-white movies on the TVs, the back bar looks like something straight out of the 1950s or '60s, the house shot is always Sambuca, and there is every cheap beer one could want. You can walk in and always feel like you're home.

—Michael Toscano, brand ambassador, Woodford Reserve Distillery (formerly of Libertine Liquor Bar) (Indianapolis)

Every American bar needs bitters. Ideally sugar to accompany said bitters, but definitely bitters. That's a bartender's salt and pepper, and you can't cook without salt.

—Ryan Gullett, bar manager, Bluebeard (Indianapolis)

BAR SNACK

Indiana passed an artisan distiller's permit law in 2013, allowing craft distillers the option to sell directly to consumers. Many other states have adopted this practice, which is why the number of craft distilleries across America has grown rapidly since 2010. If you like them apples, please do yourself a favor and try Starlight apple brandy, winner of the 2017 American Craft Spirit Awards Best of Brandy, from Huber's, a family-operated orchard that has been in southern Indiana since the 1800s.

INDIANA SPIRIT
CARDINAL SPIRITS
Bloomington

Cardinal has been around only since 2015, but it hurtled out of the gates like steam through a biodegradable paper straw, operating a distillery, tasting room, and restaurant with wonderful cocktails from day one. The company produces award-winning gins, spiced rums, coffee liqueur made with beans from local roaster Hopscotch, and various other fruit and floral liqueurs. Take a look at the website: It's sincere yet playful and rooted in philanthropy. And the canned cocktails made by Cardinal are adorable.

INDIANA'S OLDEST BAR
THE KNICKERBOCKER SALOON
Lafayette, 1835

Proudly claiming the first liquor license in Indiana, this saloon went by a few different names before turning into the Knickerbocker in 1874, when they renovated the space to offer live music (especially jazz and blues). It has accommodated such notables as Mark Twain, Ulysses S. Grant, and Al Capone over the years. A card detailing the history of the saloon reads, "Many gents spent their days in the luxury of the bar reading a good book, playing cards, or waiting on the next train that stopped directly out front." A sign above the bar offers the warming sentiment: "Enter as strangers, leave as friends."

INDIANA BEVERAGE
MILK

Lots of other states claim milk as their state beverage, but in the 1930s, Louis Meyer, the first three-time winner of the Indy 500, started a new trend by chugging milk after winning the famous race, and though it took a little while to catch on, it has now become synonymous with winning the 500.

INDIANA BUCKET LIST BAR
SAM'S SILVER CIRCLE BAR
Indianapolis

Arriving at Sam's Silver Circle was akin to entering the scene in *Dazed and Confused* at the pool hall, where everyone is hanging inside and out, drinking and laughing and checking out who's got the hot new ride with vanity plates. When your friends are singing a show-stopping version of Bowie's "Young Americans" as you're walking around the room uncertain whether to have another drink, while taking photos of 1980s *Sports Illustrated* issues on the wall and hamming it up with the locals, and your friend is yelling at you to sign him up for Tom Petty's "The Waiting," and the karaoke host is wearing an American flag button-down, a ten-gallon cowboy hat, and a scowl, obviously not enjoying anyone or his job, you consider what is most important in life. And you are right when you decide: It's asking nicely to queue up Tom Petty.

INDIANA COCKTAIL BAR
THE BALL AND BISCUIT
Indianapolis

Affectionately known as "the Biscuit" or the "B&B" bar, this is Indianapolis's original cocktail bar. *Esquire* bestowed it a spot on the "Best New Bars in America" list in 2012, and it has endured the wave of cocktail resurgence with a laid-back, casual speakeasy vibe. The cocktail menu has a few classics but mostly features original creations by the staff, such as A Dame to Kill For, a Scotch and Soda variation with green apple syrup. It's one of those menus with the right kind of variety and creativity to make you want to try everything on the list, along with some beer cheese popcorn, hummus, and charcuterie. Call the babysitter and say you might be running a little late.

SAGE GIMLET
Alyvia Cain, Cardinal Spirits, Bloomington

I'll stick with gin. Champagne is just ginger ale that knows somebody.

—Hawkeye, in the TV show *M*A*S*H*, in the 1973 episode "Ceasefire"

I love gin. I always get people who say, 'I just absolutely hate gin,' and I love to try to convince them otherwise. Some of my favorites from the States are Uncle Val's, Bluecoat, J. Rieger, Aria, Junipero, and 8th Day from here in Indy. Also, Bluebeard is right across the street from Hotel Tango. They are making big waves in the Midwest scene and growing.

—Ryan Gullett, bar manager, Bluebeard (Indianapolis)

Cardinal developed its Terra Botanical gin with spice guru Lior Lev Sercarz, of the spice company La Boîte, who calls his method of conjuring memories of scents from our past "spice therapy." The gin takes on the influences of botanicals and spices, inspired by the memories of cofounder Adam Quirk's hikes in the southern Indiana woods and Sercarz's childhood memories of zuta, a wild, prolific mint from upper Galilee in Israel. Therapy pays off, as it won American Distilling's Best in Class in 2017.

2 ounces Cardinal Spirits
Terra Botanical gin
(or another American gin,
such as Aviation, Waterloo,
or Greenhook—you will find
radical differences)

¾ ounce fresh lime juice

¾ ounce simple syrup
(1:1 sugar to water)

3 to 4 fresh sage leaves

Garnish: fresh sage sprig

Shake the ingredients with ice until chilled; fine strain into a chilled coupe or Martini glass and serve up, garnished with the sage.

BREAKFAST OF CHAMPIONS
Ryan Gullett, Bluebeard, Indianapolis

Breakfast of Champions is one of Indiana native Kurt Vonnegut's most celebrated and well-known novels. It is also the catchphrase of Wheaties cereal. In the novel, every time a female server delivers a Martini, she says, "Breakfast of Champions." It is not always on Bluebeard's menu, but I found the recipe and state influence too important to overlook, and Amaro di Angostura is a wonderful product we need more of in our lives, just as we need more voices like Vonnegut's. (Also, better eat your Wheaties.)

1 ounce Laird's Straight apple
brandy bottled in bond

½ ounce Montenegro amaro

½ ounce Amaro di Angostura

¾ ounce honey

¾ ounce fresh lemon juice

1 ounce Apple Jacks cereal–
infused half-and-half
(recipe follows)

Coupe glass rim: sugar and
crushed Wheaties cereal

Garnish: Angostura bitters

Shake the ingredients with ice until chilled; strain into a chilled coupe glass rimmed with a mixture of sugar and crushed Wheaties (run the rim of the glass with the inside of a lemon wedge, or dip the rim into lemon juice). Serve up, garnished with the bitters. If you'd like to be extra creative, draw a Kurt Vonnegut asterisk on top of the drink by dropping the bitters in the center of the cocktail and hand-carving an asterisk with a thin straw toothpick.

Apple Jacks Cereal–Infused Half-and-Half

Makes about 1 cup

1 cup Apple Jacks cereal

1 cup half-and-half

Steep the cereal in the half-and-half for 30 minutes. Strain. Store in an airtight container in the refrigerator until the half-and-half's expiration date.

Green Mill COCKTAIL Lounge

Plenty of nefarious activity occurred at Chicago's famous Green Mill since it opened in 1907. Notorious gangster Al Capone frequented the space while "alky cookers," or stills, were supplied throughout the greater Chicago area in the early days of Prohibition. People were assigned to make small batches of not-so-tasty but effective homemade liquor from their homes. They would cook up the highly potent liquid and sell the product to speak-easies for handsome profit, but before they were able to sell the boozy "gin," they needed to cut the batch with some water, and since most kitchen sinks didn't have high enough spigots, they filled bottles in the bathtub; hence, "bathtub gin." Thankfully, there are modern distilleries providing far more delicious alternatives. Letherbee, Few Spirits, and North Shore are distilleries worth seeking out when making the Illinois rounds.

Illinois

THE ICE CREAM "sundae" was named in Evanston. Influenced by piety, the community passed a city ordinance outlawing the sale of ice cream sodas on Sundays, so the drug store operators and soda store confectioners created a different spelling of "Sunday," and the rest, as they say, is served with a spoon and, hopefully, some extra whipped cream.

Chicago saw unbelievable growth in the nineteenth century, expanding so fast it was considered one of the most dangerous cities in America, specializing in crime, greed, corruption, and every other vice under the midwestern sun. One pre-Prohibition bar was called the Bucket of Blood, infamous for its nightly stabbings, fights, and the need for a constant mopping.

Chicago's cocktail history runs through its legendary hotels (the Pump Room in the Ambassador Hotel is the alleged birthplace of the celery garnish in the Bloody Mary, created when a guest was unable to find a swizzle stick) and the fact that so many people used the Windy City as a midway stopping point in coast-to-coast US travel. Nowadays, there are plenty of cocktail spots throughout Chicago, making it a destination city for today's libation enthusiasts. Logan Square in particular has some recently opened treasures: Lost Lake (a tiki bar), Billy Sunday (an amaro-focused juggernaut), and Longman & Eagle, offering an expansive whiskey and rare spirits selection.

Gin, lemon juice, sugar, and mint may not have been something Harry Caray had before the start of every Cubs game, but the classic Southside cocktail often gets associated with Illinois, and Chicago's famed South Side gang from the 1920s. If any of Al Capone's crew are still around, we don't want them upset, so let's just give it a rest for the sake of how good it feels to be in a room with people enjoying this drink, celebrating something unexpected, toasting a hard day's work, missing a loved one, or the light of the moon. One can't mention legendary Prohibition gangster Al Capone or Chicago's drinking history without speaking of the Green Mill, an iconic nightlife destination that was a favorite hangout of Capone, who had a special booth he always sat in.

And speaking of influential figures in the Chicago nightlife world, thumbs way up for Ariel E. Neal and Alexis Brown for creating Causing a Stir, an industry program dedicated to celebrating diversity, leadership, and support throughout the hospitality industry, where we can all agree inequality doesn't belong. There are still places in America where the bartenders are not given enough attention and the tutelage necessary to succeed, and a little support goes a long way.

STATE FACT

Bill Murray was born in Evanston in 1950, beating McDonald's by five years, as only Bill Murray could do. My guess? Though only five years old at the time, Bill managed to show up at that McDonald's in Des Plaines, Illinois, and most likely bought a few burgers for the staff when the manager wasn't looking. Classic Bill.

ILLINOIS SPIRIT
JEPPSON'S MALÖRT
Chicago

*What does a
punch in the
face taste like?
Just try Malört.*

—Kat Odell, author,
Unicorn Food and
Day Drinking

*But you have
to earn living
in Chicago. You
earn it by living
through those
winters. And if
Malört isn't the
liquid equivalent
of a Chicago win-
ter, I'm not really
sure what is.*

—Toby Maloney,
co-owner and head
mixologist, the
Violet Hour, quoted
in Munchies

Malört is the Swedish word for "wormwood." It was created in the 1930s by
Carl Jeppson, who brought the unique
liqueur to Chicago and developed a
cult following and niche market over
decades, curing locals of indigestion,
sweet memories, and boredom. Try as
we often might, the taste association
of Malört never really gravitates to a
place we can easily categorize. Malört
was nearly gone from history, as the
last employee of Jeppson's was about
to retire in 2018, until the CH Distillery
in Chicago acquired the company. It
will continue to produce the local
favorite spirit for the indefinite future.
As the old labels used to say: "Make it
past two 'shock-glasses' and with the
third you could be ours . . . forever."

ILLINOIS BUCKET LIST BAR
BEST INTENTIONS
Chicago

Christopher and Calvin Marty,
brothers who grew up in Illinois and
Wisconsin, opened Best Intentions on
a shoestring budget. It was the first bar
in America to serve Angostura on tap.
Drop by any night of the week (except
Mondays—they're closed) and expect
ice-cold Miller High Life bottles, the
"Damn near famous" Wondermint
Malted milkshake cocktail, ephemera
decorating the walls, and a vintage
Rock-Ola jukebox from 1978 playing
Charlie Feathers ("insert quarters
slowly or machine will jam"). And if
Chris is working, ask him to make you
the Uncle Val's peppered gin cocktail
garnished with a house-made bread
and butter pickle garnish. You. Will.
Melt. Best Intentions is a bar that is
very young, but it feels like it's been
around forever, and deserves to be
here for a long, long time. Definitely
one of my favorite bars in America.

*I'm a big fan of all the
Letherbee products out of
Chicago. I'm anxious every
spring and autumn to get a
hold of their small batch gin
releases. Their charred oak
barrel-aged absinthe is a
bottle I find myself reaching
for over and over again.*

—Morgan McKinney, Dodici at Bari (Memphis)

> ### LITTLE KNOWN
> A *New York Sun* editor coined
> the term "Windy City."

*Malört tastes like
pencil shavings
and heartache.*

—John Hodgman, humorist, who
has been known to offer shots to his
audience, because wormwood, as
we all know, makes people laugh

ILLINOIS COCKTAIL BAR
THE VIOLET HOUR
Chicago

I used to come visit family in Chicago every year and discovering Billy Sunday was one of the motivations for moving up here. I literally said to my husband, "I want to live within walking distance to this bar," and here I am many years later living in an apartment that's a five-minute walk away. It's Chicago in a nutshell to me—humble but aspirational in the same breath, elegant but comfortable and welcoming.

—Emma Janzen, author of Mezcal

In 2010, my friend Charles Joly poured me a shot of Malört, and I only just recently forgave him.

—Erick Castro, host of Bartender at Large

When you enter the Violet Hour, the space unfolds to an unexpected pre-Prohibition–imagined delight. High ceilings, marble countertops, shelves painted white to reflect a soda fountain parlor aesthetic. Toby Maloney and co. opened up this James Beard Award–winning program when every other Chicago bar was featuring two-for-ones, Jäger bombs, and pint-size vodka sodas. Violet Hour brought a thoughtful, self-proclaimed "Mr. Potato Head" approach to building nationally recognized craft cocktails, building aesthetically pleasing beverages with varying ingredients, delivered with hospitality, education, and integrity. When he first asked his bartenders who liked gin in 2007, no one raised their hand. Now they're all gin savants.

ILLINOIS COCKTAIL BAR
THE AVIARY
Chicago

One can't talk about Chicago cocktails without mentioning the Aviary, which was a midwestern trailblazer of molecular mixology, an extension of acclaimed chef Grant Achatz's breakthrough restaurant, Alinea. Drinking here, you might have memories of high school chemistry class. And bonus points: Both locations (Chicago and New York) feature the accompanying extra bar speakeasy the Office, showcasing pre-Prohibition cocktails, vintage spirit selections, and "Dealer's Choice" options, where the patron picks a cocktail based on their preferences in a range of areas: citrus characteristics to ideal vacation destination, favorite movie character to their favorite season.

> ### LITTLE KNOWN
> The first skyscraper ever constructed was built in Chicago in 1885.

ILLINOIS OLDEST BAR
THE VILLAGE TAVERN
Long Grove, 1847

Located about an hour south of Chicago, the historic family-owned Village Tavern has been serving locals fine food, drink, and nightly live music with piano songs and sing-alongs. The long mahogany bar was salvaged after it survived the Great McCormick Place Fire in Chicago in 1967.

Chicago's Charles Joly is hands-down one of the finest, most meticulous, detail-oriented bartenders I've ever met. I staged at Aviary one night with him, the same year he won world class. Watching him work in the Office was a real eye-opener. He changed the way I approached making cocktails. After twenty-five plus years of making drinks, I still feel it'll be another twenty-five before I can come close to his level of experience.

—Sean Enright, author, Pittsburgh Drinks, bar owner, Spork (Pittsburgh, PA)

HUNGRY HUNGRY HIPSTER
Toby Maloney, The Violet Hour, Chicago

My first American cocktail would have to be Grasshopper (crème de menthe, crème de cacao, and ice cream or heavy cream) when I was a kid. I also tasted a frozen Daiquiri in the 1960s made with Minute Maid concentrated frozen Limeade. I'm sure that will horrify some modern bartenders. I didn't really drink at all until I started college. I drank Cuervo and OJ in early 1980s because that was cool...still kind of grossed out by that...but good tequila and fresh orange juice is a beautiful combo.

—Todd Appel, bar and cocktail consultant (Chicago)

The Violet Hour gets associated with some incredible modern classics, such as Sam Ross's Paper Plane and the Bitter Giuseppe. This recipe pays homage to modern cocktail classics and the rich tradition of drinking cold beer on warm midwestern summer days and nights. (It's the only recipe in this book with beer, so feel free to sip some cold, refreshing High Life while mixing up the recipe for friends!) It was first published in *PUNCH* and is derived from the classic mimosa recipe (sparkling wine and orange juice). Despite its name, this drink isn't garnished with a sideways "Von Dutch" trucker hat, but it might try to take a selfie for Instagram without asking for your approval.

2 ounces Zwack (or another amaro—I recommend experimenting; Campari, Aperol, and Ramazzotti are great starts)

1 ounce fresh orange juice

½ ounce fresh lemon juice

Miller High Life beer

Garnish: half orange wheel

Shake the amaro, orange juice, and lemon juice with ice until chilled; strain over fresh ice in a chilled Collins glass, top with the beer, and garnish with the orange.

PAPER PLANE
Sam Ross

New York's Sam Ross created the Paper Plane for Toby Maloney's Chicago bar The Violet Hour (a place he never worked) while listening to M.I.A.'s "Paper Planes," which is a song we should all listen to at least once a day. M.I.A. was scrutinized for performing live while being pregnant. I challenge anyone to not feel the groove of her song whenever it comes on or of this drink when you take your first sip.

¾ ounce Bourbon

¾ ounce Aperol

¾ ounce fresh lemon juice

¾ ounce Amaro Nonino

Shake the ingredients with ice until chilled; strain and serve up in a chilled cocktail glass.

* * *

I encountered something in Chicago called the "Mouth Manhattan," where you take a bottle of Angostura bitters (dasher lid removed) and a bottle of rye and shoot them both simultaneously.

—Joy Buehler, assistant general manager, The Roosevelt Room (Austin, TX)

AB NEGATIVE AND AB POSITIVE
Christopher Marty, Best Intentions, Chicago

*The Midwest
is famous for
down-to-earth
hospitality,
deep and real
friendships, and
a welcoming
nature border-
ing on naïveté.
Chicago remains
my favorite of the
large American
cities for offering
the diversity
and culture that
comes with a
major metropol-
itan area, while
maintaining a
great majority of
the authenticity
that's the calling
card of this part
of the country.*

—Christopher Marty,
co-owner, Best
Intentions (Chicago)

This cocktail actually has two iterations, the AB Negative for spring/summer and the AB Positive for the fall/winter. The drink celebrates Best Intentions's stead-fast efforts to keep the versatile, irreplaceable, and unforgettable Angostura in the foreground, while using a softer tea in the warmer months and a smokier, formidable Souchong to keep you warm during the colder season. Both versions will save your life.

AB Negative (Spring/Summer)

1 ounce Angostura bitters

1 ounce Bärenjäger honey liqueur

1 ounce Todd Appel's lemon cordial (recipe follows)

1 ounce cold-brewed Dragonwell green tea (Steep 1 tea bag in 6 ounces cold water for 4 hours; strain and store in a nonreactive container in the refrigerator for up to 1 week)

AB Positive (Fall/Winter)

1 ounce Angostura bitters

1 ounce Bärenjäger honey liqueur

1 ounce Todd Appel's lemon cordial (recipe follows)

1 ounce cold-brewed Lapsang Souchong tea (see above for method)

Shake the ingredients with ice until chilled; strain and serve up in a chilled coupe glass.

Todd Appel's Lemon Cordial

Todd Appel is a Chicago-based bar instructor and consultant with some nice tricks up his sleeves. His cordial is quite magical. A cordial is often categorized as a syrup but is far more versatile, as the concentrated flavor of a cordial packs a lot more punch than your typical watered-down syrups.

Makes approximately 15 ounces

8 organic, unwaxed lemons   Sugar

Zest the lemons. Set the zest aside.

Cut the lemons in half and squeeze for juice. Strain the lemon juice. You should have 6 to 8 ounces of juice, depending on the lemons. Add the juice along with an equal amount of sugar (by volume) to a small saucepan.

Heat over medium heat, whisking steadily. When the mixture is hot but not boiling (175°F /80°C on a candy thermometer) and the sugar has dissolved, remove from the heat and let cool to room temperature.

Add the lemon zest to the syrup and let steep in the refrigerator overnight, or up to 24 hours. Transfer to a clean bottle and store in the refrigerator for up to 3 weeks.

Old Fashioneds are so popular in Wisconsin, the first morning milk from cows actually comes out with brandy, sugar, and bitters. I have to give credit where it is due: Wisconsin is the state that raised me, and its unique drinking traditions were the genesis of wanting to write a book about our drinking traditions throughout America. So thank you, good people of Wisconsin. Your efforts to out-unique everyone else is why I love you so much. I'm not saying I'm playing favorites, but I'm playing favorites.

Wisconsin

DOES THE STATE of Wisconsin have strange habits? You tell me, weirdo. I am from Wisconsin, so at any given moment there are "strange" things running through my veins, such as Friday night fish fry, pull tabs (basically, pull tabs are like playing slots, but are available in vending machines in many neighborhood bars), summertime tractor pulls and demo derbies and Bossy Bingo (where a Bingo board is spray-painted on grass and festivalgoers place bets on where Bossy the Cow will make her first dropping), rolling dice, drinking more brandy than the rest of the country combined, saying "Oh, sure" and "U betcha" and "Ya see?" on a regular basis, packing both shorts and a winter coat when vacationing somewhere in the state, calling water fountains "bubblers," grilling in February, laughing at the thought of anyone using an umbrella when it snows, and serving a beer chaser (aka "snit") with every Bloody Mary. We take our Bloodys very seriously, so much so that Sobelman's in Milwaukee, known for its legendary Bloody Mary garnishes, serves one with nine skewers of varying garnishes and a whole three-pound fried chicken on top. The Bloody Beast at Sobelman's is such an epic Bloody Mary that the bartenders provide you with a pitcher of Miller Lite while they work on making it! And don't even get us started on how we ask how you like your Old Fashioneds. (Spoiler alert: That comes later in this chapter.)

The state that raised Harry Houdini, Liberace, Frank Lloyd Wright, and Harley-Davidsons also boasts lots of Capitals of the World, such as:

Toilet Paper Capital of the World (Green Bay, also Wisconsin's oldest city)
Bratwurst Capital of the World (Sheboygan)
Inner Tubing Capital of the World (Somerset)
Troll Capital of the World (Mt. Horeb)
Ginseng Capital of the World (Wausau)
Butter Capital of the World (Reedsburg—my hometown, woot woot!)

Bratwurst wasn't invented in Wisconsin, but we sure do act like it, and if you want a true Wisconsin food experience, look no further than beer-battered deep-fried cheese curds, available at nearly every bar serving food, or fresh cheese curds from the factory, which squeak when chewed when they're one to two days old.

Supper clubs rule the roost of dining culture throughout the state. They are places where people go mostly for dinner, and wind down with family or loved ones with a Martini, an Old Fashioned, or a nice bottle of wine—but not without dessert and the option of an ice cream–based Grasshopper, Brandy Alexander, or Pink Squirrel. Following the Brandy Old Fashioned and beer chasers with every Bloody Mary, ice cream cocktails finish out the Holy Trifecta of the Wisconsin cocktail canon.

Not only has food grown more artisanal here, but bars are celebrating more local ingredients. Great cocktail dens in Milwaukee, such as Boone and Crockett, the Phoenix, and Lost Whale are measuring creative collaborations with terrific neighborhood restaurants such as Bay View's Goodkind, with such unforgettably named cocktails like "Get Out of My Room, Mom!"

Madison, the state's capital, has developed a healthy cocktail community in the past ten years, with the Robin Room, Gib's, Mint Mark, and Merchant shaking the shackles of a beer-focused community (don't get me wrong, though, I always love visiting the Great Dane brew pub, which gave me my start in the bartending world), and there are some truly innovative cocktail programs attached to wonderful restaurants, such as L'Etoile, Heritage Tavern, the Tornado Club Steak House (where I highly recommend starting with a cold, bone-dry Martini). Visit the Old Fashioned on the capital square for—wait for it—Old Fashioneds until the cows come home, and Natt Spil, an essential downtown spot specializing in "Chinese Pizza Disco," offering dim sum, terrific DJs, and endless neighborhood bar warmth.

Now let's see which one of the kids wants to get lucky on the pull tabs.

WISCONSIN SPIRIT
BRANDY

Long ago, people started pouring brandy in their Old Fashioneds, and the trend mushroomed into a state-wide cocktail worn with pride on its sleeve. Korbel produces one-third of its brandy for Wisconsin alone. Wisconsin is smack dab in the middle of the Brandy Belt (Minnesota, Wisconsin, and Michigan), and people are also happy to mix it with their Manhattans, their coffee, and their euchre card games.

WISCONSIN'S OLDEST BAR
1847 AT THE STAMM HOUSE
Middleton, 1847

The historic 1847 at the Stamm House has recently been renovated to preserve the integrity of its nineteenth-century architecture, while offering some welcome upgrades. The space once served as an inn and stagecoach stop on the Old Sauk River Trail from Milwaukee to Minneapolis, and now it serves lake-caught fish, pierogies, and fine steaks, with a cocktail menu offering contemporary updates to well-known classics, such as the Stamm House Sidecar, a variation of a New York Sour.

WISCONSIN'S PRETTY OLD BAR
DICK'S BAR
Hudson, 1860

While not quite the oldest bar in the state (it's pretty close), I had to mention this gem. One can watch the Packers play on a Sunday, crank the jukebox or catch some live music in the Walnut Room, play some bar dice, or grab a basket of free, fresh, tasty popcorn. If you meet a Bartels while you're at the bar, chances are that's my brother. He lives just down the road. He's probably drinking a beer and playing Golden Tee.

> **STATE FACT**
> The badger, Wisconsin's state animal, doesn't actually refer to the badger animal, but the miners in the 1820s who dug holes and burrowed inside to keep warm.

You can always spot a Wisconsin bartender by looking at their red-stained fingertips from grabbing cherries in the cherry juice.

—Troy Rost, co-owner, 1847 at the Stamm House (Madison)

WISCONSIN BUCKET LIST BAR
NELSEN'S HALL & BITTERS CLUB
Washington Island

WISCONSIN
BUCKET LIST BAR #2:
CARIBOU BAR
Madison

What does it mean when kids say, "That's dope"?

—Ma Bartels (Reedsburg)

Nelsen's Hall & Bitters Club on Washington Island (upstate and next to Lake Michigan) pours shots of Angostura for its customers, stemming from founder Tom Nelsen's efforts to avoid Prohibition and offer the high-alcohol-by-volume Trinidadian bitters as tonic for stomach issues. If you take a shot while attending the Hall, you earn the privilege of adding your name in a fifty-year ledger and receiving a card denoting club membership, and what looks like a stain from the bartender's filthy hands on the edge of the card is actually an intentional bitters thumbprint. Once initiated into the Bitters Club, you are "considered a full-fledged islander and are entitled to mingle, dance, etc. with all the other islanders."

Nelson's Bitters Club Certificate reads as such:

This certifies that YOUR NAME has taken 'the cure' by consuming the prescribed measure of bitters and as such is a fully initiated member of the Bitters Club. You are now considered a full-fledged Islander and entitled to mingle, dance, etc., with all the other Islanders.

—*Bitters Pub & Restaurant*

Every great state worth its weight in snow salt needs a steady local bar or two to keep us warm when the winter wind picks up, and for this, look no further "The 'Bou." Apart from being the bar where I was accidentally punched in the head by an ex-Navy Seal when trying to break up a kerfuffle, the Caribou is located on Madison's near east side and situated next to a Laundromat. The Caribou bartenders there take care of a long line of drinkers seated and standing at the bar, all Wisco-thirsty, and on top of keeping the peace and slinging the beverages, they work the grill. There is a bartender who works there named Winslow, the mustachioed marvel with a healthy Wisconsin accent, who treats everyone with quintessential hospitality whether there are two people in the room or it's a packed house of four or five dozen people, and he does it alone, with 'bou burgers, French fries, and cheese curds for the whole fam damily.

My first cocktail was a vodka and cranberry juice. I was on a boat on Lake Michigan. I thought it was the height of sophistication. That doesn't count the sips of Tom and Jerrys I had growing up as a youngster in Milwaukee.

—Robert Simonson (born in Milwaukee), author of *The Martini, A Proper Drink, The Old Fashioned,* and *3-Ingredient Cocktails* (Brooklyn, NY)

*My goals are:
To eat without looking hungry
To drink without acting drunk
To love the way I first loved
And to dance in a way that looks like I can hear the music.*

—Adam Benedetto, friend, bicycle superhero, a sheriff who fights crime, and a damn fine poet (Wausau)

Wisconsin is the holy of weirdness. I tried to make a whiskey Old Fashioned at a guest shift in Milwaukee once, and the guest looked at me like I was the son of Satan. Green Bay drinks more rye per capita because a local doctor wrote an editorial about its health benefits. Pretty sure Madison still holds the record for the most Old Grand-Dad bonded per capita. Nelsen's Hall was slinging shots of Angostura through Prohibition. When I was on the spirit expo loop, all the reps would double the amount of product they brought for Wisco. The state goes hard.

—Marco Zappia, bar director, Martina and Colita (Minneapolis, MN)

WISCONSIN BEVERAGE
ANGOSTURA BITTERS

There's just nothing like Bryant's Cocktail Lounge in Milwaukee. I love the fish tank behind the bar. It feels like you're going to a cocktail party at your grandma's house in the 1960s.

—Jeremy Oertel (born in Wisconsin), co-owner of Donna (Brooklyn, NY)

Not only is Wisconsin famous for Nelsen's Hall & Bitters Club, where shots of Angostura bitters are de rigueur, Wisconsin is the US headquarters of the Brandy Old Fashioned cocktail, which requires a couple of dashes of bitters in every drink, thus catapulting Angostura's popularity throughout Wisconsin. Angostura bitters—arguably the only bitters bottle perched on every bar in America—has an alcohol base and is 44.7 percent ABV, but it's actually considered a food additive and flavoring agent. I don't know what kind of numbers they're using in Trinidad and Tobago, but keep 'em coming.

WISCONSIN BEVERAGE
TOP NOTE TONICS

Top Note has been creating top-notch tonics since 2015, with owner and botanist Mary Pellettieri using her years working in brewery labs as inspiration to continue working with the sociability of beverage through nonalcoholic mixers, creating tonic syrups, such as ginger and bitter orange, and sparkling beverages like the award-winning Indian tonic, made with gentian root. Mary is constantly working on levitating the flavors we celebrate, and providing healthful and mindful nonalcoholic alternatives so people can enjoy special beverages when the moments arrive. As the signs and T-shirts say: "Drink Wisconsinbly."

We like it here.

—Ad from Larry's Drinking Establishment, the bar my uncle Larry owned (Reedsburg)

WISCONSIN COCKTAIL BAR
BRYANT'S COCKTAIL LOUNGE
Milwaukee

Bryant's gets consistent recognition as one of the best cocktail destinations in Wisconsin for a reason. It's amazing! The menu is enormous! Drinking there feels like you have one foot in cocktail history, before craft cocktails started turning corners in every little city in America over the past ten years, and the bartenders there execute their cocktails with masterful deftness and enduring Wisconsin hospitality. My experiences at Bryant's make me think of surgeons performing for an audience. They're skilled enough that the operations could be executed blindfolded—but always with an effortless smile.

Maybe I have been in Wisconsin too long, but I would say the most American cocktail is the Old Fashioned. You can get it anywhere, but the differences are diverse and regional, just like America itself.

—John Dye, owner, Bryant's Lounge, At Random, and Jazz Estate (Milwaukee)

WISCONSIN BRANDY OLD FASHIONED
Brian Bartels

Being steeped in Wisconsin culture, I grew up with cocktail hour. My grandfather brought a whole bar kit when they visited us and he acted as the bartender…always Manhattans, Old Fashioneds, Gimlets, Martinis, and Kiddie Cocktails, etc. Wisconsin really is a time capsule for old school cocktail tradition even if some technique and ingredients have become frayed. But resurgent Supper Clubs are cleaning it up. There's nothing better than after-dinner ice cream drinks at the supper club: Pink Squirrels, Grasshoppers, Brandy Alexanders. So great.

—Todd Appel, bar and cocktail consultant (Chicago, IL)

A Wisconsin Brandy Old Fashioned is made with brandy, bitters, muddled orange and cherry, and sugar. The true test of a properly ordered Wisconsin Old Fashioned is having the bartender ask, "Sweet, sour, or press?" If you take it sweet, that's a splash of 7Up on top, sour is a pre-packaged sour mix or Squirt (widely used in many Wisconsin bars), and press, well, here is where we get regional. Press is half soda, half 7Up, and that is where Wisconsin is a step above other states in its unique drinking tradition. Lake Delton's Ishnala Supper Club (Wisconsin's number-one supper club and my first job working in a restaurant) and Madison's Old Fashioned on the Capitol Square make about a billion Old Fashioneds every year. All of those Wisconsinites can't be wrong, so why not give this recipe a try?

1 to 2 maraschino cherries

1 orange wheel

1 sugar cube, or ¼ ounce simple syrup (1:1 sugar to water)

3 dashes Angostura bitters

2 ounces brandy (Korbel is a Wisconsin classic, or elevate the game with Bertoux)

A splash of sour mix, soda water, and/or 7Up

Garnishes: 1 maraschino cherry and 1 orange wedge

Muddle the cherries, orange wheel, sugar, and bitters in a chilled double Old Fashioned glass until the sugar dissolves, adding a splash of water, if desired. Fill the glass with ice and add the brandy. Top with the soda water, sour mix, 7Up, or press (half soda, half 7Up). Skewer the cherry and orange and add to the drink.

In 2018, after visiting Lambeau Field, I visited Roepke's Village Inn in Charlesburg, Wisconsin, and got the best Brandy Old Fashioned Sweet I'd ever had. The bar manager had done something extraordinary and made this kind of "Angostura Syrup," and it was incredible. Not only was the cocktail great, but the bartender working cranked out an entire round for our group in less than a minute. Oh, and they were $4.50 each…Only in Wisco.

—Mike Henderson (born in Wisconsin), beverage development specialist, Breakthru Beverage Group (Denver, CO)

MISSED FLIGHT HEARD

Thor Messer, Merchant, Madison

Merchant opened the cocktail floodgates in Madison, and every time I visit I am continually impressed with its creative cocktails and engaging bar staff. Thor created this cocktail for the fall 2014 menu at Merchant. Scarlet Tea, which offers blueberry-cherry-floral-hibiscus notes, is not an ingredient often seen in cocktails. A nice feather in the cap of this drink is the Bittercube bitters, from a Wisconsin-based company founded in 2009. Go Bucks! Go Brewers! Go Pack Go!

1 ounce Del Maguey Vida mezcal

¾ ounce Bonal Gentiane-Quina (or Punt e Mes)

¾ ounce Scarlet Tea syrup (recipe follows)

¾ ounce fresh lime juice

1 dash Bittercube Blackstrap bitters

Garnish: lime peel curl or lime wheel

Shake the ingredients with ice until chilled. Strain into a chilled coupe glass and serve up, garnished with the lime.

Scarlet Tea Syrup

Makes about 4 cups

5 grams scarlet tea (Rishi preferably)

1 cinnamon stick

2 cups hot water

2 cups sugar

Combine the tea, cinnamon stick, and hot water in a medium saucepan and place over medium heat. After 5 minutes, add the sugar and stir until it dissolves. When the mixture reaches its boiling point, remove from the heat and let cool to room temperature. Strain and store in an airtight container in the refrigerator for up to 2 weeks.

The first time I was really impressed with a cocktail was at Bryant's Cocktail Lounge. I never had a bartender just ask me about flavors before asking me what I wanted. He made me a Last Word and it was delicious. It was at that moment that I had been bartending for several years and realized I didn't know a lick about making a proper cocktail. I really started to learn what it meant to make cocktail from Bryant's.

—Thor Messer, bar manager, Merchant (Madison)

Plenty of different species of fish are swimming through the wonderful lakes of Minnesota. Northern pike, crappie, bull trout, lake trout, steelhead, muskie, sturgeon, catfish, walleye, bluegill, perch, salmon, burbot, and smallmouth bass, which reminds me of my favorite *Onion* headline: "Largemouth Bass Has Largemouth Sass." I think I laughed for three years straight after reading that.

Minnesota

Our state is famous for Paul Bunyan, hockey, Prince, hot dish, ice fishing, and deep frying every type of food at our State Fair and putting it on a stick. And we talk with funny accents. We're also home to Senator Andrew Volstead, who is credited with the constitutional prohibition of alcohol in the United States from 1920 until 1933. (We don't like to be associated with him, though.)

—Dan Oskey,
cofounder
Tattersall Distilling
(Minneapolis)

WE ARE IN the Land of 10,000 Lakes. *Minnesota* is Sioux for "water that reflects the sky," so not surprisingly, perhaps, there are plenty of places to fish, and plenty of fishing poles attending those spots. The Ice Hole Bar on Lake Lida even allows fishing from the bar.

Also called the Bread and Butter State, for its abundance of flour mills and butter factories, and the Gopher State, not for its abundance of furry rodents but for an 1857 railroad scandal, Minnesota is known for funny accents and people saying things like "Up north," "Go Vikings!," and "Jeet," which we all know is short for "Did you eat?" Minnesota started the Adopt-a-Highway program, which is probably why the state continues to have the cleanest roads. They do meat raffles, love hockey and glogg (Scandinavian mulled wine), nosh on Juicy Lucys, drink "pop," say "Booya!" a lot (which is not only a celebratory exclamation, but also a meat and vegetable stew), and given how cold it gets, they make plenty of "hot dish," a casserole-like assembly of beef, green beans, another vegetable, and a can of cream of mushroom soup, often topped with cheese and—because why not?—tater tots.

Minneapolis is home to some wonderful neighborhood bars, such as Palmer's, Jimmy's, and my personal favorite, Bull's Horn, a location that has been a bar since 1935 but does a wonderful job of keeping one foot in history and one foot modernized. Just ask the antique Grain Belt Beer sign outside, the Indeed Brewing Company sign inside, the meat raffle sign, the vintage Zodiac jukebox, the amazing portrait of Yoda in the back room, or the gender-neutral restroom signs, which say: "Whatever. Just wash your hands." Love this place and all the people inside.

King Cocktail Dale DeGroff created a cocktail to honor home state scribe F. Scott Fitzgerald in the 1990s. The Fitzgerald operates as a gin sour without the egg white and has become an adopted addition to many Twin Cities cocktail menus in recent years.

Minneapolis is running wild with wonderful cocktail programs such as Spoon and Stable, the Marvel Bar, Constantine, Young Joni (which does themed menus as well as any I have seen), and places like Martina, with a beverage program run by Marco Zappia, who rolls up his sleeves and digs deep when creating cocktail menus, spiritually, physically, and anarchically, going so far as to combine multiple spirits of the same category for the same cocktail, all while avoiding brand labels. He enjoys working with fermented beverages, which help elevate botanicals and lower ABV, providing a more balanced approach to experiencing new cocktail frontiers. Rumble, young man, rumble.

BAR SNACK

There might be a reason why the Upper Midwest has such a convivial nature come wintertime. Scientists have found that when one holds a warm drink in their hands, they view others more favorably. When one holds a cold drink there is always going to be a less favorable opinion. Temperatures affect our disposition, inside and out. Perhaps that's why the Tom and Jerry (always served hot) is so celebrated in Minnesota and Wisconsin.

Bob Dylan once said there's a Mason-Dixon line that cuts through our state. The North is hard, industrial, ship horns cutting fog. When you go north there's a serene feeling of isolation and self-reliance. The southern part is farmland, agricultural communities, the Twin Cities a bohemian lighthouse that our state assembles on for rock and roll concerts. We didn't invent the potluck, but I'm pretty sure we perfected it. Going with that, the flowing bowl and communal libations go hand in hand.

—Marco Zappia, bar director, Martina and Colita (Minneapolis)

TATTERSALL DISTILLING
Minneapolis

Depending on where you are, a lot of people order shots of "Polish." Actually, they'll just say, "I'll take a Polish." This means Polish blackberry brandy. This is probably a tradition started in the Northeast neighborhood of Minneapolis. The hangover is not fun.

—Dan Oskey, co-owner, Tattersall Distilling (Minneapolis)

I'm just saying: there's a lot of wonderful combos out there when it comes to beverage and food, but an Old Fashioned and a burger are a classic combo. Also, go Vikings!

—Kevin Quiring, brother-in-law, (Minneapolis)

Launched in 2015, Tattersall began by producing four different spirits, and had moved past thirty by the year 2018; the company is now distributing its product in more than twenty states. Tattersall makes an amaro that's so good I would pour it over my corn flakes in the morning. Minnesota state liquor laws allow distilleries to have their own bars—which is great, because Tattersall's horseshoe-shaped bar is a very comfortable one to have a cocktail at, and even has a nice little outdoor patio next to the BNSF railroad tracks—but the catch is they can only serve their own spirits only at the bar, and that limitation becomes a refreshing challenge, as the cocktails they make are 100 percent Tattersall.

NEUMANN'S
St. Paul, 1887

Neumann's deserves more recognition—it's only been around more than 125 years, no biggie! Neumann's—the bar, not the *Seinfeld* character—takes pride in the fact that it has been open continuously since 1887, even serving people upstairs during Prohibition. Post-Prohibition, then-owner Jim Neumann decided the bar needed something every great bar is missing: frogs! Neumann built a small pond (now an aquarium) in front of the bar and invited the neighborhood and locals to come see the frisky amphibians. (Is that a great name for a cocktail? I can't decide.) The original back bar (thanks to Theodore Hamm's Brewing Company, founded in St. Paul in 1865) is still there, a clock from 1892 still works, and chances are one of the regulars might be able to tell you something that happened here long ago, as the Neumann's following is nothing but loyal, and pass on traditions and stories with the best of historic bars.

CC CLUB
Minneapolis

Me (to bartender): "Are you guys famous for anything special here?" CC Club Bartender: "We're known for being the CC Club, so there's that." The CC is as neighborhood as any bar will ever be in the Midwest. Great music on the jukebox, affordable drink specials, and a casual, relaxed, tattooed sensibility that doesn't take itself too seriously. The Minnesota music scene has been hanging out there for decades, as bands like Soul Asylum, the Replacements, and various Minnesota punk rock musicians kept a steady attendance there in the '80s. It's the kind of place I can have a "hearty" Gin and Tonic with my sister, or a shot and beer with my brother-in-law, or a brunch Bloody Mary with my niece. It's so comfortable, in fact, you should have left three hours ago, and yet there you still are, ordering another round for your family and friends.

PARLOUR
Minneapolis

It's easy to point a person in a multiplicity of directions in the Twin Cities cocktail revival scene. There are *many* excellent cocktail bars here! And I would give a handful the honor if I could. But the staff at Parlour did something better than the rest of the places I visited: They greeted us with warm hellos when we walked in, and they said thank you and acknowledged us when we walked out. Those little gestures were everything. And of course it did not hurt that their cocktails were consistent and delicious. Oh, I almost forgot: Parlour has a burger that demands you ignore anyone you are with, including your favorite loved one. I would know. I sat there with my family and had a bite of my sister-in-law's, and I couldn't speak to anyone until I finished. Bonus: There's a location in Minneapolis and one in St. Paul. Everyone wins.

BOOTLEG (AKA BOOTLEGGER)
Brian Bartels

I've always said that Minnesota was the Florida of the Midwest. The Bootleg is a wonderful confirmation of the claim, as it's a choppy hybrid of a Mojito and a Mint Julep. There are several stories of the origin of the Bootleg, including that it was first made at the Woodhill Country Club in Wayzata, but one thing's for sure: The drink has made its way around country clubs, swimming pools, and ice shanties in and around Minnesota since the days of Prohibition.

2 ounces rum, vodka, bourbon, tequila, or gin

2 ounces Bootleg mix (recipe follows)

1 to 2 ounces club soda

Garnish: fresh mint sprig or lemon wheel

Shake the ingredients with ice until chilled; strain over fresh ice in a chilled rocks glass, and garnished with the mint or lemon.

Bootleg Mix

Makes 8 ounces (enough for 4 drinks)

½ cup fresh lemon juice (from about 3 large lemons)

¼ cup fresh lime juice (from about 1 large or 2 medium limes), or additional lemon juice

¼ cup light agave nectar or honey

3 packed tablespoons fresh mint leaves

Combine all the ingredients. Store in an airtight container in the refrigerator for up to 1 week.

. . . .

One of my favorite American bartenders is Bennett Johnson at Tattersall Distilling Cocktail Room. Bennett can make a wicked cocktail, but he has a lot of that old-school bartender in him—the banter component. Bennett has the gift of relating with guests and getting to know them, their names, their tastes, their interests. All too often in the modern bartending world the conversation between bartender and guest isn't where it was some twenty years ago, when everyone was more or less making the same standard drinks. What differentiated a good bartender from a great bartender then was the personal touch that took hospitality to the same level of inviting people into your home and being an entertaining host.

—Dan Oskey, co-owner, Tattersall Distilling (Minneapolis)

AQUAVIT BLOODY MARY
Brian Bartels

Take between thumb and forefinger of the right hand with your largest old-fashioned glass. Half fill this with vodka, holding the glass up to the light to see if it leaks. Add half this amount of tomato juice. Now mix in a little lemon juice, the Tabasco and Worcestershire. If there is room, drop in an ice cube and, if there is still room, a couple of sprinkles of salt and pepper. Down all this without pausing for a breath, and in a few minutes, if you see a burnt matchstick on the floor, you will jump over it three feet in the air.

—Errol Flynn, actor, describing his Bloody Mary recipe in Ted Saucier's *Bottoms Up* (1951)

As the author of *The Bloody Mary* book, I have traveled and tasted many a Bloody Mary throughout the country, and some of the best still hail from the Midwest, an area famous for adopting celebratory weekend drinking at a level on par with any college kegger. The Twin Cities deserve praise for having an especially strong Bloody Mary game. Just ask Ike's, an airport bar that has a famous Bloody. Aquavit is a grain or potato distilled aperitif often associated with Scandinavia, and often flavored with caraway and/or dill. Given Minnesota's healthy Nordic heritage, the spirit has long been celebrated as an opportunity to connect with the Old World. People in Minnesota are gifted in their ways of family, community, and culture, and there is no cocktail better associated with that practice than the Bloody Mary, which stands on the Paul Bunyan shoulders of the Upper Midwest in triumphant glory. This is my first attempt at naming a Bloody Mary mix after the hallowed Bartels family, but as I previously mentioned, I am lucky enough to know the person who wrote *The Bloody Mary*. He was kind, courageous, and clearly humble enough to share.

1½ ounces aquavit
   (or gin, tequila, or mezcal)

4 to 5 ounces Bartels Bloody
   Mary mix (recipe follows)

Garnishes: celery stick, lemon
   wedge, and olive or pickle

Combine the ingredients in a chilled pint glass with ice, briefly stir, and add the garnishes.

Bartels Bloody Mary Mix

Makes about 32 ounces

24 ounces tomato juice
   (R.W. Knudsen,
   Sacramento, or Campbell's)

2 ounces fresh lemon juice

2 ounces Worcestershire
   sauce

2 ounces Tabasco chipotle
   sauce

1 tablespoon steak sauce

1 tablespoon freshly ground
   black pepper

2 teaspoons celery salt

Combine all the ingredients in a nonreactive container. Cover and store in the refrigerator for up to 10 days.

....

My dad used to drink Manhattans on ice. I grew up thinking that was the standard, always associating Manhattans in rocks glasses instead of the classic up version.

—Nick Fauchald, co-author, *Death & Co.* and *Cocktail Codex* (Minneapolis)

Some famous Iowans include artist Grant Wood, who painted American Gothic in 1930 (modeled after a house in Iowa, and the man in the painting was his dentist, and the woman was his sister), movie star John Wayne (born Marion Robert Morrison), iconic actress Donna Reed *(It's A Wonderful Life*, people), and Ashton Kutcher, who was unable to comment, as he was busy filming *Dude, Where's My Cocktail*? (#sorrynotsorry).

Iowa

ANYONE WHO'S SEEN *Field of Dreams* probably knows that is exactly what Iowa stands for ("Is this heaven?" "No. It's Iowa.") and the rolling fields and corn taller than a basketball hoop convince anyone passing through. The Ayuxwa Indians called this place Iowa for "the one who puts to sleep," which aptly communicates the Buddhist-like tranquility you can find in some of the more remote areas. When I think of Iowa, I think of having sweet corn and iced tea on a sleepy Sunday afternoon, reading the paper or a good book, going for a walk, or watching the sky unfurl from blue to white to pink and introduce a bright poster of stars across a dark blue canvas.

Quaker Oats, the largest cereal company in the world, is located in Cedar Rapids, the National Balloon Museum is in Indianola, and Red Delicious apples were created in Peru, Iowa. "The greatest thing since sliced bread" is an expression that acknowledges how wonderful modern conveniences can be, and we can thank inventor Otto Frederick Rohwedder of Davenport, who built the first bread slicer in 1912.

One of my favorite root beers I had while traveling across America hails from Millstream. Based in Amana, Millstream opened as a brewery in the mid-1980s, and didn't start producing its legendary root beer until 1995. It's especially creamy, with long notes of vanilla and a touch of anise and mint. The High Life Lounge in Des Moines proudly serves the Root Down shot—Millstream root beer and Jägermeister. Old-time root beer. Big-time high-five flavor.

The cocktail scene in Iowa (Clinton Street Social Club in Iowa City, Juniper Moon in Des Moines, and Cobble Hill in Cedar Rapids are some state notables) has been steadily progressing over the past few years, and with rye whiskey reentering the fold in the last decade, that means one thing: lots more delicious Manhattans for all those Busch Light beer drinkers.

I believe it was a strategic move to associate Al Capone with Templeton Rye Whiskeys as campaigns, but "The Good Stuff" was undoubtedly a feather in Iowa's cap, known to operate in the basement of a Catholic church during Prohibition, while amens and hallelujahs were taking place upstairs.

One unique note about Iowa: The temperature is wildly unpredictable. If you're away for the day, bring a short sleeve T-shirt and a sweatshirt. And wear waterproof shoes. And bring a hat. And mittens. And a snack. And maybe a blanket. And of course a flask.

....

Iowa is solid whiskey sour country. But there's a big Scandinavian population, which is why I think there are pickle-backs. I remember farmers drinking pickle juice. I like to think there's guys taking a nip of whiskey and then downing it with sauerkraut juice. Iowa is simple like that in the best possible way.

—Andre Darlington (grew up in Ames), author of *The New Cocktail Hour* and *Booze & Vinyl*

IOWA SPIRIT
TEMPLETON RYE
Templeton

I'm all for the highest degree of hospitality, regardless if there's a dress code or peanuts on the ground. There's nothing worse than a staff annoyed by the presence of guests, especially in the final hour of business. That separates the true professionals from those just on the clock. That's a bucket list bar for me.

—Joy Buehler, assistant general manager, the Roosevelt Room (Austin, TX)

I got a job here by trying the entire cocktail menu in one sitting. No lie.

—Nick, bartender, Hello, Marjorie (Des Moines)

Though first produced in the shadows of small-town Templeton (population as of 2016: 349), Prohibition curtailed Templeton's production. Allegedly a favorite of notorious gangster Al Capone, Templeton rye was brought back into production and bottled in Iowa starting in 2006, and quickly became a popular shelf item for many bars and restaurants, subsequently winning a gold medal in 2009 at the World Spirits Tasting and *Whisky Bible*'s "Whisky of the Year." Templeton has developed a brand-new distillery, aging warehouse, and museum, dedicated to its history in Iowa, ensuring that "the good stuff" will be around for a good, long while.

IOWA'S OLDEST BAR
BREITBACH'S COUNTRY DINING
Sherrill, 1852

Jacob Breitbach got a liquor license from President Millard Fillmore in 1852 and six generations later this family-owned and -operated bar and restaurant is still going with gusto. The original building burned down not once but twice in 2007 and 2008, and the community banded together to help the Breitbach family restore the space so the good people of Iowa could drink and eat in proper community fashion. And if that isn't a story celebrating America, I don't know what is.

IOWA BUCKET LIST BARS
HIGH LIFE LOUNGE AND EL BAIT SHOP
Des Moines

Appropriately nicknamed "the Champagne of Bars," the High Life Lounge is covered in wood paneling, antique beer lights, and vintage Miller High Life memorabilia. It serves (surprise, surprise) Miller High Life and bacon-wrapped tater tots, and is known for its unique shots, such as Tangermeister (Tang and Jägermeister), and accordingly it was voted one of *Esquire*'s "Best Bars in America." El Bait Shop has an endless list of craft beers available (and more than 180 on tap! How is that possible?) and celebrates all things bicycle, as the location is connected to many of Des Moines downtown bike paths.

IOWA COCKTAIL BAR
HELLO, MARJORIE
Des Moines

Hello, Marjorie is a spacious lounge featuring retro furniture, and when you enter it you might think you're visiting a relative, which is exactly the point. Marjorie was owner Nick Tillinghast's grandmother, whose husband unexpectedly passed away early and who raised her three daughters on her own. At Hello, Marjorie, you will be treated like family and served delicious cocktails, and you can catch a glimpse of the famous superhero matriarch herself in a painting, where she is smiling and drinking her famous favorite beverage: sloe gin on the rocks. On top of all this, the bar has Templeton six-year whiskey on tap, an unusual practice but a welcome homage to the state's drinking history.

STATE FACT
Register's Annual Great Bike Ride Across Iowa (RAGBRAI), an annual week-long bike ride across the state which started in 1973, is the largest bike tour in the world. It starts from Iowa's west side and the Missouri River and finishes on the east with the Mighty Mississippi.

THE MARJORIE
Nick Tillinghast, Hello, Marjorie, Des Moines

The Marjorie is named after owner Nick's grandmother, Marjorie, who loved drinking sloe gin on the rocks more than anything else. Stop by Hello, Marjorie any time and view the prominent portrait of Marjorie to the left of the bar, cigarette in one hand and a full glass of sloe gin and ice in the other. You gotta love the 1970s, baby.

1½ ounces Absolut Pear
  vodka

¾ ounce Plymouth sloe gin

¾ ounce simple syrup
  (1:1 sugar to water)

¾ ounce fresh lemon juice

Garnish: lemon wheel

Shake the ingredients with ice until chilled. Strain over fresh ice in a chilled rocks glass and garnish with the lemon.

IOWA FLANNEL SHIRT
Marcus Owens, Clinton Street Social Club, Iowa City

This is Clinton Street's take on Oregon bartender Jeffrey Morganthaler's modern classic, the Flannel Shirt (an autumnal-focused cold cocktail made with Scotch, Averna amaro, lemon, apple cider, bitters and St. Elizabeth Allspice Dram, a wonderful accent to any fall or winter cocktail). The drink features apples from Wilson's, a local orchard, and red pears to make an apple-pear cordial, but seek out fresh cider from your local farmers' market and make it easy on yourself—and what's more, better for the farmers. There's really no substitute for St. Elizabeth allspice dram, but be warned: A little goes a *long* way.

1½ ounces Templeton rye

½ ounce CioCiaro amaro

¼ ounce St. Elizabeth allspice
  dram

¼ ounce fresh lemon juice

¾ ounce pear cider

¾ ounce apple cider

2 dashes Angostura bitters

Shake the ingredients with ice until chilled. Strain over fresh ice in a chilled rocks glass.

BAR SNACK
Though it sounds like something between a pinch runner and a double play in baseball, switchel is a drink made with apple cider vinegar, fresh ginger, and water, with a sweetener that depends on whatever region it hails from. In Vermont, it would be maple syrup. In Iowa and other places in the Midwest, honey syrup is not uncommon. In the South, sorghum syrup. Some places use molasses. The medicinal value shouldn't be overlooked, as ginger contains anti-inflammatories, vinegar wields microbial benefits, and the sweetener provides a little energy kick (and molasses is rock solid with potassium). Switchel was everyone's Gatorade from the 1700s through the 1900s. Play ball.

Butterflies have sustained their beauty over the years by subsisting on a steady diet of the Rendezvous cocktail, which debuted in Kansas City in the 1940s. St. Louis' Gateway Arch, which debuted in 1965 as a model of territorial expansion and development of these United States, was influential for our pioneering spirit, our historic reverence, and embracing new frontiers, not unlike the way a bartender approaches creating a new cocktail.

Missouri

What does every American bar need? Purse hooks and foot rails.

—Ryan Maybee, co-owner, Manifesto and J. Rieger & Co. (Kansas City)

THERE'S ONLY ONE Show Me State in the finer fifty. This nickname is often associated with Congressman Willard Duncan Vandiver, who in 1899 stated, "I'm from Missouri, you've got to show me."

The word *Missouri* means "wooden canoe people," which is an ideal vessel for reclining in after eating at one of Missouri's famed barbecue locations (Arthur Bryant's in Kansas City has a spicy house sauce to die for, and I will happily join you there for lunch any old time.)

Kansas City, the "Paris of the Plains," is special, mainly for being one of the cities to pretty much ignore Prohibition, so let's toast to its defiance. There's lots of great bars and restaurants in the Crossroads District, home to many independent businesses and little to no corporate elevations, thanks to a heroic former mayor. Swing by the boiler-room basement coziness of Swordfish Tom's and revel in co-owner and bartender Jill Cockson's nightly classes on keeping it real. SoT Social and Novel are also worthwhile cocktail destinations, and do not miss the Green Lady Lounge, one of the hippest happenings in the Midwest for live jazz, cocktails, and cutting a rug. TikiCat put Old Westport on the Kansas City cocktail map, and Country Club Plaza's Monarch Bar, awarded Cocktail Bar of the Year by the Nightclub & Bar Media Group, succeeds in elevated hospitality and bar design at its finest, with more than a thousand acrylic butterflies adorning the central marble-topped bar, and a separate VIP room and bar with a completely different cocktail menu and high-end spirits.

St. Louis has a wonderful history of bartenders and watering holes; our esteemed godfather Jerry Thomas spent a little time there on his way across America, and so did Tom Bullock, a legendary St. Louis barman who published his first cocktail book in 1917—the first by an African American. When you're not playing the fiddle or square dancing (both well-documented state pastimes), you can't sneak by the state without hearing the whispers of Budweiser and its King of Beers clout, as Saint Louis's Anheuser-Busch brewery is the largest beer-producing plant in the country.

There are ample great cocktail destinations in St. Louis. Blood & Sand has a wildly inventive cocktail menu, with signature cocktails inspired by a wide variety of musicians, Sanctuaria holds one of the most impressive bourbon selections in the country, and don't miss Taste for a feel-good balance of delectable kitchen snacks (yeah, you, tempura-fried bananas). Taste was the last place I visited in St. Louis, and it will be the first place I go upon returning to the city. The Bartender's Choice at Taste is always a great move, which makes me think of Gentleman Jim Gates, a radio DJ from East St. Louis who, for the first time in America, in 1979, made a funky move to put a little song on the airwaves called "Rapper's Delight," by the Sugarhill Gang, and the rest, as they sing, goes a little something like . . .

. . . To the rhythm of the boogie the beat . . .

Guess what, America? We love you. (I hope you appreciate how I needed to find a way to celebrate St. Louis cocktail legacy through the eyes of the Sugarhill Gang and bring it all home with the "America, we love you" reference. "It's the little things, kids," as my lovely brother Tim would say.)

Jeremy Roth of Harry's Bar & Tables in KC is one of my favorite American bartenders. Twenty years behind the same bar. Remembers everyone's name. Treats everyone the same and is happy to mix you a cocktail, pop open a beer, or pour you a shot.

—Ryan Maybee, co-owner, Manifesto and J. Rieger (Kansas City)

MISSOURI'S OLDEST BAR
J. HUSTON TAVERN
Arrow Rock, 1834

When Joseph Huston realized his private residence would be a fine destination for cross-country travelers seeking sanctuary, J. Huston became a tavern and inn, and has never looked back. Open since 1834, J. Huston is the oldest restaurant west of the Mississippi. It has three dining rooms and a tap room, and some say the fried chicken will make you a believer. Arrow Rock is also famous for being the home of George Caleb Bingham, one of America's great nineteenth-century artists.

MISSOURI BUCKET LIST BAR
HARRY'S BAR & TABLES
Kansas City

Harry's Bar & Tables has been around since before any of us were born, and it's where the locals go any time of day to unwind, because it's just so damn comfortable and inviting inside, and the whole damn staff is downright polite, no matter what damn time of day. Not only do they make a mean Horsefeather cocktail (page 189), but they make any classic cocktail with the right kind of execution, and they do it with class. Restaurant and bar industry staff head to Harry's when they're done working at their own places because Harry's stays open until 3 A.M. every night. With an extensive Scotch menu, an all-star staff, and a kitchen open until 2 A.M., let the good times roll.

MISSOURI SPIRIT
J. RIEGER & CO.

There was no such designation as Kansas City whiskey until J. Rieger started to champion the cause in 2014. After lying dormant for decades, the brand was reestablished by Ryan Maybee and Andy Rieger, the great-great-great-grandson of J. Rieger, famed Kansas City hotelier and distiller until Prohibition, and in doing so created a new spirit designation: to be considered a Kansas City whiskey, the whiskey must contain 2 percent sherry—in this case Williams & Humbert oloroso sherry. J. Rieger's Caffé amaro, a coffee liqueur made with locally sourced Kansas City beans, is a spirit to stock on the shelf, and one I have unapologetically used in many cocktails. J. Rieger also makes an annual limited-edition Monogram whiskey, aged in one-hundred-year-old oloroso sherry barrels, and the wonderful house gin is distilled by Tom Nichol, former longtime master distiller of Tanqueray. The company's new distillery—a theme park of epic scale and history celebrating the civic pride of Kansas City—opened to the public in 2019 and is alone worth a trip to the city.

In 2014, J. Rieger & Co. were two guys making whiskey and everything by hand, with forty barrels to begin their process. They reached their one-year goal in seven weeks. Now they have over seven thousand barrels and counting in their new distillery.

> ### BAR SNACK
> Kansas City has more miles of boulevards than Paris and more fountains than any city except Rome.

MISSOURI BEVERAGE
ICED TEA

The 1904 World's Fair took place in St. Louis (aka "the Gateway to the West"), and at that very spot a merchant named Richard Blechynden served tea to everyone—which of course was not an unusual thing to do—but he served his tea with ice, which was not the first time tea ever mixed with ice (as documented in an article from 1890 out of Nevada, Missouri). Legend has it he was going to serve hot tea, but the weather in St. Louis was so warm he made a last-minute decision to add ice, and the drink became an overnight sensation. While he did not create iced tea, Blechynden gets all the credit to this day.

MISSOURI COCKTAIL BAR
MANIFESTO
Kansas City

It's important to recognize the little engines of our small business world. When Manifesto opened in 2009 in what's now known as the Crossroads District of Kansas City, nothing else was surrounding it, so Ryan Maybee needed it to be special enough to be a destination for people who wouldn't otherwise be in the neighborhood. At the time, no other craft cocktail bars were operating in Kansas City, and the bartenders at Manifesto take great pride in cocktail history and their community. It's the ideal hybrid of a place to get a well-balanced, thoughtful cocktail, coupled with friendly conversation. J. Rieger's Ryan Maybee created Caffé Amaro, their fantastic coffee amaro, while standing behind the bar of his seminal speakeasy Manifesto, located in the basement of the Rieger Hotel. They use Thou Mayest coffee roasters, a local roaster stocked with fishing poles, house plants, and boxes of cereal (yes, they carry Kix, Reese's Puffs, and Fruit Loops, in case you were wondering) and they play King Gizzard and the Lizard at ten in the morning, which is exactly the right time to play them.

MISSOURI COCKTAIL BAR
PLANTER'S HOUSE
St. Louis

Planter's House is a space inside what feels like a former church or medieval quarters. It has original cocktails and themed menus. On my visit they were celebrating roller derbies: Every cocktail celebrated a roller derby term—Hip Whip, Skater Tot, Ghost Points—and there was even a featured cocktail for which the bar donated $1 of each sale to St. Louis's roller derby teams. My favorite cocktail was Skate Left, Turn Right, which had El Mayor añejo tequila, matcha-agave syrup, Licor 43, and lime juice. And it was served in a cute little porcelain tea cup. And I felt pretty swell after sipping on it.

> ### STATE FACT
> If a woman was caught bartending in Missouri in the early 1900s, she was charged with a felony.

When you're traveling, you are what you are right there and then. People don't have your past to hold against you. No yesterdays on the road.

—William Least Heat-Moon, *Blue Highways* (born in Kansas City, MO)

I fell in love with bars because of the uninhibited, disordered, and surprising way life unfolds at the bar. The only logical progression in my life has been the wealth of characters who have crossed my path, leaving their sweet, sour, strong, and weak for me to ponder.

—Dale DeGroff, aka King Cocktail, author of *The Craft of the Cocktail* and *The Essential Cocktail*, and arguably the most important bartender in the world

---

BAR SNACK

Legend has it that Clara Bell Walsh of St. Louis invented the first ever cocktail party in 1917. Given that men frequented and gallivanted long into the night at many a tavern, and Owen Johnson's 1913 The Salamander stated, "New ideas are stirring in [the modern woman], logical revolts—equality of burden with men, equality of opportunity and pleasure." Mrs. Walsh wanted to bring some dignity to a social circle, so she decided to throw a "cocktail party" on a Sunday in St. Louis, updating the concept of afternoon tea into evening imbibing. A social crusader, to say the least.

RENDEZVOUS
Brian Bartels

I came across a Rendezvous recipe in Ted Saucier's *Bottoms Up*, and Ted had retrieved it from the famed Hotel Muehlebach in Kansas City, most likely named after the Rendezvous restaurant and lounge located inside the historic hotel. I think it's worth noting to the home bartender: Don't skimp on Luxardo maraschino; it should be one of your bottles available when making cocktails for friends. It gets plenty of love from the craft cocktail crowds, but you can wow a lot of new cocktail drinkers by smartly incorporating it into your cocktail repertoire. This recipe is my updated version of the original, adding more gin and allowing the maraschino to step up on the dance floor.

1½ ounces J. Rieger gin
(or another American
option, like St. George,
Aviation, Dorothy Parker, or
Letherbee)

¾ ounces Luxardo maraschino
liqueur

¾ ounces fresh lime juice

Garnish: lime wedge
(optional)

Shake the ingredients with ice until chilled; strain into a chilled cocktail glass and serve up, garnished with the lime, if using.

PENDERGAST
Ryan Maybee, Manifesto, Kansas City

Ryan Maybee, *Imbibe*'s 2013 Bartender of the Year, created this cocktail on Kansas City soil in his heralded speakeasy, and the rest is modern history, which is appropriate, as this is named after Tom Pendergast, who may or may not have been a little "influential" during Prohibition in Missouri. In addition to creating wonderful cocktails, Ryan also happens to be one of the most hospitable human beings I know, and is the kind of person who is nothing short of gracious when learning of people visiting his city and looking for recommendations. Also, his Great Dane is named Moose.

1½ ounces bourbon

¾ ounce sweet vermouth

½ ounce Bénédictine

2 dashes Angostura bitters

Garnish: lemon twist

Stir the ingredients with ice cubes until chilled; strain into a chilled double rocks glass without ice and garnish with the lemon.

BAR SNACK

Have you ever heard of a pawpaw? Neither have I, until I was given a Boomerang (when a bar makes a cocktail for another bar, then the other bar presumably makes a cocktail to send back to them, though I have never actually witnessed this accomplishment) at Corvina in Kansas City, to take with me to the Monarch Bar. They have me a pawpaw Bee's Knees cocktail. Pawpaw is not unlike a mango and is otherwise known as "hillbilly mango" around Missouri. Pawpaw is indigenous to North America. Just like hillbillies.

We're in Kansas, Toto, so be mindful of tornadoes and their aptitude to make unrivaled impressions that can last a lifetime. First impressions are known to make a difference in our bar culture. There is much to learn from greeting someone as they enter your establishment. In social climates, greetings have impact. Greeting someone is a tool which engages the atmosphere. So if you're stirring a cocktail, I hope you're keeping an eye on something else, like the door. I'm a big believer in the matter between properties and how they interact in a contained atmosphere, such as a bar, or a dining room, or a kitchen, office, places a lot of us live and work when we're not sleeping. What's more: that's how great cultures begin.

Kansas

Drinking culture everywhere I've been is unique. In Wisconsin, it's all about sharing the experience with others. In New York, it's haut and minimalistic, more about the drink than the drinker. In San Francisco, it's hip and hipster, searching for the least known and next best thing. In Kansas, drinking in public bars wasn't allowed after Prohibition ended (1933) until 1986. Cocktail culture here is just starting to blossom, so there's a lot of variability.

—Gabrielle Korb,
outlet supervisor,
Ambassador
Hotel (Wichita)

"HOME ON THE Range," from a poem written by Dr. Brewster Martin Higley IV, an otolaryngologist (ear and throat doctor), is the state song of the Sunflower State; the music that later made it a song was added by Daniel E. Kelley, a carpenter. Put an ear doctor and a carpenter in the same room, and you get an American classic.

Traveling from Oklahoma to Missouri on Kansas's good ole Highway 35, you'll see almost nothing but wide open prairies and "horizons only seen in big screen movie pictures," as travel writer and Kansas City, MO-born William Least Heat-Moon has said. The state's healthy amount of flatland is home to Tornado Alley, wheat is grown everywhere, and if you head to Liberal, you can see an identical replica of Dorothy's house in *The Wizard of Oz*.

The first-ever Pizza Hut opened in Wichita, White Castle started burgers flying across America in 1921, the first Payless Shoe Store arrived in 1956, and the first-ever Icee drink arrived in 1960 at a Dairy Queen in Coffeyville. Customers loved the frozen concoction so much the owner developed a specific machine to serve the Icee. The magic all started when the owner's soda machine broke, so he placed bottles of soda in the freezer to keep them cold, and when he sold the bottles of soda, they turned to slush as they opened, and people kept commenting on how much they loved the slushy goodness. I knew them as "slush puppies" as a kid.

Kansas inventors include Almon Strowger, of El Dorado, who invented the dial telephone in 1889; William Purvis and Charles Wilson, of Goodland, who invented the helicopter in 1909; and Omar Knedlik, of Coffeyville, who invented the first frozen carbonated drink machine in 1961.

The first woman mayor in the United States was Susanna Madora Salter, who was elected to office in Argonia in 1887.

Kansas held the longest alcohol ban of all fifty states; it was dry for sixty-eight years (between 1880 and 1948), though saloons were still finding ways to serve alcohol. Six-foot-tall temperance warrior Carrie Nation started walking through illegal Kansas saloons in 1899 with a hatchet and a chip on her shoulder, and was arrested and fined thirty-two times over the course of ten years. She once claimed, "You have put me in here a cub, but I will come out roaring like a lion, and I will make all hell howl!" She must have been a real hoot at holiday parties. As a result of this sober past, cocktail culture is just starting to blossom throughout Kansas, so expect a healthy amount of unbridled enthusiasm when visiting.

Check out the Bourgeois Pig in Lawrence if you like all-day casual coffee spots that turn cocktails into a nightly reason to stay and keep drinking, and find time for its popular Bloody Mary. Vorshay's Cocktail Lounge and Dockum are two great spots to get your Wichita cocktail set in a groovy direction, and everyone loves Kirby's Beer Store, featuring live music in a small space, with a jukebox when there isn't a band, and a rotating list of rascals and merry regulars who smile for anyone walking through the door or leaving with or without their hat on.

AUNTIE MAE'S PARLOR
Manhattan

My hometown, Atchison, Kansas, is the birth-place of Amelia Earhart and Midwest Grain Products (known to those in the biz as "MGP"). It's on the Lewis and Clark trail and is rumored to be the most haunted town in Kansas. And you can't drink a beer in Atchison without leaning on a truck.

—Kevin Denton (from Atchison), senior advocacy manager, Pernod-Ricard, (Manhattan, NY)

Dora Mae Walters took over her recently deceased husband's plumbing business in 1929, during the Great Depression (*and* Prohibition, of all double whammies), and though she knew very little about plumbing, she knew the dusty little town of Manhattan, Kansas, needed a drink, so on February 21, 1930, Dora Mae opened a little speakeasy in her basement. On any given night, Auntie Mae's features live music, art shows, trivia night, a meat raffle (a traditional event, where meat is raffled for charity while attendees sip on libations), open mic comedy shows, and horrible movie night, offering a little something for everyone in and around Manhattan.

LARK A FARE
Lawrence

It's not easy being casual and elegant at the same time (and on top of that, having a unique name that can catch pretty much everyone off guard). The name *Lark a Fare* is an homage to the Kansas state bird, the meadowlark. The menu is an impressive balance of Highballs, Old Fashioneds, punches and sours, classic cocktails, and mocktails. The cocktails at Lark a Fare build off the classics and manage to wrangle heightened creativity into delicious offerings, such as the Heartland Highball, made with Kansas City whiskey, lemongrass, wheat syrup, citrus, and ginger soda.

BOOT HILL DISTILLERY
Dodge City

Boot Hill opened in 2014 as Kansas's first-ever distillery and operates as the only soil-to-sip distillery in Kansas, producing 100 percent of the grain used in 100 percent of its products. They produce vodka, gin, bourbon, whiskey, white whiskey ("One of the finest—if not the best—white whiskeys around," according to *F. Paul Pacult's Spirits Journal*), and a prickly ash bitters, which is an amaro made with prickly ash bark, coriander, senna, and cubeb pepper, offering round, earthy layers of mint and citrus to dance with the bitter botanicals. They have a beautiful tasting room to boot. (Pun not intended, but we'll take it.)

HAYS HOUSE RESTAURANT
Council Grove, 1857

Seth Hays, Daniel Boone's great-grandson, decided to build a log cabin on the Santa Fe Trail right on Main Street in Council Grove. Hays would serve locals and travelers through the weeknights and weekends, then cover up the bottles after Saturday evening so they could respectfully conduct church service in the space on Sunday mornings. Stop by and visit the half-moon bar for the breakfast Railroad Special meal (meaty sausage gravy over fluffy biscuits) and a sip of history.

STATE FACT
Smith County is the geographical center of the lower 48 United States, and Kansas was the first place scientists discovered helium in America, but another interesting fact about the state: It. Is. Flat. Scientists once compared the topography of Kansas to a pancake from iHOP and found that an iHOP pancake had more rolling hills.

BAR SNACK
Dodge City is known as the windiest city in the United States, and speaking of wind, the first black woman to win an Academy Award? That would be Kansan Hattie McDaniel, who won the award for her role in—yep—*Gone with the Wind*.

HORSEFEATHER
Brian Bartels

Though it's now associated with Kansas City, Missouri, and originally served with club soda instead of the modern-day ginger beer or ginger ale, history points to Lawrence's now-closed Paradise Café consistently serving this modern icon through the 1990s, expanding with such popularity that bars in Kansas City eventually claimed the Horsefeather as its own. The drink is a riff on the 1800s classic Horse's Neck cocktail, a bourbon-based cooler made with ginger ale or club soda and bitters, and often garnished with a long lemon peel in the style of a horse's long neck. Similar to a Moscow Mule, a Horsefeather gains extra spice from the rye whiskey (and a spicy ginger beer, if I may recommend) and extra dashes of bitters. That's a kick to the system.

1½ ounces J. Rieger Kansas
    City whiskey

4 ounces Fever-Tree ginger
    beer

3 dashes Angostura bitters
    (orange bitters also work)

Garnish: lemon wedge

Pour the ingredients over ice in a chilled highball glass and briefly stir. Garnish with the lemon.

HOME ON THE RANGE
Brian Bartels

Kansas was the home of genius George Washington Carver, who developed more than three hundred different products that could be made from peanuts. This Old Fashioned riff is not one of them, but it does give us another excuse to use peanuts, as opposed to just standing in the kitchen, three in the morning, eyes closed, with an upside-down peanut butter–covered spoon on your tongue.

2 ounces peanut and coffee
    bean–infused rye whiskey
    (recipe follows)

¼ ounce Demerara syrup
    (1:1 Demerara sugar to
    water), or 1 brown sugar
    cube, muddled

2 dashes Hella aromatic
    bitters (or Angostura)

2 dashes orange bitters

Garnish: orange and lemon
    peels

Stir the ingredients with ice until chilled; strain over fresh ice in a chilled rocks glass and garnish with the orange and lemon.

Peanut and Coffee Bean–Infused Rye Whiskey

Makes about one 750 ml bottle

One 750 ml bottle rye whiskey
    (above 90 proof, ideally)

1 cup unsalted peanuts

½ cup whole decaffeinated
    coffee beans

Combine the whiskey and peanuts in a nonreactive container. Set aside to infuse for 2 days.

Add the coffee beans and continue to infuse for 2 hours. Taste to make sure the flavor is to your liking and steep longer if a stronger coffee flavor is desired—but be warned: Coffee will overpower the infusion if it sits too long. Strain out the solids and store in a nonreactive container at room temperature for up to 6 months.

Nebraska

Nebraska earned the nickname the "Cornhusker State" in 1945 from the University of Nebraska athletic teams, which called themselves "the Cornhuskers" in honor of the state's leading vegetable crop. Before the invention of husking machines, husking corn was done by hand. Which reminds me: as a kid, I detasseled corn for one day, which is a job I wish upon no one. So please make sure you appreciate the corn we eat in the future. That said, I probably would have enjoyed detasseling corn a little more if I had a bottle of Becherovka with me. I also probably would have been sent to jail as a minor.

Interesting fact: if you are from Norfolk, we pronounce it "Norfork." The town was supposed to be named North Fork (pertaining to the north for of the Elkhorn River in northeast Nebraska) but was mis-transcribed to Norfolk. Also, Johnny Carson grew up in Norfolk after moving from Iowa at the age of eight.

—Keith Hamm, bar manager (Lincoln)

YOU HAVE TO love a state with "Equality Before the Law" as its motto. It's no surprise Nebraska constantly gets picked as one of the happiest places in the country.

The Reuben sandwich (which my brother-in-law orders at every restaurant in America) was created in Omaha, the 911 system of emergency communications was created in Lincoln, and there are more miles of river in Nebraska than in any other state. The strobe light was invented by Harold "Doc" Edgerton, of Aurora, Nebraska. We tried reaching him for comment, but he was still dancing at the all-night rave, shirtless, sweating, and smiling for no apparent reason.

In Lincoln, circa 1958, Clifton Hillegass bought a series of extensive guides to Shakespeare from a Canadian book company owner named Jack Cole. Hillegass then condensed these long tomes, eventually calling them CliffsNotes, which subsequently became every high school student's favorite invention of all time.

Arbor Day started in 1854 when an agriculture and tree enthusiast (which I hope we all are today) moved from Detroit to the Nebraska prairie and immediately realized that the open space needed more trees for the sake of forest and fruit. That year, on the first Arbor Day, more than one million trees were planted in Nebraska alone, and Arbor Day later inspired one of Nebraska's great nicknames, "The Tree Planter's State."

Once you set down in the Heartland, make way for the cocktail bars in Omaha and Lincoln, which are conveniently very close to one another. In Omaha, Nebraska's largest city, the Berry & Rye started things off in 2013, followed by Wicked Rabbit, Laka Lono Rum Club, and Mercury. The Berry & Rye takes its ice game seriously, hand-sawing blocks of ice and serving cocktails with perfect rounded ice ball spheres, a technique adopted from Japanese bartending methods.

Nebraska is famous for its chili, cinnamon rolls, and cheese frenchees, which are basically deep-fried grilled cheese sandwiches.

—Spencer Long, NFL player, born and raised in Nebraska

NEBRASKA COCKTAIL BAR
THE OTHER ROOM
Lincoln

The best bars are the hardest to find, right? When seeking them out, we need to feel excitement about the possibility of discovering something new, anxiety when we realize the destination might not be in the direction we're heading, dread that we may looking entirely in the wrong area, and overwhelming relief when we find that it's right under our noses. (Maybe that's why I love Indiana Jones movies.) The Other Room is a gorgeous, hidden, nondescript, James Beard semifinalist speakeasy in an alley in Lincoln's Haymarket district. The Other Room creates its own bitters (jalapeño, fig, allspice, and so on), can accommodate only twenty-five people at a time, and serves some of the most well-balanced cocktails in the middle of America. As Omaha native Marlon Brando might say, "I'm gonna make you a cocktail you can't refuse."

NEBRASKA SPIRIT
BECHEROVKA
Karlovy Vary, Czech Republic

Nebraska has the highest population of residents of Czech descent in the United States. While that might mean there is plenty of Pilsner Urquell being poured in tap rooms throughout the state, it's long overdue that we talk about Becherovka ("beck-urr-oave-kuh"), a Czech liqueur with ginger, cinnamon, and cloves. Not only is Becherovka a dynamite option in cocktails, if you keep a bottle of it in your freezer to sip on during special occasions, chances are I might be stopping by your place soon to say hello. And if you're wondering, yes, there is a Prague, Nebraska, population: 303, home of the World's Largest Kolache (a famous Czech pastry).

BAR SNACK

Hiccups happen, but you don't have to go into that great hiccup abyss alone. Most bartenders swear soaking a lemon wedge in bitters, dipping it in sugar, and then biting into the mixture as an antidote, but I have something more unique, and it has never failed. My college roommate Will Enright shared this recipe with me while attending medical school (which to my recollection requires endless study sessions and a bottle of vodka in the freezer). Note: This requires a friend to help.

DR. WILL ENRIGHT'S RUSHMORE HICCUP CURE

Step 1: Grab a clear water glass and fill it with 10 to 15 ounces water.

Step 2: You (Hiccupper) hold the glass of water.

Step 3: Have your friend hold a pen or similar object directly under the glass, so you, the Hiccupper (Is that a word? Who cares? You've got the hiccups!), can see it through the bottom of the clear glass.

Step 4: Steadily drink all the water in the glass without stopping. Don't slam it. Make sure to finish the contents before you stop drinking.

Step 5: Put the empty glass down.

Step 6: High five a stranger. Hiccups gone! Now you can focus on really making a go of it at Grover Cleveland. (Sorry. *Rushmore* reference. Classic film.)

NEBRASKA
BUCKET LIST BAR
THE HOMY INN
Omaha

Jill Cockson is one of my favorite American bartenders. She was the manager at Other Room for the first two years of business. I learned a lot of real information about the industry from Jill. She taught me the correct way to open a bar. Since then, she has moved and opened Swordfish Tom's in Kansas City. I am indebted to her for showing me the right way to enjoy this industry. Thank you, Jill.

—Keith Hamm, bar manager (Lincoln)

The Homy Inn is located outside downtown Omaha, just around the bend from Saddle Creek Road, and features some very nice bartenders in the cozy cabin-like space. Bonus points for the location, which seems to be in its own little neighborhood, making it a destination for most people and a welcome walking retreat for neighborhood locals, as the Homy is located in a more residential area. Plenty of beer signs, steins, and novelty items decorate the walls, giving the intimate space a lived-in feel, but the true draw of the Homy is abstract: They serve Champagne on tap and peanuts in dog bowls, rather uncommon features for a classic dive bar.

BAR SNACK
A "Red Beer" is half beer, half tomato juice, and way too easy to drink to have just one. Many people make and can their own mix with the fall harvest. Though its origins are unknown, Red Beers are popular in Nebraska, appearing regularly at football tailgates, which makes sense, as they are user-friendly versions of brunch favorites such as Micheladas (beer, tomato juice, spices, and seasonings) and Bloody Marys, which often have up to ten different ingredients.

NEBRASKA'S OLDEST BAR
GLUR'S TAVERN
Columbus, 1876

Named after its second owner, Louis Glur, this old reliable corner tavern has been serving Wild West charm long enough to have its own Buffalo Bill Cody stories swimming around the historic space. Owners have come and gone, but today Glur's maintains its reputation of being a go-to spot for family reunions and chatting with the locals. Try the Major Peters Bloody Mary, which goes well with Glur's famous no-frills burger and listening to the nearby train moving through town. Close your eyes and you might believe it's 1938.

NEBRASKA BEVERAGE
KOOL-AID

Of all the beverages to come out of Nebraska, I present to you the American Dream come true: Kool-Aid, a beverage I was most definitely over-served as a child. Edwin E. Perkins, of Hastings, Nebraska, invented Kool-Aid in 1927 (during the Great Depression, no less), and Perkins (not a chemist, per se, but undoubtedly a "mixologist") essentially reconstituted Fruit-Smack, a four-ounce soft drink served in bottles, and dehydrated the contents into six unforgettable flavors: cherry, grape, lemon, orange, root-beer, and raspberry (Mr. Perkins's favorite). Bravo, Mr. Perkins. My cavities forever curse you but my heart will always applaud.

The three-martini lunch is the epitome of American efficiency. Where else can you get an earful, a bellyful and a snootful at the same time?

—President Gerald Ford (born in Omaha)

STATE FACT
The world's largest porch swing is located in Hebron, Nebraska. Twenty-five adults can sit on it at one time.

THE LAWN CHAIR
Keith Hamm, the Other Room, Lincoln

The Lawn Chair is a summer seasonal at the Other Room, and is a fan favorite whenever the warmer months start rolling back. Mixing vodka and gin might freak some vodka purists out, but fear not—Keith has a message: If you like vodka, use all vodka. If you like gin, use all gin. Now who's going to the grocery store for an ice run?

1 ounce vodka

1 ounce gin

½ ounce fresh lemon juice

½ ounce simple syrup
(1:1 sugar to water)

6 fresh mint leaves

3 large dashes Fee Brothers
peach bitters

Garnish: fresh mint sprig

Shake the ingredients with ice until chilled; fine strain into a chilled coupe glass and serve up, garnished with the mint.

EARLY BIRD BLOODY MARY
Early Bird, Omaha

I love Bloody Marys. I like that they're kind of like tiramisù, how everyone has their own recipe.

—Murray Stenson, bartender and bar legend (Seattle, WA)

The Early Bird Bloody Mary was one of the best Bloody Marys I had while traveling across America for this book. Swell vodka, house Bloody Mary mix, and Cholula. I ordered it with a can of PBR, because you can take the boy out of Wisconsin, but you can't take Wisconsin out of the boy, America. This place is fun and worth the visit. If I lived in Omaha I would be a breakfast regular. The early bird gets the ~~worm~~ pancake.

1½ ounces Swell vodka (or
you can substitute gin,
mezcal, or tequila)

4 to 5 ounces Early Bird
house Bloody Mary mix
(recipe follows)

2 to 4 dashes Cholula hot
sauce (optional)

Garnishes: lemon wedge,
celery stick, and olives

Combine the ingredients in shaker glasses or pint glasses with or without ice and roll the ingredients back and forth at least three times. Pour over fresh ice in a chilled pint glass and add the garnishes.

EARLY BIRD HOUSE BLOODY MARY MIX

When preparing Bloody Mary mix, it's always best to err on the side of caution with spices. Also, the salt content of canned juice and canned tomatoes varies greatly from brand to brand, so be mindful, and do taste tests as you build. Too much salt or spice can be offensive, while blandness can be fixed.

Makes about 20 servings (4 to 5 ounces each)

One 46-ounce can tomato
juice

Two 6-ounce cans whole
tomatoes

2 cups Worcestershire sauce

1 cup soy sauce

¼ cup celery salt

¼ cup chili powder

¼ cup garlic salt

½ cup fresh lime juice

¼ cup freshly ground black
pepper

Combine the ingredients in a large mixing pitcher. Working in batches if necessary, pour into a blender and blend until completely smooth. Return to the container and store in the refrigerator for up to 2 weeks.

The ring-necked pheasant is the state bird of South Dakota, and while one might think it favors a quality-made Aviation cocktail (gin, crème de violette, maraschino liqueur, and lemon juice), I feel the colder South Dakota temps might enable this pheasant's colorful plumage reason to fly with a Perfect Manhattan (2 ounces rye whiskey to equal half ounces sweet vermouth and dry vermouth.)

South Dakota

I am not sure that we have an odd or unique drinking tradition in "So Dak." We are a pretty young state and barely had our feet underneath us before Prohibition, and post–World War II, industrialization of everything did away with anything that could have become a cocktail tradition here. From what I have observed, it has pretty much been the same homogenous drinking culture that permeated everywhere before the cocktail revolution of the last decade. But we're growing now. Dave Arnold's Liquid Intelligence, *for example, was an incredibly eye-opening introduction into what is possible with cocktails.*

—Cody Horan, bar manager, Blind Lion (Rapid City)

WE HAVE FINALLY arrived in coyote country, a tricky subject on any geography quiz. Sadly, most people can't even begin to guess the state capital, or they get it wrong and say Fargo. It's actually Pierre ("peer"), located smack-dab in the middle of the Coyote State, and the second-tiniest capital in the United States at approximately fourteen thousand residents.

Mount Rushmore, a sixty-foot-high granite monument of four US presidents (Thomas Jefferson, Abraham Lincoln, George Washington, and Theodore Roosevelt), was completed in 1941 and is located in the Black Hills. Crazy as it sounds, the mountain's name comes from a New York lawyer, Charles Rushmore, who visited the Black Hills in 1884 to investigate legal titles on properties, and when he asked what the name of the mountain was, no one had it, so someone said, "From now on we'll call it Rushmore." And *that* is why you are holding this book, America. The Sundance Kid spent time in a Deadwood jail cell in 1897 for a bank robbery attempt in Belle Fourche. A few weeks later, he had escaped and became one of the most wanted outlaws known in the West (although we eventually caught him on page 219).

At most bars in South Dakota, you could order a "Beertini" and find a couple of olives arriving on the edge of a glass of beer. And if the Beertini isn't working wonders for you, try the Red Beer Deluxe on for size; it's beer, tomato juice, olive brine, 4 or 5 olives inside the glass, and a pinch of salt, mixed and then garnished with some pickles. Essentially, this is a Michelada cocktail, or a Bloody Mary without the spices, citrus, and extra seasoning. Oh, and somewhere inside that Red Beer Deluxe is the beer, too.

Sioux Falls's Carpenter Bar is a great spot to sip on a Paloma cocktail made with Patrón Silver tequila; swing by Parker's Bistro for the house Parker's Martini, made with cucumber-forward Hendrick's gin, but if you're looking for bolder flavors, don't miss the American Whiskey Bar at Saloon #10 in Deadwood, which has more than 150 whiskey selections behind the bar and cowboys hanging 'round the poker tables.

BAR SNACK

Niki Ganong's wonderful book, *The Field Guide to Drinking in America*, features a terrific anecdote on the Wild West days of Deadwood: "The tradition of spreading sawdust on a barroom floor reportedly began in Deadwood. It was an attempt on the part of saloonkeepers to hide all of the falling gold dust, which would be swept up, sifted, and rendered at the end of the day."

SOUTH DAKOTA SPIRIT
DAKOTA SPIRITS DISTILLERY

Dakota Spirits was started in 2011 by two brothers who grew up in South Dakota and who could agree on a couple of things: Source from local fruits and grains, and ferment using purified waters from the nearby Missouri River. Everything else was a friendly sibling disagreement, and what endured while they bickered were their spirits: Ringneck vodka, a blended whiskey, an unaged whiskey named Coyote 100 Light whiskey ("might not be your grandma's whiskey, but it used to be!"), and their award-winning neutral brandy, Couteau des Prairies brandy, named for the French explorers who labeled that particular area of South Dakota grasslands.

SOUTH DAKOTA'S OLDEST BAR
BUFFALO BODEGA
Deadwood, 1877

Though there are no longer any lawless shootouts in Deadwood like those that occurred in the late 1800s, the Buffalo still embraces its wild side whether the sun is shining or the moon is howling. The space is big enough to house a little something for everyone. Have lunch in the Stockade or dinner in the steakhouse, grab some games in the casino, or catch live music in the outdoor courtyard, and while you're at it say hello to the wandering ghost of former regular Buffalo Bill, and stay late for the tasty musical samplings of DJ Cowboy. Giddy up!

SOUTH DAKOTA BUCKET LIST BAR
FULL THROTTLE SALOON
Sturgis

Do you like motorcycles? Check. Beer? Check. Adults? Check. Mechanical bull? Sure. Zip line? Body paint? Live music? Burlesque? Hey, it's Friday somewhere! The Full Throttle is the epicenter of the famous annual Sturgis Motorcycle Rally, a ten-day rally with live music. Past performers have included REO Speedwagon, Sheryl Crow, Bob Dylan, and Aerosmith. When I was doing research for this book, I saw that the band Jackyl was performing in the summer, which was a sign: The first music concert I ever attended was Aerosmith, and the opening band? Jackyl. Now who's got the first round of Boilermakers?

SOUTH DAKOTA COCKTAIL BAR
BLIND LION
Rapid City

Sometimes, the journey is as great as the destination: Park in downtown Rapid City and make your way to Ninth and Main Street, where the Blind Lion speakeasy is waiting for you underneath Murphy's Pub and Grill through a basement door. Behind that door is a bar with vintage furniture, live music, a fireplace, and some well-crafted cocktails featuring liquid nitrogen and cold-smoking technique. The Blind Lion handles the notion of throwback traditions by emphasizing the little things that tend to disappear all too quickly in our modern age. Observe the first house rule, as it should probably be the first house rule in any fine establishment: Slow down (live in the moment).

STATE FACT
The Badlands have fossils dating back thirty-five million years ago, when different animals roamed the earth. The largest T-Rex ever found came from the Badlands and is now on display at Chicago's Field Museum.

THE COLONEL
Cody Horan, Blind Lion, Rapid City

This is a cocktail that has been on the Blind Lion menu since its inception. It was put together for a colonel who used to come into the Blind Lion's sister bar.

2 ounces Catdaddy spiced
  moonshine (or Fireball, if
  it's easier to find)

½ ounce Grand Marnier

½ ounce honey syrup
  (page 89)

½ ounce fresh orange juice

Garnish: flamed orange peel

Shake the ingredients with ice until chilled; strain over a good amount of fresh ice into a chilled rocks glass. Flame an orange peel by holding the colored side toward the glass, with the lit wooden match between the peel and the drink. Squeeze the peel so the oils cause a flame and caramelize over the drink, then wipe the peel around the glass before placing it in the drink.

BADLANDS NATIONAL PARK
Brian Bartels

This Hot Toddy variation was created to honor the dramatic landscape of South Dakota, where bison, prairie dogs, and bighorn sheep live among canyons and grasslands. When I was in college, and all the other students wanted to head to Florida or somewhere warm for spring break, I was the weirdo who wanted to visit the Badlands. Also, that's when I started drinking whiskey. Any coincidence?

1½ ounces cinnamon, clove,
  and star anise–infused rye
  whiskey (recipe follows)

½ ounce brandy

¾ ounce ginger syrup
  (page 51)

¾ ounce fresh lemon juice

3 to 4 ounces hot water

2 spritzes of absinthe from an
  atomizer (optional; if you
  don't have an atomizer,
  fear not. It's okay to drop a
  couple drops on top of the
  drink for aromatics, but not
  necessary)

Garnishes: lemon peel and
  cloves

Pour the whiskey, brandy, ginger syrup, and lemon juice into a coffee mug and stir. Top with the hot water. Spritz the absinthe over the top of the glass. Garnish with the lemon and sprinkle with a few cloves.

Cinnamon, Clove, and Star Anise–Infused Rye Whiskey

Makes one 750-ml bottle

One 750-ml bottle 100-proof
  rye whiskey

Three 3-inch cinnamon sticks

8 whole cloves

4 star anise

Combine the ingredients in a large Mason jar or nonreactive container and steep at room temperature for 4 days. Taste to see if the mixture has achieved your desired spice. You can steep for another day or so, but be careful to not oversteep, as the spices will overpower the intended balance. Strain and store at room temperature for up to six months.

Some say you can judge the mood of one of the state's most iconic animals, the bison, by the way it moves its tail. If it is standing straight up, it is ready to charge, which makes sense, as I know some people who feel like that after their first Martini. Though there are more bars per capita in North Dakota than any other state in the country, one of my favorite aspects of the state would be the names of some cities: Voltaire, Prairie Rose, Nome, Grace City, Mantador, Jud, Fort Ransom, Maxbass, Starkweather (which sounds like the name of a *Game of Thrones* episode), Noonan (any relation to *Caddyshack*?), Pick City, Wing, Buffalo, Dwight, Zap, Bowbells, Buelah (*Anyone? Anyone? Bueller?*), Wahpeton, and Hope.

North Dakota

North Dakota has one of the most extreme temperature ranges in the United States. Nevertheless, that doesn't stop us from enjoying the outdoors and venturing out to socialize. Bismarck, the state capital, has a vibrant downtown community filled with many different types of restaurants, bars, breweries, and boutiques.

—Tristen Hoffer, bar manager (Bismarck)

NORTH DAKOTA MIGHT have my favorite nicknames in the United States. In addition to the Roughrider State, North Dakota is the 701, Peace Garden State, Norse Dakota, and, for the win, Heaven. Polka—a German dance accompanied by an accordion (and usually older people), bingo games, and beer—is very common in North Dakota, due to the state's many inhabitants with German ancestry, and the fact that polka king Lawrence Welk is from North Dakota.

Flickertail ground squirrels are everywhere in North Dakota. They flick their tail up and scurry every which way and are commonly celebrated throughout the Flickertail State (yes, another nickname for North Dakota) but don't tell Turtle Lake, famous for its annual turtle racing championships. Rutland is famous for being home to the largest hamburger ever constructed, according to the Guinness Book of World Records, topping out at 3,591 pounds, forming a whopper of indigestion. Stop by the Myra Museum in Grand Forks and experience the nineteenth-century way of life of pioneer women, touring one-room schools and the original log cabin post office. Or grab some famous knoephla soup (aka potato dumpling soup), coffee, and pie at Kroll's Diner. Plenty to see and do, and watch the buffalo, too!

Cocktail bars are gaining in popularity throughout North Dakota, so it wouldn't hurt to stop by Fargo's Boiler Room and Mezzaluna, Bismarck's Lüft rooftop bar, and Grand Forks's Brick and Barley, known for some knockout Bloody Marys featuring a top-secret homemade spice blend.

North Dakota has helped make bars even more entertaining for decades. Fans of trivia might be interested to know that "Think and Drink" began in Grand Forks in 1973 at the Westward Ho peanut bar, and subsequently spread through the nation to become what we now know and love as "bar trivia night."

My favorite piece of trivia about the state? North Dakota grows more sunflowers than any other state. One for each of you.

NORTH DAKOTA'S OLDEST BAR
PEACOCK ALLEY
Bismarck, 1933

The oldest bar in North Dakota also features an extensive cocktail selection, which is a nice accompaniment to its sprawling bar. Located in the lobby of the historic Patterson Hotel and opened the year Prohibition ended, the Peacock hosted politicians, wayfarers, gamblers, and all sorts of ne'er-do-wells in its prime, and still manages to get people riled up with its modern-day Espresso Martinis, and the prices are spookier than the ghosts haunting the old space!

NORTH DAKOTA BUCKET LIST BAR
TOASTED FROG
Fargo, Bismarck, and Grand Forks

Yes, Toasted Frog does sound like a bar in Times Square that's been open for forty-plus years, one tourists go to after seeing the famous episode on *Bar Rescue* about the older, wise-cracking New York owner who fought the mafia, the cops, and, well, even the tourists, and somehow made the place lovable. But the Toasted Frog turns out to be a small chain of great restaurants with creative cocktail programs in Bismarck, Fargo, and Grand Forks. Their cocktail menus feature a nice balance of craft American distilleries and international standbys.

NORTH DAKOTA SPIRIT
PROOF ARTISAN DISTILLERS
Fargo

Our drinking tradition is steeped in community and craftsmanship. The US is home to hundreds of great craft cocktail bars that have paved the way. If it wasn't for Americans wanting to enjoy the company of our friends and community, we would not be able to create amazing cocktails and trends inspiring others across the world. The cocktail industry is like one massive family. Everyone knowns everyone, and we learn and adapt from each other, and we get inspiration from our fellow bartenders. Every bar needs passion. Passionate staff drive your business's success, and if your bartenders love what they do, it spreads to the patrons and their subsequent enjoyment of a truly well-crafted cocktail.

—Tristen Hoffer, bar manager (Bismarck)

Award-winning distillers of whiskey, vodka, gin, and varying liqueurs, Proof has been serving Fargo only since 2016, but it's housed in plenty of North Dakota tradition, headquartered in a building that is nearly a hundred years old, and the tasting room has a bar from 1892 Grand Forks, rescued by friends of the distillery who affectionately call themselves "minions," so beloved and devoted to the distillery that Proof has named their house gin, Minions gin, in their honor. They recently produced North Dakota's first bourbon, Crooked Furrow, named after the furrows created when you plant corn; as distiller Jeremy Meidinger told *Fargo Monthly*, "Grandpa always said corn grows better in a crooked furrow. Of course, he just said that because he drove crooked."

NORTH DAKOTA COCKTAIL BAR
HUMPBACK SALLY'S
Bismarck

Humpback Sally's was opened by a wife-and-husband team, one of those great American business stories that proves that not only can a couple stay happily married, they can also achieve life goals together. As my good friend Gabriel Stulman would say, "Yahtzee!" Their menu features variations on classics (Grasshopper with coconut milk? Two, please), a fall Old Fashioned with sweet potato–infused bourbon, and a separate list that makes my little juniper-soaked heart go pitter-patter: Gin and Tonic variations with house-made 510 tonic. And if you like the drinks they're making at Humpback Sally's, don't be afraid to sneak into 510.2, their speakeasy in the same building. It's a No Dak win-win, yes yes.

NORTH DAKOTA BEVERAGE
THE SMITH AND CURRAN

In April 1951, a farm in Tioga struck oil, and the state was inundated with wildcatters, land speculators, geologists, and roughnecks. Wendell Smith and James Curran were partners during the North Dakota oil surge, and their office was on the second floor of the Prince Hotel in Bismarck. However, they spent plenty of time downstairs imbibing at the Blue Blazer Lounge. One day in 1952, they challenged the bartender at the Blue Blazer, Gebert "Shorty" Doebber, to come up with a soothing "hair of the dog" concoction for them. It quickly became a favorite drink of the oilmen. And because oilmen tend to travel, they spread word of the drink around the world. So these days, anywhere you find oilmen, you'll probably find the Smith and Curran (under one of its many modified names like Smith and Kearns, which was the result of a bartender not hearing "Curran" over the loud din of a drinking crowd). The original recipe is crème de cacao, heavy cream, and club soda, but the recipe was modified in the 1960s once Kahlúa started popping up. Either way you wrangle it, you're basically drinking a milkshake—or, I drink your milkshake, or Daniel Day Lewis will drink your milkshake like he does in *There Will Be Blood*.

STATE FACT
Although North Dakota's official state flower is the wild prairie rose, the state grows more sunflowers than any other. Nearly 90% of North Dakota is farmland and ranches, leading the country's agricultural charge with flaxseed, durum wheat (pasta), canola, and honey production.

BLACK MARKET NEGRONI
Mezzaluna, Fargo

This Negroni variation is exactly what I would want to drink on a cold, wintry North Dakota night. Make sure your spiced orange black tea has cinnamon in it, which is a terrific ingredient when mixing these flavors. Fords is one of my favorite gins on the market, and it also boasts one of the best packaging labels ever produced, listing not only each ingredient that goes into the gin, but its origin and flavor profile—and it isn't just four or five ingredients. Most Negroni recipes call for equal parts of savory, sweet, and bitter for their ideal balance, but Mezzaluna goes the way of cocktail historian and *Negroni* cocktail book author Gary "Gaz" Regan, who notoriously prefers a little more gin for the win. And now, we dance!

1½ ounces Fords gin

½ ounce sweet vermouth spiced orange black tea (recipe follows)

½ ounce Tattersall bitter orange liqueur (Combier or Cointreau also work)

½ ounce Cynar amaro

Garnish: orange peel

Stir the ingredients with ice until chilled; strain into a chilled rocks glass with fresh ice. Garnish with the orange.

Sweet Vermouth Spiced Orange Black Tea

Makes one 750 ml bottle

2 tablespoons spiced orange black tea

One 750 ml bottle sweet vermouth

Combine the ingredients and steep for half an hour. Taste before straining, but be careful not to oversteep: Leaving the tea in the vermouth for any extended period of time will cause the tannins to overpower the vermouth. Strain and refrigerate for up to 1 month.

THUNDER ALLEY
Proof Artisan Distillers, Fargo

Thunder Alley is not only the name of my next bluegrass-folk album, it is one of Proof's cocktails that combines 2 Docks cream liqueur, a variation on Baileys Irish cream, with 2 Docks Fire by Proof, a cinnamon-flavored whiskey in the vein of Fireball. What's great about this drink is that you can have it hot with coffee (winter-friendly in North Dakota) or iced for the summertime (August in North Dakota ☺).

1 ounce 2 Docks cream liqueur (Bailey's or Amarula also work)

1 ounce 2 Docks Fire by Proof (or Fireball, if you don't live in North Dakota)

3 to 4 ounces hot coffee or cold brew coffee (store-bought, or see page 39 for homemade concentrate recipe)

Combine ingredients in a heat-resistant cup (if using hot coffee) and stir. If you would like to have it iced, combine ingredients in a chilled rocks glass with the diluted cold brew, add ice, stir and serve.

When people assign little ceremonies or traditions to their boozing, no matter how mundane or silly they might seem, that's when drinking becomes elevated to this much more important thing.

—Jeffrey Morgenthaler, Oregonian and author of *The Bar Book* and *Drinking Distilled*

The West

Alaska *Washington*
Montana *Wyoming*
Idaho Oregon
Nevada Utah *Colorado*
New Mexico *Arizona*
California Hawaii

Alaska

Bars stay open until 5 A.M. throughout Alaska, which is probably a little risqué for people in June, when the sun stays out for nearly ninety days. Which reminds me of a great joke: "So a salmon and a bear walk into a cocktail…"

ALASKA IS ONE-FIFTH the size of the Lower 48, and "America's Last Frontier" is mighty impressive for its sheer area alone: 571,951 square miles. Did you know there are more than three million lakes in Alaska? And that there are more than one hundred volcanoes there? And think about this: You could fit the state of Rhode Island into Alaska 425 times. Great gobbledygook! Mt. Denali, the highest peak in North America, is 20,320 feet high. That's a lot of steps on your Apple Health program. Take a stroll through Glacier Gardens and behold one of the most curious sights around, that of hundreds of upside-down spruce and hemlock trees, the result of a landscaping mishap, but a beautiful accident nonetheless. Yes, the wild forget-me-not is the state flower, which would be a great name for a cocktail if cocktails in general were better at helping to improve our memory.

Alaska has come a long way since drinking evergreen shrubs (a local mixture of evergreen, sugar, and vinegar imbibed for its medicinal properties), Labrador tea (a medicinal herbal infusion made from the shrubs of evergreens and conifers, no doubt originated by the First Nations and Inuit people hundreds of years ago), and, eventually (I'm sorry), Duck Farts—a hypnotic and unwelcome shot mix of Kahlúa coffee liqueur, Baileys Irish cream, and whiskey. Some tales point to this shot originating at the Peanut Farm in Anchorage, and though that is debatable, one fact remains: Duck Farts somehow exist, and we are all worse for it.

Though gold is the official state mineral, you can't talk about Alaska without celebrating moose, wolves, bald eagles, beluga whales, grizzly bears, and salmon. The Alaska Distillery apparently agrees about the last item in that list, anyway, finding a way to infuse its potato vodka with wild smoked salmon, which is an eye-opening ingredient to add to your Bloody Mary. That's a vast improvement from when gold miners used to put unwashed foot rags into their mash when making whiskey.

Cocktail bars in Anchorage and Fairbanks are sprouting up left and right. Whiskey fans should try the Spenard Roadhouse, or have a cask-aged Old Fashioned with the talented staff at Simon & Seafort's Saloon, and don't miss Tequila 61°, because if I'm going to freeze to death, I'm going to do it drinking mezcal and beer, and ideally I'm going to do it on Taco Tuesday; otherwise I have failed in this life.

There has never been a better time to be a bartender. Advances in production, packaging, distribution, and storage have improved the quality and safety of our ingredients. But perhaps more important, bartenders have an increased awareness of which methods should be unsentimentally left behind and which should be preserved, unaltered, for posterity.

—From *Meehan's Bartender Manual* by Jim Meehan

ALASKA BEVERAGE
THE SOURTOE

For those of us willing to subscribe to Let Your Freak Flag Fly Magazine, I give you the Sourtoe. Since 1973, the good people of the Yukon Territory in Dawson City have been serving one kick of a tradition: They have a dehydrated human toe they use to garnish a drink of one's choosing. There have been numerous toes used in this process, starting with one from a legendary rum runner named Louis Liken, who lost his frostbitten appendage in the 1920s (Prohibition-related, perhaps?) and preserved the toe in a jar of alcohol. It was found fifty years later by Captain Dick Stevenson, who brought the toe over yonder to the Sourdough Saloon and challenged wayfaring miners and mountaineers to drink their beverages with the toe floating in their glasses. Hence, the Sourtoe cocktail was born. It lasted long enough for someone to have a baker's dozen of Sourtoe Champagne cocktails, and on the thirteenth cocktail, the drinker fell back on his chair and swallowed the original toe. The owners have now decided a fair price of toe consumption should be $2,500. Know this: "Toe time" is between 9 P.M. and 11 P.M., and there's one consistent rule: "You can drink it fast, or you can drink it slow—but the lips have gotta touch the toe."

ALASKA BUCKET LIST BAR
SALTY DAWG SALOON
Homer

The Salty Dawg Saloon was first built as a cabin, and served the citizens of Homer (the "cosmic hamlet by the sea") as a school, post office, railway station, and grocery store until 1957, when the building was turned into the Salty Dawg Saloon, and here is where the locals descend for a healthy pint, hearty conversation, or the signature cocktail, the—wait for it—Salty Dawg Martini, a vodka and grapefruit mixture shaken and served up with some salt on the lip of the glass. The ceiling and walls are covered with countless dollar bills; long ago, a customer visited the saloon and left money for a friend who would be arriving later so they could buy them a drink. It's humbling to know of places where people continue to congregate, in hopes of connecting with friends, new and old, and leaving a little something for them, whenever they may arrive. Bonus humanity points for the Salty Dawg, as well: Each year, most of the dollar bills are removed and donated to charity.

BAR SNACK
Hooch is a word for illegally made or low-quality liquor. It was introduced to the United States by miners coming back from the Klondike Gold Rush in the late 1800s and was a shortened form of *hoochinoo*, a Tlingit word for rum and molasses.

ALASKA COCKTAIL BAR
THE SPEAKEASY
Anchorage

THE Speakeasy is a (surprise, surprise) hidden gem inside the Williwaw, a multifaceted gathering spot in downtown Anchorage. Once inside, there will be house cocktails waiting, but I have a soft spot for any menu featuring an actual Blue Blazer cocktail, a pre-Prohibition Intro to Bartending Theatrics, which is prepared by taking Scotch whiskey and boiling water, lighting it on fire, then mixing that arc of fire back and forth between two metal mugs (you know, like they taught you in third-period junior high science class). Featuring a properly made Blue Blazer on any menu is paying homage to the man who invented it, "Professor" Jerry Thomas, who knew a thing or two about showmanship, spirits, and decorum—but he also knew you probably shouldn't try this cocktail on your own at home, old sport. Let THE Speakeasy ride the lightning.

BAR SNACK

An Alaskan icehouse is a common space for fishermen to keep warm from the frigid Alaskan air, but the icehouse, where ice was kept cold before there were electric freezers, is also an integral part of our cocktail history. Ice started to make its way into American drinks and bars in the early nineteenth century, courtesy of Frederic Tudor, a New England entrepreneur, and even then, ice was usually only available in port towns, larger cities, and for the wealthy, as it was difficult and expensive to obtain and keep. Ice was frowned upon by nineteenth-century dentists, as they claimed it was bad for the teeth, which is fine, because someone then invented the straw, but then, later, we all invented ways to destroy the environment, so we stopped using straws—or at least plastic straws. Right? (Please don't use plastic straws. Use metal or biodegradable straws, or do what they did back in the day: Sip from the glass.)

ALASKA SPIRIT
50 FATHOMS GIN, PORT CHILKOOT DISTILLERY
Haines

Located in a former army outpost, Port Chilkoot is a good enough excuse to pull the car over and taste true small-batch, artisanal spirits being made with local herbs and house-milled organic grains. Head distiller Heather Shade is not only gifted at making spruce sing inside the bottles of juniper-forward gin, she is the founding president of the Distillers Guild of Alaska, and responsible for 50 Fathoms gin, which received a double-gold medal at the World Spirits Competition in San Francisco.

ALASKA'S OLDEST BAR
B&B BAR
Kodiak, 1906

B&B is actually a tiny little watering hole on an island, featuring cold bottled beer, salty regulars, drink specials, a pool table, and fishing antiques, and it's open late. There may be boats parked nearby waiting to participate in the next *Deadliest Catch*, but there's nothing that can take the pole position of sitting in the oldest bar in Alaska and seeing the bar rules listed on the mirror: (1) Know what you want, (2) Cash only, and (3) No whining.

STATE FACT

Vegetables in Alaska are enormous. Though they see only one hundred days of sunlight per year, the best days receive over nineteen hours of sunlight, which results in cabbages that look like Cadillacs.

THE ALASKA
Brian Bartels

This pre-Prohibition drink was not created in Alaska, but it was created in homage to Alaska becoming a part of the United States. The original recipe appeared in 1913 in Jacques Straub's *Manual of Mixed Drinks* and later in *The Savoy Cocktail Book,* and most recipes call for Old Tom gin, which was unavailable in the United States until recently, but Old Tom is a sweeter gin, and since yellow Chartreuse is also sweet, I volunteer a citrus and cardamom-forward spirit as a base, like Amass gin from California. Or best me by combining two different American gins and see where the botanical experiment can take you. Who knows? You might strike gold.

2 ounces Amass gin (or
1 ounce each of two
American gins)

½ ounce yellow Chartreuse

½ ounce amontillado sherry

2 dashes Regan's orange
bitters

Garnish: lemon peel

Stir the ingredients with ice until chilled; strain into a chilled coupe glass and serve up, garnished with the lemon.

GOLD RUSH
T. J. Siegal, Milk & Honey, Manhattan, New York

On a tip from fellow prospector Robert Henderson, a sourdough (aka a prospector) named George Cormack and his two Native American brothers-in-law, Skookum Jim and Dawson "Tagish" Charlie, found gold in Alaska's Klondike River valley at Bonanza Creek on August 17, 1896. As the Gold Rush was a keystone movement involving the sourdoughs of yesteryear, so too was this Whiskey Sour variation, created by T. J. Siegal in the halcyon days of New York's Milk & Honey. "Claim your stake" with a dash of Angostura, if you're feeling lucky.

2 ounces bourbon

¾ ounce fresh lemon juice

¾ ounce rich honey syrup
(recipe follows)

Shake all the ingredients with ice until chilled; strain over fresh ice in a chilled rocks glass.

Rich Honey Syrup

Makes approximately 1½ cups

1 cup honey

½ cup water

Heat the honey and water in a saucepan over medium heat, stirring occasionally, until the ingredients have integrated. Remove from the heat, let cool, then transfer to a tightly sealed container and store in the refrigerator for up to 1 week.

Washington

Is it any surprise that Seattle's own Bill Nye, the Science Guy, once said: "Technically, alcohol is a solution."

WASHINGTON HAS CAPTIVATING geographical landmarks, such as Mount Rainier, the Puget Sound, and the Space Needle, and though grunge music, serious coffee, and Microsoft have storied tradition through Seattle's historic bar scene (one of Microsoft's founders, Robert Hess, also co-founded the Museum of the American Cocktail and wrote *The Essential Bartender's Guide: How to Make Truly Great Cocktails*), the person who deserves more credit is Murray Stenson, who put Seattle's Zig Zag Café on the map as a tourist destination strictly for his reputation as being the consummate bar professional.

Walking around Seattle with Murray Stenson is like church-hopping with the pope, only the churches are bars. Everyone knows him. Everyone respects him. He has elevated bartending through his steadfast reputation for being a polite, efficient (his nickname was "Murr the Blur," as he was known for speedy service), thoughtful bartender (he remembers everyone and their drinks) who leads by the best example: hospitality first.

There is no shortage of wonderful bars and cocktail destinations throughout the Emerald City, and the balance of traditional spots and new cocktail havens keeps me on my toes each time I visit. For example, I started my odyssey with Murray by having a bone-dry Martini at Oliver's Lounge, located inside the Mayflower Park Hotel. Oliver's is famous for being the first daytime bar in Seattle, as windows were outlawed in adult drinking establishments and liquor could not be served in view of the street until 1976, so when Oliver's opened, they made sure to do it with style: The view from the bar is floor-to-ceiling windows, and I assure you, it's worth sitting there and having a Martini if a seat is available.

*Brian Bartels:
What's your
favorite cocktail
to make?*

*Murray Stenson:
Jack and Coke.*

(months later)

*Brad Thomas
Parsons: Brian
told me your
favorite cocktail
was a Jack
and Coke.*

*Murray Stenson:
Oh, I was just
goofin' with him.*

Make time to visit Damn the Weather, a gastropub in Pioneer Square offering a little something for every palate; Life on Mars is not only a great David Bowie song, it's a don't-miss destination in Capitol Hill with thousands of records available to shop and play while imbibing; and if there's a wait at Canon (and there probably is), you are just a hop, skip, and jump from Tavern Law, which has never steered me wrong.

Chef Renee Erickson has not only brought significant culinary acclaim to the Seattle scene, but her cocktail programs flourish as much as her food programs. All of her restaurants showcase creative cocktail menus, and one of my favorite stops, which I can't recommend enough, is the Walrus and the Carpenter, located right next to Barnacle, Erickson's small plates bar specializing in a wide variety of amari (and drink selections accompanied by such proclamations as "gitchie gitchie ya ya da da, friends," because, yes, always)—but do not miss Deep Dive, her newest spot, which opened in South Lake Union, full of deep-sea tchotchkes and illuminating nooks and crannies from which one may never want to return.

Belltown is the Seattle neighborhood people have been flocking to for the past few years. Places like Bathtub Gin & Co. (a well-hidden speakeasy tugging at the juniper-covered heartstrings inside each of us) has a lovely house cocktail menu; and Navy Strength, owned by Anu Apte and Chris Elford, are reaching new audiences for their appreciation of all things rum and tiki-focused, winning "Best New Bar" at Tales of the Cocktail 2018. Anu is also responsible for Rob Roy, a wonderful cocktail bar with a wide list of cocktails created to command respect, such as the Sharpie Moustache, made with 100-proof rye, gin, amaro, tiki bitters, and orange oil. Don't fall asleep on that puppy.

Beyond Seattle, there is Dillinger's Cocktails and Kitchen, a worthwhile cocktail destination in Olympia holding all the riches with its extensive classic and contemporary cocktail menu. Dillinger's is located in a former bank, constructed in 1926, when famed bank robber John Dillinger was robbing twenty-four banks, avoiding and aggravating enough lawmen to spawn the Federal Bureau of Investigation.

*Zig Zag Café is
the American
cocktail bar I tell
everyone to visit.*

—Jeffrey Morgenthaler,
Clyde Common
and Pépé Le Moko,
(Portland, OR)

WASHINGTON BUCKET LIST BAR
ZIG ZAG CAFÉ
Seattle

The Zig Zag Café, tucked inside the Pike Place Market, has long been a must-visit destination for anyone looking to have a quality cocktail from its talented team of bar professionals. Murray Stenson bartended there for over twelve years, but many of its bartenders shape the legend that has made Zig Zag a necessary bar destination. Their take on the classics is exemplary, and the warm and welcoming space makes one want to sit and sip forever.

WASHINGTON BEVERAGE
RACHEL'S GINGER BEER

I had my first bottle of Rachel's ginger beer at its location next to the legendary Pike's Place Market, and if you like a spicy ginger beer like I do, you'll keep coming back for Rachel's simple yet oh-so-refreshing ginger magic. Operating since 2009, Rachel's not only features the classic ginger beer, it now has approximately one dozen flavored ginger beers, such as white peach, caramelized pineapple, and black currant.

WASHINGTON'S OLDEST BAR
THE BRICK
Roslyn, 1889

To quote Brad Thomas Parsons (a former resident of Seattle) in his brilliant seminal book, Bitters, *as he waxes so proficiently: "So what, exactly, are bitters? Bitters are an aromatic flavoring agent made from infusing roots, barks, fruit peels, seeds, spices, herbs, flowers, and botanicals in a high-proof alcohol (or sometimes glycerin). Long reputed to possess medicinal properties, bitters were billed as the cure for whatever ailed you, whether it was a headache, indigestion, stomach cramps, or constipation." As Brad is one of my favorite spirits, cocktails, all-around writers, and genuine people on the planet, I find it's best to follow his lead. Thank you, Wildcat.*

The Brick is famous for its 45,000 bricks, a basement jail cell, a beautiful one-hundred-year-old bar, being a regular bar scene in the TV show *Northern Exposure* (one of Ma Bartels's favorite shows), and having a twenty-three-foot running water spittoon along the bar, which hosts the annual Brick Regatta every March, when people race tiny homemade boats down the old-time saloon's spittoon. It's nice to know there are places in America where people aged twenty-one to a hundred and one can congregate over some drinks, shoot a little pool and catch a live music performance on a weekend night.

WASHINGTON SPIRIT
OOLA DISTILLERY
Seattle

OOLA, named after "the greatest German Shepherd who ever lived," opened in 2010 in the heart of Seattle's Capitol Hill neighborhood, and was one of the first Washington distilleries to open post-Prohibition. It provides a wonderful new American gin, winter wheat vodka, four-grain bourbon, and some terrific flavored vodkas, such as rosemary, citrus, and chile pepper, which are all wonderful choices for Bloody Marys. Owner Kirby Kallas-Lewis is a staunch advocate of sourcing locally and maintaining eco-friendly practices, and it shows on a daily basis at the distillery. Check out the website for some wonderful cocktail recipes.

WASHINGTON'S COCKTAIL BAR
CANON
Seattle

Entering Canon does not feel like entering Canon. The front doors perform a wonderful smoke-and-mirrors act, hiding what awaits, and the façade might look like what lies inside won't be much to brag about—but that's a rookie mistake. Once inside, try not to stand and stare with your mouth agape: The right side of the darkened bar holds shelves and rows of spirits, festooned in a way that might make you believe you've just entered a graduate program for spirits awareness and appreciation. "Professor" Jamie Boudreau is the person to thank for creating this School for Gifted Imbibers. Open since 2011, Canon holds an impressive spirits selection, hovering somewhere around four thousand and counting, which is a healthy number for a thirty-two-seat cocktail bar, but their vintage spirit offerings are what impresses this author the most, particularly a Calvados aged for sixty years in a barrel, which Boudreau has claimed tastes like "unicorns squirting rainbows ... with an insanely vibrant finish that *will* end you."

Jamie Boudreau (from Canon) has one of the best palates on the planet. He can taste the nuances and details in just about anything. Remarkable.

Murray Stenson, bartender and bar legend (Seattle)

TRIDENT
Robert Hess, Seattle

In my opinion, the Trident doesn't get enough attention or respect, as instead of sugar, it successfully wields more savory components than most cocktails. The Trident very much is a Negroni variation, but thanks to cocktail crusader Robert Hess, it was testing the Negroni variation waters long before any modern bartenders or mixologists were riffing their own recipe saxophones.

1 ounce Krogstad aquavit

1 ounce Cynar amaro

1 ounce fino sherry

2 dashes peach bitters

Garnish: grated lemon zest and a strip of lemon peel

Stir the ingredients with ice until chilled; strain into a chilled coupe glass and serve up, sprinkled with the grated zest and garnished with the lemon peel.

CLEAN SLATE
Jermaine Whitehead, Deep Dive, Seattle

Have you heard of Amazon? Word on the street is they have money. And lots of employees. And in Seattle, on the ground floor of Amazon's headquarters, there is Deep Dive, where Jermaine Whitehead is running things with historic reckoning and attention to detail. This low-alcohol, nutty, and refreshing Clean Slate recipe was first published in 2019 in *Imbibe*. Seattle's Scrappy's makes some of the best bitters in America. (Love you, Celery.) Manzanilla sherry is not only a wonderful and underappreciated cocktail ingredient, but I will happily visit your home if you keep a bottle in the fridge. (P.S.: Your fridge is the large white box in your kitchen next to all the flattened empty Amazon boxes you need to recycle.)

1 ounce Manzanilla sherry

1 ounce bianco vermouth (Whitehead uses Mancino, but Carpano or Dolin work)

¼ ounce Salers aperitif (Lillet also works)

2 dashes Scrappy's Orleans bitters (or substitute Peychaud's)

Garnish: edible flower (Whitehead uses nasturtiums, which grow in abundance in Seattle)

Stir the ingredients with ice until chilled; strain into a chilled coupe glass and serve up, garnished with an edible flower.

. . . .

Oliver's has got some history to it. It used to be a carousel room, and they had an actual carousel with horses inside, and in Washington in the 1970s, the law was, if you sold beer and wine, you could have windows, but if you sold cocktails, you could not have windows looking out into the street. So Oliver's was the first cocktail place to have windows installed. It's one of my favorite bars.

—Murray Stenson, bartender and bar legend (Seattle)

Is it time for another good bar joke yet? Okay. An elk walks into the Sip 'N Dip in Great Falls, where there is a mermaid tank located behind the bar, and people are sipping colorful cocktails and listening to Piano Pat play the hits. The elk says to the Mermaid sitting next to him, "Did you hear about the bailiff who moonlighted as a bartender? She served subpoena coladas."

Montana

I love it if you get a drink at a bar, and upon the first sip, it is so enjoyable, you have to say (pounds hand on table), "That is a pounder!" I love pounder drinks.

—Dave Arnold, author, *Liquid Intelligence*, co-owner, Existing Conditions (Manhattan, NY)

THE MONTANA STATE motto is "The Last Best Place," and it is nicknamed the Treasure State for its natural beauty. These claims are hard to refute, as anyone who drives the Going-to-the-Sun Road in Glacier National Park will attest that it happens to be one of the prettiest drives in America.

Grizzly bears, Lewis and Clark, and the country's largest collection of dinosaur fossils (at the Museum of the Rockies) are a big part of Big Sky Country. And that's when people aren't talking about spotting elk, antelope, pelicans, sage grouse, moose, wild buffalo, snow geese, golden eagles, loons, deer, and swans. There are more cattle in Montana than there are people. And I haven't even mentioned the fish! Which reminds me—*creek* is pronounced "crick" in Montana. The word *spendy* means "expensive" here, used the same way as the word *pricey*.

Don't forget to swing by the historic Montana Bar, a beautifully preserved western bar in downtown Miles City, or Charlie B's in Missoula, open pretty much all day, serving Cajun food next door at the Dinosaur and offering what *Esquire* says "is the nicest place in the country to find a beautiful woman who can gut her own trout."

Bozeman is a wonderful college town with many choices for food and drink, notably Plonk, Haufbrau House, Crystal Bar, and Copper Whiskey Bar & Grill. (Plonk also has a location in Missoula, and both are worth a visit.)

Enbär in downtown Great Falls specializes in house craft cocktails highlighting state distilleries (Gulch in Helena, Montgomery in Missoula, and Spotted Bear in Whitefish, to name a few), and incorporates celebrated philanthropic endeavors into its lively bar atmosphere, such as Toast to a Tuesday, where 10 percent of the drink sales go toward a local nonprofit.

Silver Star Steak Company in Helena balances a list of impressive classic cocktails with a wide variety of Martinis, and don't miss out on Gulch Distillers's wonderful portfolio of hand-crafted spirits, offering a varied list of creative spirits such as a reserve gin with elevated citrus and apricot notes, a bourbon cask spiced rum, and a fernet made with chamomile, saffron, rhubarb, mint, and Montana grains. The celebrated tasting room offers cocktails with house-made syrups, fresh citrus, and locally grown herbs.

If you're stopping by a distillery also known for its cocktails, such as Montgomery Distillery in Missoula, fair warning: Montana law dictates that only two drinks are allowed during any distillery visit. Make 'em count!

BAR SNACK

Virginia City, founded in 1863, is still considered one of the more complete original towns of its kind in the United States. While it is known as a backyard to Yellowstone today, it was a destination spot at the turn of the nineteenth century for theatre and vaudeville, mining for gems and gold, shopping at the mercantile exchange to try on eighteenth century wardrobes and mining gear, and hanging out at the Bale of Hay Saloon, the oldest bar in Montana.

MONTANA SPIRIT
GLACIER DISTILLING COMPANY
Coram

It's worth noting that Glacier Distilling Company was conceived during a Montana snowstorm in the winter of 2009–10. The founders took inspiration from a Glacier National Park bootlegger named Josephine Doody, who produced an un-aged rye whiskey around the 1900s. They now assemble a wonderful variety of organic and GMO-free corn-based alpine whiskies and fine spirits such as Trail of the Cedars absinthe, made with pot-distilled Montana wormwood.

MONTANA'S OLDEST BAR
BALE OF HAY SALOON
Virginia City, 1863

Virginia City is only 198 people, and the Bale of Hay Saloon, located on the western side of town next to the Opera House, keeps its locals happy with microbrews, original period artwork, live music, billiards, and ghost tours. The bar is absolutely beautiful. Bale of Hay is open only from mid-May through September, so get there while the summer sun is working its magic.

MONTANA BEVERAGE
"DITCH"

I wish this was more complicated. But it's not. The word *ditch* means "with water." Most places in Montana will know what you want right off the bat if you order a whiskey ditch. It's whiskey. And water. And that's about it.

MONTANA BUCKET LIST BAR
SIP 'N DIP
Great Falls

There's no question this is one of the great bucket list bars in America. Open since 1962 and famous for its tiki-themed décor, swimming mermaids, and Piano Pat, the octogenarian piano virtuoso who brings the crowds to their feet when she gets a chance to tickle the ivories in a rendition of "Ring of Fire" for all the Mai Tai drinkers. The Sip 'n Dip's signature drink is the Fishbowl, a sweet, boozy blue cocktail served in a fishbowl for a group of friends. Piano Pat performs Wednesdays through Saturdays. And she can play the hits, but she has her own request: No more "Sweet Caroline," if you please.

MONTANA COCKTAIL BAR
COPPER WHISKEY BAR & GRILL
Bozeman

Given the states proximity to fresh mountain water and hearty grains, whiskey holds a special place in Montana's history, with female homesteaders getting involved with making spirits as a means to supplement their limited farm income. Copper celebrates the nostalgia with a nice blend of more than 150 selections, combining international whiskies with local Montana-based distilleries. But don't let the name derail you: Copper is a well-known restaurant destination as well, and serves elevated pub food—and yes, it even has fried cheese curds, which makes this Wisconsin boy proud. The cocktail menu is playful and inventive, featuring Old Fashioned, Manhattan, Flip, and Moscow Mule variations, and notable Highballs such as "Best Whiskey Coke Ever," with a cardamom-infused bourbon.

STATE FACT
In Montana, it is illegal for married women to go fishing alone on Sundays, and illegal for unmarried women to go fishing at all. Sheesh.

EVEL MULE
Brian Bartels

Inspired by Evel Knievel, Butte, Montana's hometown son, and Moscow Mules across America, this spicy sipper is here to bring out your inner daredevil. Evel Knievel was many things: insurance salesman, con man, fashion icon, purported kidnapper of his future wife of forty years, painter, and danger-seeking stuntman who attempted riding motorcycles over cars, buses, and bridges. If this cocktail could be a message, it would say: "Welcome to Danger City, population: you."

1 ounce Glacier Distilling
  Cabin Fever (or Fireball)

1 ounce Gosling's dark rum

½ ounce fresh lime juice

3½ ounces Fever-Tree ginger
  beer (classic or smoked)

2 dashes Angostura bitters

Garnish: lime wheel or lime
  wedge

Combine the ingredients in a chilled Old Fashioned or highball glass with ice. Garnish with the lime.

BLACK DIAMOND
Caroline McCarty, Montgomery Distillery, Missoula

Montgomery Distillery is the kind of family-run place you might hope to own and/or work in at some point in you life, because the people surrounding the company seem just too wonderful to ignore. This cocktail diamond elevates a simple Vodka Sour variation with honey and herbal notes and runs the table with the black pepper—an underappreciated cocktail ingredient—at the end.

¾ ounce fresh lemon juice

Leaves of one 3- to 4-inch
  fresh rosemary sprig

1½ ounces vodka

¾ ounce honey syrup
  (page 89)

3 to 4 turns freshly ground
  black pepper

Garnish: fresh rosemary sprig

Put the lemon juice and rosemary leaves (about 10) in a shaker and muddle them. Add the vodka, honey syrup, pepper, and ice, cover, and shake until chilled. Fine strain into a chilled coupe glass. Feel free to add a couple more twists of pepper to the top. Garnish with the rosemary.

BAR SNACK

Yellowstone is largely in Wyoming, but actually spreads into the southern part of Montana. Don't miss Boiling Springs, located at the northern part of Yellowstone, where hot springs flow into a cold ass river. You can actually be wading through water that is making one half of your body heat up while the other side can feel as though it's freezing. I don't believe there's a cocktail that wields similar characteristics, but if you ever see Dave Arnold, ask him. The confluence of temperatures are drastic enough that one's body temperature radically changes when moving a few inches, which is important to recognize, as all the elk surrounding you on the shoreline are shaking their heads and silently judging you, like a Geico commercial.

Wyoming

Cowboy Etiquette 101: Don't wave at another cowboy on a horse, as the horse might be distracted by the Margarita in your other hand. When entering a bar, tip your hat to greet the bartender. Be honorable. If you're ordering whiskey, and you're uncertain of which brand you would like, asking the bartender their advice is a sign of respect and admiration. Don't call the bartender "Chuckwagon." Be hospitable. Be grateful. And when ordering an Old Fashioned, never steal another patron's garnish. That's just gross.

WYOMING WAS THE last state in the union to raise the drinking age, making all Wyoming teenagers in 1988 the last coolest teenagers in the country. Cooler than the *Stranger Things* kids. But we might never meet them, as Wyoming is plenty big but the least populated state in America—which actually makes for some truly great appreciation of preserved land.

Yellowstone was the first national park in America (1872), with Devils Tower (a butte made of igneous rock) the first national monument, and geysers for all the kids. Geysers are quite the rage in Wyoming, with none other than "Old Faithful," the most popular geyser of them all, erupting approximately every hour and a half in Yellowstone. Wyoming is known for its wilderness and rugged frontier life: It has not just Yellowstone but the Grand Tetons, and all

In an interview with Taste the Dram's *Gene Kizhnerman, Wyoming Whiskey cofounder David Defazio captures the magic in the bottle: "When we set out to make America's next great bourbon, we settled on the following mission statement: 'The Wyoming Whiskey Mission is to produce Wyoming's first premium whiskey, using regional ingredients, through a select process that promotes Wyoming's natural and human resources.' All of our corn, winter wheat, winter rye, and malted barley is grown at high elevation and is all non-GMO. And our water is the best in the business. We're told that this limestone water hasn't seen the light of day in over 6,000 years, which dates back to the Bronze Age. Such a water source is unique because it needs no filtering."*

the hunting, fishing, skiing, hiking, and camping you could want. All the more reason to walk into a bar and Wyoming, nod to the bartender, and politely ask, "Can you make a Negroni?"

Jackson Hole's cocktail culture does a nice job of balancing pre–craft cocktail culture with the modern-day movement. Drop by the Bridger Deck for what some locals believe to be the best Margarita in Wyoming for more than fifteen years and counting, snag some cheese and charcuterie with a spicy For Whom the Well Tolls (bourbon, spicy Ancho Reyes liqueur, and lime) at laid-back favorite the Local, or save some room for handmade pasta and *aperitivo* cocktails at Glorietta inside the Anvil Hotel. In addition to skiing the slopes around Jackson Hole, people corral the bar (don't forget, little buckeroos, rodeo is Wyoming's state sport), with places like the historic Wort Hotel's Silver Dollar Bar & Grill, with a bar made up of 2,036 silver dollars minted in 1921, featuring bluegrass music on Tuesdays.

The Mint Bar in Sheridan, Wyoming, is a historic western bar open since 1907, with one of the coolest neon bar signs outside, featuring a cowboy riding a bucking bronco. The space inside is beautiful, and while they don't feature a cocktail menu, the bar staff does a fine job of making Old Fashioneds next to frothy pints of beer. The real draw of the Mint is the space itself, and how remote it is from other major cities.

Downtown Cheyenne has been keeping everyone fulfilled through the multifaceted Paramount Ballroom, a welcome meeting space for cocktails, coffee, live music, and classic movies, operating with the almighty philosophy:

*We want everyone to leave a little
happier than when they came in
Because we all need to just chill sometimes.*

WYOMING SPIRIT
WYOMING WHISKEY
Kirby

Wyoming Whiskey, which opened in 2012, was the first legal post-Prohibition distillery in Wyoming. Its revolutionary whiskeys run the gamut of single barrels to small-batch bourbons, and from bonded rye to a caramel-rich, orange-toned five-year private stock. Each whiskey uses a pure water source, custom-grown grains, and yeasts hand-picked by head distiller Sam Mead. *Esquire*'s Aaron Goldfarb called it "the absolute best American craft whiskey," and *Whiskycast*'s Mark Gillespie called its bourbon "one of the best bourbons I have ever tasted." This lauded liquor is distilled, barreled, and bottled in Kirby.

WYOMING'S OLDEST BAR
MINERS AND STOCKMEN'S STEAKHOUSE AND SPIRITS
Hartville, 1862

Everyone in the little town of Hartville knows about Miners and Stockmen's—which is probably not surprising, since there are only sixty people in town. Miners and Stockmen's is open year-round, from Thursday through Sunday, between 5 P.M. and 10 P.M. Come by for some Prime USDA, one of the whiskies from its extensive collection, or a glass of Goats Do Roam wine. Stay long enough and you might catch a glimpse of the ghost of one of the notorious bank robbers who used to hide out in the basement in the late 1800s—which is ironic, because the place looks like an old bank.

WYOMING BEVERAGE
SLOSHIE

We've got one ringer of a drinking tradition here - it's called Gelande Quaffing and it's a sight to be seen. Originally invented in the Bear Claw bar in the basement of a ski shop in Jackson Hole, word has it there was a blow down day (when there was so much snow and wind they couldn't operate the lifts), so the apres ski party started early. The bartender slid a beer down the bar to a patron, where it went OFF the edge of the bar, the patron caught it and threw it back on the spot. And Gelande Quaffing was born! You really need to just search YouTube for video of the world championships (held in Jackson every year). There are qualifiers, tricks, fire, and the occasional girls in bikinis.

— Brittany Fells, General Manager and Bartender, The Rose (Jackson Hole)

One cocktail that is very regionally specific is the sloshie, which loosely translates to a flavored frozen cocktail, and is often consumed in and around Jackson Hole. Sloshies are available not only in bars and ski resorts but at gas stations, food courts, steakhouses, and hotels, sold to go in clear plastic cups with the lid taped over. They come in many unusual flavors—and equally creative names, such as Bodega's Wu-Tang Cran. One of the more popular choices is the Hound, at Creekside Market & Deli, a greyhound made with fresh-squeezed grapefruit juice and vodka.

WYOMING COCKTAIL BAR
THE ROSE
Jackson

If you are in the great state of Wyoming and looking for the cocktail light-house, look no further than the Rose in Jackson. It features tasty vittles and a classic cocktail menu as well as house originals, such as Eve's Temptation, made with Jameson, Pierre Ferrand dry Curaçao, Noilly Prat vermouth, grapefruit, and lemon. Bonus points: The Rose features nightly enter-tainment, such as salsa, DJs on the weekends, and cultured-AF trivia, and it happens to be conveniently located next to the Pink Garter Theatre, Jackson's best live music venue.

WYOMING BUCKET LIST BAR
MILLION DOLLAR COWBOY BAR
Jackson

To understand the Million Dollar Cowboy Bar a little better, picture the setting: The neon sign outside depicts a wild cowboy riding a bucking bronco, and there are horse-drawn carriages and motorcycles passing by outside as you enter the old saloon gates, where, upon entering, you're greeted by a giant stuffed grizzly bear and bound-less bottles of Jack Daniel's single barrel, which can be further enjoyed while sitting on one of the many bar-stools waiting for weary travelers. The barstools are my favorite part of the Million Dollar Cowboy Bar: They hap-pen to be leather saddles. Giddy up!

BAR SNACK
One of the first dude ranches in America was the Eaton Ranch, near Wolf, Wyoming. Originating in the late 1800s and believed to be derived from "Yankee Doodle Dandy," a "dude" on the ranch was a city slicker, or someone mocked by the ranchers for being too dressed up for cattle wrangling. Years later, "dude" transformed into the surfer culture as a form of familiarity, and eventually made its way into movie magic with 1998's *The Big Lebowski*, forever changing the way we order and celebrate White Russians. This dude abides.

STATE FACT
This is one of my favorites: The Wind River actually changes its name in the middle of its stream. It becomes the Bighorn River close to the Owl Creek Mountains, which was named by two different Native American tribes, and each year local tribes hold a ceremony celebrating the "Wedding of the Waters." Amazing.

THE SUNDANCE KID
Brian Bartels

Harry Alonzo Longabaugh was in Sundance, Wyoming, when he was jailed for stealing a horse at the age of fifteen, which was his claim to fame, until he changed his nickname to honor the town that jailed him, eventually becoming "the Sundance Kid." This drink honors Sundance's wild escape to Bolivia with Butch Cassidy and the wonderful Bolivian brandy I always keep in my home, Singani 63, made by a company owned by filmmaker Steven Soderbergh, whose first film (foreshadowing alert) debuted at the Sundance Film Festival in 1989. Singani is floral and fruity and simply great on ice, and like Robert Redford's Sundance says in the movie, it's enjoyed even better when it can be on the move.

1 ounce Singani 63 brandy

1 ounce dry white wine
(Sauvignon Blanc is
a winner)

¾ ounce fresh lime juice

½ ounce honey syrup
(page 89)

2 dashes absinthe

Garnish: lime wheel

Shake the ingredients with ice until chilled; strain into a chilled coupe glass and serve up, garnished with the lime.

RYE IN SIDRE
Brittany Fells, The Rose, Jackson

This delicious recipe not only found its deserving place on a menu, but it was featured in *Town and Country*'s Best Whiskey Cocktails in America 2019. As Fells stated, "It is complex enough to keep you interested until the last sip, and easy enough to nurse while you party." Eric Bordelet's ciders are some of the best on the planet, so if you can use this product, you're playing to win.

1 ounce Wyoming Whiskey
Outryder

½ ounce fresh lemon

2 dashes orange bitters

4 ounces Eric Bordelet Sidre
Tendre

½ ounce yellow Chartreuse

Combine whiskey, lemon juice, and orange bitters in a wine glass with crushed or pebble ice. Add more ice, then add the Sidre. Add more ice, then top with the yellow Chartreuse. Serve with a paper straw.

....

Prohibition not only changed what Americans drank, it also changed the way they drank. It put a nudge and a wink into the experience. It encouraged the massive binge, the hangover worn as a badge of honor, the barely hidden hip flask, proof that the owner belonged to a daring fraternity. Because a drink was denied by law, those who did drink were determined to do it up right when the opportunity arose.

—William Grimes, in *Straight Up or On the Rocks*

Idaho is well-known for its potatoes, but it's nickname happens to be the Gem State, as it's known to have an abundance of precious and semi-precious gemstones, one of the most-famous being garnet. Other state gems include the many craft distilleries, such as 44 North, making use of their local potatoes to provide superb vodkas.

Idaho

Idaho is obviously famous for its potatoes, but it's also one of the very best places to grow hops. My hometown in particular is known for smelling like onions. It even has its own breed of onion—the Fruitland Super Sweet. My first cocktail was an Appletini on my 21st birthday.

—Sara Lynch, bar manager, Red Feather Lounge, Diablo and Sons Saloon, and Bittercreek Alehouse (Boise)

LIKE THE UNIVERSE, Idaho only seems to be expanding. Oregon and Washington get all the attention, but Idaho is the Little Engine of the Pacific Northwest. State motto: "Let It Be Perpetual." (I think "Let It Be Potato" was already taken.)

Idaho is derived from a Native American word meaning "land of many waters," which would explain all those trout we hear about when dining out in restaurants, but it's no secret that the potato runs deep in the soil of the state, as Idaho spuds account for one-third of America's potatoes.

Idaho has a surprising number of Basque inhabitants who settled here decades ago, forming the second-largest population of Basque residents outside of Spain. Apparently, Idaho was leading the pack for sheep herding in the early twentieth century, and so Basques found work in and around Boise in the sheep herding game, which led to them settling in the state. The 600 block of Boise's Historical District is the Basque Block, and many locals convene at the culture center and Bar Gernika for olives, meats, cheeses, Rioja wine, and the unmistakable, unofficial cocktail of Idaho: the Kalimotxo ("call-ee-moach-oh"), or, as we Americans like to simply say, "Red wine and Coke." In the United States, it is often served with a lemon, and since we are not a society in which looks are important, we drink our cocktails with our eyes wide open.

The Bardenay distillery makes vodka, gin, rum, ginger rum, and every flavored liqueur under the sun. There's a restaurant connected to the downtown Boise distillery with a monthly menu offering more than sixty cocktails, an impressive feat and not often accomplished by craft distilleries.

Boise's cocktail scene has been on the upswing over the past few years, with the Modern Hotel and Bar being one of the pioneers, along with Diablo and Sons and the Red Feather Lounge, which served me one of my favorite cocktails while traveling through Idaho—my memory of the Long Goodbye, a spirit-forward cocktail made with Del Maguey Vida mezcal, Cognac, Punt e Mes, and Cherry Heering, brings a smile to my face. Red Feather wields a very creative menu layout, highlighting the philosophy behind its bar program, the bar friends (aka local purveyors) who help make the menu a little more special, and the bartenders at the Red Feather, each with a unique little inside joke bio (e.g., "Sharktanksy—better late than never"). I asked the guy at the coffee shop if the locally made BuckSnort ginger beer was legit, and his response: "Oh yeah, brother, oh yeah. She is legit. She's a real one, boy." That collection of words alone made me go crack open a can and sip the magic. Was I the happiest ever? No. But I was sipping a real one.

BAR SNACK

In colonial times, the bar was not what we commonly view today as a counter where we sit and sip the time away. The colonial tavern had "cage bars," which were small rooms located in the corners of main rooms. In places like Colorado, Nevada, and Idaho, the tavern-keeper would enter the cage bar from his private quarters and raise a counter into place, which signaled he was ready to serve drinks. Essentially, it was a protective measure to ensure that the valuable ceramic punch bowls would not be damaged by a bunch of unscrupulous hooligans. That's why Mom and Dad are not allowed to have nice things.

IDAHO SPIRIT
44 NORTH HUCKLEBERRY VODKA
Boise

For me, the most American cocktail is the Old Fashioned. For many bars and homes, it's a personal love story about their favorite mid-shelf American whiskey. How it's made is a reflection of era and the part of the country you're in. There's a fierce ideology to its variables. It's the pizza of cocktails.

—Sara Lynch, bar manager, Red Feather Lounge, Diablo & Sons Saloon, and Bittercreek Alehouse (Boise)

Neurolux was the first bar I went to when arriving in Boise. Great jukebox, live music, stiff drinks, and many games of pool, which comes in handy after a long shift. But one of my favorite American experiences surrounding drinking tradition was when I shotgun beer playing golf at night.

—Remi Courcenet, bar manager, The Modern Hotel (Boise)

Distilled five times from 100 percent Idaho potatoes and filtered with Rocky Mountain spring water, 44 North proudly represents the premium Idaho vodka society. An interesting side note is that it's bottled at 70 proof, which you don't often see in a vodka. Though it's a smooth sipper, the real hero here is the slight hint of huckleberry, which is a cousin to the blueberry. Native to the Pacific Northwest (and the state fruit of Idaho), huckleberries thrive in elevated mountain ranges with more acidic soil, and though they are small, they retain a unique spread of tart to sweet characteristics. If you are serving this at a party, to paraphrase Doc Holliday in *Tombstone*, I will totally be your huckleberry. Which means your friend. Or it means you're Tom Sawyer. And I'm Huck Finn. Either way, you win.

IDAHO'S OLDEST BAR
WHITE HORSE
Spirit Lake, 1907

This bar does have an air of *Deadwood* about it due to the name, the location, and the fact that it's been around since 1907—the weathered interior and hardwood floors are as seasoned as any ole prospector you'll find out west. Part saloon, part restaurant, and part boutique historic hotel, the White Horse wears its vintage memorabilia in plain sight, as evidenced by the iron prison bars that separate the hotel and restaurant from the old Spirit Lake jail. And yes, it's been known to be haunted: Some people have affectionately nicknamed one of the ghosts "Big Girl," and she apparently loves room 2 in the hotel, though of course she likes to spread the haunt around, as people have confirmed reports of slamming phantom doors, echoes deep through the hallways, footsteps from unknown areas, and

dishes falling and breaking without anyone nearby. While you're braving the ghost, try some of that famous tomato-basil soup, which may be a tongue-in-cheek reference to the thickness of the house Bloody Marys.

IDAHO BUCKET LIST BAR
PENGILLY SALOON
Boise

Walking into Pengilly's is akin to taking a trip back in time. The décor alone—paintings of deer, fair maidens, and waterfalls; stuffed bison; a Stroh's Beer light over the cardinal-felt pool table; and the 120-year-old Brunswick bar—will keep you distracted enough to wonder how many stories the space could tell. No one's ever in a hurry at Pengilly's, and that's the point: Take your time, appreciate where you are, where you have been, and don't get too anxious about where you're going. But the late-afternoon regulars will keep you coming back, and perhaps you will become one yourself.

IDAHO COCKTAIL BAR
PRESS & PONY
Boise

Press & Pony's staff take a great amount of time in preparing the ingredients for their curated cocktail menu, but they also know it's important not to take themselves too seriously. I applaud this to no end. Fresh-pressed juices, homemade cola, and various tinctures are important, but putting a cocktail on the menu called Denim Blazer (High West bourbon, coffee syrup, Angostura bitters, and a flamed orange peel) obtains that necessary balance. They pay homage to Tom Cruise in *Cocktail* with his photo, enlarged and framed, above the bar, and the night I attended, the bartender dipped his fingers in a glass of 151-proof rum, lit a match, then blew a fireball when no one was paying attention. There's also an old-school arcade bar underneath the ground floor. Sorcery!

RYE AND PEPPER COCKTAIL
Sara Lynch, Diablo & Sons Saloon, Boise

Diablo & Sons is a relatively new spot in downtown Boise, and has one of the most smile-inducing cocktail menus I came across during all of my research for this book. It's clever, playful, and full of content. I particularly like Sara's beginning recommendation, which is to swirl a little peaty, smoky Scotch in the Martini glass before making this beauty.

Everyone in Boise has their own preference for measuring the Kalimotxo ingredients, but there is one similarity: you will have the best hangover of your life the next day.

—Boise resident seated next to me at Press & Pony

Peaty Scotch
(I use Lagavulin)

2 ounces Woodford Reserve rye

½ ounce Ancho Reyes liqueur

¼ ounce Cynar amaro

2 dashes spicy chocolate bitters (recipe follows) (or use Bittermens Xocolatl Mole or Bittercube Corazón)

Garnish: a high-quality cherry such as Luxardo or amarena

Swirl a little bit of Scotch in a chilled Martini glass and dump it out (or drink it).

In a mixing glass, combine all the ingredients, add ice, and stir gently for about 10 seconds. Strain into the prepared glass and serve up, garnished with the cherry.

Spicy Chocolate Bitters

Makes about 5 ounces

One 5-ounce (148 ml) bottle chocolate bitters (Diablo & Sons uses Scrappy's)

2 teaspoons red pepper flakes

In a small bowl, combine the bitters with the red pepper flakes. Let infuse for about 30 minutes. Strain and rebottle; the bitters will keep for up to 6 months.

Every American bar needs bartenders that are passionate about sharing stories and flavors, and a few particular spirits that each bartender has a personal connection to, such as American style gin, which is only getting more popular; each one has such unique flavors that you can play off of, and that's always exciting.

—Sara Lynch, bar manager, Red Feather Lounge, Diablo and Sons Saloon, and Bittercreek Alehouse (Boise)

FRAU HOLLE
Samuel Bishop, Modern Hotel, Boise

Frau Holle is a character in a famous Grimm Brothers German fairy tale from 1812, who apparently appears as a toothless hag, scaring children and adults to this day. In Scandinavia, however, Frau Holle is a feminine spirit, honored as the sacred embodiment of earth and home, and is often associated with snowfall, making this an optimal name for a welcome winter sipper to keep the bones warm. Ron Zacapa is a feel-good, smoky twenty-three-year-old rum aged in solera casks, with chocolate and vanilla notes.

1½ ounces Zacapa 23 rum

¾ ounce Dolin dry vermouth

¾ ounce Cynar amaro

¼ ounce Smith & Cross Jamaican rum

Garnish: fresh rosemary sprig

Stir the ingredients with ice until chilled; strain over fresh ice in a chilled rocks glass and garnish with the rosemary.

BAR SNACK

If you're wondering the person you're talking to is from Idaho or not, try getting them to say Boise. Longtime residents and natives tend to pronounce the word "boy-see" and everyone else generally opts for "boy-zee." See?

Oregon

This is just clean, free advice: If you get a chance to visit Oregon, I insist you drive from Portland to Bend for the three hours of three different terrains. And if you're friends with any local beavers, there's a good chance they'll have one of Jeffrey Morgenthaler's barrel-aged Negronis nearby, so stay close! And be polite. Beavers appreciate good manners.

I LOVE OREGON, for if it is anything, it is unapologetic—in its natural beauty, its woodsy charm, and its insistence on unusual, eccentric gatekeepers celebrating individuality and expressionism. Oregon offers endless outdoor activities in pretty much every direction. One of my all-time favorite drives in this country is the three-hour journey from Portland to Bend, where you move through one hour of rolling hills and valleys, one hour of open prairie with the Sisters Mountains and wild horses in the distance, and one hour of lush, thick forest and rivers with trees taller than fairy tales.

Oregon is worth its weight in ghost towns, hazelnuts, bicycle paths, and Douglas firs. *The Goonies* was filmed here, as was *Portlandia*, and Springfield, is the inspiration for the town of Springfield in *The Simpsons*. And shout out to Eugene for being the first city with one-way streets, which have driven my parents and other older people up the wall in many other cities since they were developed.

Bend has seen some nice cocktail programs cropping up on the wings of its notable breweries. Stihl Whiskey Bar, which has more than 350 labels, is a great place to start. And it only takes stepping inside the Brown Owl to make one wanna hoot.

The cocktail scene in Portland (aka the City of Roses—check out the International Rose Test Garden sometime, which features some five hundred varieties of roses) has been running strong for years. When the craft cocktail movement was taking shape in New York, Chicago, and San Francisco in the early 2000s, Portland was the little engine making waves up in the modest northwestern corner of the United States. Thanks to people like Jeffrey Morgenthaler at Clyde Common, Daniel Shoemaker of the Teardrop Lounge, the staff at Multnomah Whiskey Library, and the staff at many other bars

I was never really a drinker until I started working in bars. By the time I became a bartender it was the mid-90s and the whole swing revival thing was happening, and people were starting to discover cocktails again. So at one point I became enamored with bone dry Sapphire martinis with a twist—basically a giant cold glass of gin. My first "cocktail" was probably a big splash of gin from a plastic handle of cheap stuff my friend Adam and I stole from a party and mixed with Mountain Dew.

—Jeffrey Morgenthaler, bar manager, Clyde Common and Pépé le Moko (Portland)

and restaurants, Portland has an abundance of well-deserved fame for its commitment to improving its surroundings. Terrific destination bars such as Rum Club, Angel Face, and Expatriate are assembling cocktails and hospitality as well as any in the country. And food-focused restaurants like Tusk, Holdfast's Deadshot, and Jacqueline are combining unforgettable food options with well-crafted cocktails, forcing people like me to lose sleep at night. I will not forget the Piggy Back at Hamlet any time soon: a shot of smoky mezcal served with a side of prosciutto ham. The two get along like they're sharing a clean, crisp high five with each sip and nibble.

A modern Oregon cocktail that deserves some recognition is the Barrel-Aged Negroni, created by Jeffrey Morgenthaler at Clyde Common. This was arguably one of the most talked-about cocktails in the early part of the twenty-first century, and if Jeffrey Morgenthaler had been living in San Francisco, Los Angeles, Chicago, or New York, he would be a household name by now. But the funny thing is, the serious bartenders in those cities were all talking about *him*, and more specifically, his aged Negroni, which was inspired by a trip to 69 Colebrooke Row in London. Morgenthaler put the classic equal-parts Negroni inside a used, charred whiskey barrel and let it age for a few weeks. The barrel aging allows the harsher elements in the cocktail to settle a little more, and the result was a rounder, textured, softened, Cadillac version of the original Negroni.

Oregon is also the home of some terrific distilleries these days, such as Aviation American Gin, Krogstad Aquavit, Crater Lake Spirits, and New Deal Distillery, which makes a wonderful assembly of liqueurs and a knockout pear brandy. "Founder Tom Burkleaux is someone you're always happy to see at the bar," says local author Jacob Grier about New Deal, "no matter which side of it you're on." Grier is a big fan of New Deal's Cascadia liqueur, a bittersweet gentian made with wild lavender, rose petals, and a variety of Pacific Northwest botanicals.

OREGON SPIRIT
CLEAR CREEK DISTILLERY
Hood River

Clear Creek started distilling in 1985, long before most of the other modern-day distilleries were taking shape and developing their own spirit wares. Clear Creek makes a fine assembly of brandies, liqueurs, grappas, and single-barrel whiskey. The Bartlett pear brandy has been a staple for many years, and the Douglas fir brandy, paying homage to the Oregon state tree, is not only unique, but versatile in cocktails as well. Jim Meehan pays respects to the company's craft distillation in *Meehan's Bartender Manual*, where he calls it one of the more venerable distilleries in America.

BAR SNACK

"Safety meeting" is a term for taking a quick nip of liquor or a shot of something to get through a busy or challenging shift. Bartenders in Portland, Oregon, are not allowed to do this, as it is against the law. A business's first violation within being open for a two-year period results in a thirty-day liquor license suspension, which can cripple most small businesses. A bar in Old Town even sued one of its bartenders to the tune of $115,000 in January 2019 for being drunk on the job.

OREGON'S OLDEST BAR
HUBER'S
Portland, 1879

Huber's, an upscale tavern with stained-glass skylights, palm trees, warm wooden booths, and a happy-go-lucky staff, has been in business since 1879, when every drink served was accompanied by a turkey sandwich. Though the free turkey sandwiches have flown away, the Spanish Coffees, created in the early 1970s, are here to stay. One can't visit the iconic Huber's without having a Spanish Coffee, which is not in fact Spanish but Portlandian, as it originated in Rip City, gathering enough accolades you might believe Kahlúa was invented in Oregon: Huber's sells more of it than any bar in the country.

OREGON COCKTAIL BARS
CLYDE COMMON AND PÉPÉ LE MOKO
Portland

These spots should be part of every tourist map and *Lonely Planet* guidebook to the Pacific Northwest. Go to Clyde Common for the Barrel-Aged Negroni, and go to Pépé Le Moko (located right around the corner) for a modern version of the Grasshopper. Go. Just. Go. The staff are all knowledgeable, tattooed, and gracious, and Jeffrey Morgenthaler is a consummate professional. If you get a chance to sit at Morgenthaler's bar, go and do it. He's the quintessential bartender in so many ways, and truly cares about the integrity of researching and executing the best versions of cocktails we have come to know and celebrate in the past few decades, along with inventing new ones. He has fun while bartending. And you're having a blast because the drinks are fantastic. Everyone wins. Just don't freak him out by gawking at him.

OREGON BUCKET LIST BAR
HOLMAN'S BAR & GRILL
Portland

Do you want everything in your bucket list bar? Then, at Holman's, everything you shall have! Holman's has endless wall tchotchkes, decorative ceiling lamps, Coca-Cola signs, classic beer signs, multiple pinball machines, mac and cheese, a wide variety of whiskey options (and a Whiskey Club), and an outdoor garden patio—and what's more, they are the ambassadors of the Bloody Mary Bar, operated Saturdays and Sundays from 8 A.M. to 3 A.M., featuring vodkas infused with basil, garlic, horseradish, habanero, jalapeño, cucumber, and Thai sriracha. Luke Dirks (co-owner of Tusk and my former colleague at Happy Cooking Hospitality), thank you for showing the way!

BAR SNACK
There are more than eighteen hundred bottles at Multnomah Whiskey Library, which is on the second floor of a building and easy to miss if it's raining (which it is on any given Portland day). But when you find it, oh boy. Rows and rows of shelves resemble a library in one of the opening scenes of an *Indiana Jones* movie, right before the action kicks in, which makes *me* feel a little bit like Indiana Jones, only I'm not cool enough to wear the hat, or crack the whip, but that's okay, because everyone working there makes you feel as though you are, so watch them whip, then watch me nae nae.

AMARETTO SOUR
Jeffrey Morgenthaler, Clyde Common, Portland

Morgenthaler created this version of a classic sour because he felt most Amaretto Sours were too sweet, and for once in his life, he was right. *Difford's Guide* rated Morgenthaler's Amaretto Sour the fourth-most-ordered cocktail in 2017, which is a tremendous accomplishment, and deservedly so. When Morgenthaler began making the Amaretto Sour with egg white, the rest of the bartending country followed.

1½ ounces Amaretto

¾ ounce cask-proof bourbon

1 ounce fresh lemon juice

1 teaspoon rich simple syrup (2:1 sugar to water)

½ ounce fresh egg white

Garnishes: lemon peel and brandied cherry

Shake the ingredients *without ice* for a healthy 10 to 15 seconds. Add ice to the shaker and shake again until chilled. Strain over fresh ice in a chilled rocks glass and garnish with the lemon and cherry. "Serve and grin like an idiot as your friends freak out," as Morgenthaler himself says.

STUMPTOWN BOULEVARD
Brian Bartels

This is a spin on the Boulevardier, which is a spin on the Negroni, which we can already agree is a delicious cocktail everyone should try. The outstanding J. Rieger's Caffé amaro uses Sumatran coffee mixed with orange peel, cardamom, vanilla, and gentian, flavors that play quite well with the maple and vanilla in bourbon and the bitter, herbaceous brightness of Campari. And if Simon Kelly, proud son and devotee of the heralded Boulevardier cocktail, is anywhere near where you are while drinking this cocktail, then you are having a great night.

1 ounce bourbon

1 ounce J. Rieger's Caffé amaro (if not available, bummer, but try upping the Campari to 1 ounce and adding a bit more cold brew, about ¾ ounce)

½ ounce sweet vermouth

½ ounce Campari

½ ounce cold brew coffee (preferably Stumptown, as I owe them my focus, hustle, and sanity while writing this book, or the homemade version on page 39)

Garnish: orange peel

Stir the ingredients with ice until properly diluted; strain over a large ice cube in a chilled double rocks glass and garnish with the orange.

BAR SNACK
The Bone Luge shot was created by Jacob Grier one night at Portland's Laurelhurst Market steakhouse in a light bulb moment of drunken inspiration. Grier and friends had a plate of bone marrow and shots of tequila at their table. Someone started the challenge of drinking the shot as it cascaded down the bone marrow tube, like an ice luge—that is, downing it from the other end of the bone after it passed through the remnants of marrow. After the experience was Instagrammed and tweeted, it soon became an international drinking trend. The *Wall Street Journal* featured the Bone Luge on its front page, and if that's not making it in America, I don't know what is.

I'd be lying if I said I wasn't almost arrested in the first two hours of being in Las Vegas, and no I wasn't there for a bachelor party, or to audition for *The Hangover 4*, or to try my hand at the roulette tables at the Mirage (though I did eventually do that, and failed miserably, as expected). Remind me to tell you the story if we see each other. Hopefully it's over gin Martinis at the Golden Steer, and we're toasting under a photo of Sammy, Dean-O, and Frank, in the company of an Elvis impersonator or two.

Nevada

NEVADA GETS PIGEONHOLED by its Vegas-ness all too often, when there are many wonderful things happening throughout the state, like the Hoover Dam (built in 1936), the Great Basin National Park (with the route dubbed the "Loneliest Road in America," from Carson City to Lake Tahoe to the Mojave Desert—where I spent one night sleeping in my car), Burning Man, and the longstanding National Cowboy Poetry Gathering in Elko, Nevada (a six-day festival of poetry, music, dancing, and folk art, where one can rawhide braid, swing dance, and spit cook while reciting some open-hearted love of the written word).

Northern Nevada's Basque population has enabled many to associate that area with the Picon Punch, a cocktail made with grenadine, club soda, brandy, and Amer Picon, a nutty-flavored orange liqueur that is not very easy to come by. (So, just like true love, if you find some, hold on to it for dear life.)

In 1931, the Pair-O-Dice Club was the first casino to open on Highway 91, which would eventually become the Las Vegas Strip, and yes, Las Vegas is worth visiting if you like all-you-can-eat buffets, bright lights, hanging out with one million strangers in the middle of a dry, hot desert, getting married by an Elvis impersonator, being surrounded by more hotels than anywhere else in the world, and watching people walk around with their mouths agape. But it also has really nice museums.

Contemporary Vegas cocktail spots have blossomed over the past few years, with Frankie's Tiki Room, the Downtown Cocktail Room, and Oak & Ivy keeping score with the popular and noteworthy resort cocktail bars, such as the NoMad (with a beverage program helmed by the talented Leo Robitschek), Parlour Cocktail Lounge at the Mirage, and the Lily Bar & Lounge at the Bellagio, all gifted in the art of keeping one distracted from the beckoning outside world. One of my favorites that I visited in Las Vegas was Velveteen Rabbit, owned by Pamela and Christina Dylag, who both grew up in Las Vegas and opened this art-inspired gem in the Arts District. Not only is the artwork on the walls done by locals, each cocktail menu is original content from local artists and writers, perfectly matching the quality of crafted cocktails coming from the talented staff.

Vegas is also home to the flair bartender, which gained popularity in the 1980s and was stored in cinematic history by Tom Cruise in *Cocktail*. One can attend flair bartending classes in Vegas, which is not unlike being at the circus as bartenders flip, balance, twirl, and toss bottles and barware with cocktail theatrics. They manage to look like ringleaders and clowns at the same time, and you, dear drinker, are always the tiger.

STATE FACT
The town of Rachel is located near "The Extraterrestrial Highway," and Area 51, regarded for being "The UFO Capital of the World."

NEVADA SPIRIT
LAS VEGAS DISTILLERY
Henderson

My first true cocktail experience started with a Dark 'n Stormy at Downtown Cocktail Room in Las Vegas. And seeing that I have returned since then, do yourself a favor and visit Dino's, which can be the nightcap of many crazy nights. Karaoke and anything goes.

—Nick Tillinghast, owner, Hello, Marjorie (Des Moines, IA)

It seems absurd that a Nevada distillery would take so long to open in a state where public intoxication is not illegal, but Nevada's Prohibition-era rules limited distilleries from letting their freak flag fly until Romanian-born George Racz founded Las Vegas Distillery in 2010, sourcing most of his grains from a farm upstate. Las Vegas Distillery produces a wide variety of spirits—notably the first-ever Nevada rum-whiskey hybrid, aptly called "Rumsky." LVD opened an adjacent bar, the Hooch, in 2016, and hosts events there regularly. As the distillery's slogan suggests, "Follow your heart and raise your spirits!"

NEVADA'S OLDEST BAR
GENOA BAR AND SALOON
Genoa, 1853

This diamond in the desert rough has been there, done that, and seen enough history to be considered a historic landmark. The Diamond Dust Mirror behind the bar is from Scotland, and was shipped to Nevada in the 1840s; legend has it, if you shine a flashlight into the mirror, you can see the diamond dust. Impromptu dance parties spill onto the street when the weather is nice enough. The bar's slogan? "You may walk in here a stranger, but you will leave here a friend!"

NEVADA BUCKET LIST BAR
ATOMIC LIQUORS
Las Vegas

Atomic Liquors opened the same year the atomic bomb was created, and was famous for being *the* bar to visit back in the Old Vegas heyday, where you could rub elbows with the Rat Pack while watching mushroom cloud bombs going off sixty miles away. The "Atomic Liquors Cocktails" sign outside the establishment is as classic as the "Welcome to Fabulous Las Vegas" image everyone sees when entering Sin City. The bar is long and beautiful and the stools are just like large couch cushions. They still feature a signature cocktail, Hunter S. Mash, made with Old Crow bourbon and honoring Hunter S. Thompson, author of *Fear and Loathing in Las Vegas.*

NEVADA COCKTAIL BAR
HERBS & RYE
Las Vegas

Herbs and Rye has been open only since 2009, but it already feels legendary. The cocktail menu dips into recipes dating all the way back to 1776, and there is plenty of Rat Pack influence throughout the hallowed space, even singling them out on the cocktail menu (1958–68) with the Piña Colada, Vesper, and Harvey Wallbanger, and although none of these cocktails was directly linked with the famous group of celebrities, everyone and their cousin was drinking them through the 1960s. I was there at 6 P.M. on a Monday and the long bar and all the tables were packed, the room was jumping, and Joy the bartender was shaking and pouring a Ramos Gin Fizz with a big smile on her face, and no wonder: The bar hosts two happy hours a day, when the steaks are half-off and cocktail prices reduced. A modern classic. Tell superhero Giuseppe Gonzalez, inventor of the Trinidad Sour cocktail, Bartels sent you.

BAR SNACK
Wayne Newton (aka Mr. Las Vegas and the Midnight Idol) is three hundred and seventeen years old.

THE NEVADA
Brian Bartels

This recipe was extracted from David Embury's *Fine Art of Mixing Drinks*, from 1948, though it was first published in W.C. Whitfield's *Here's How* in 1941. How it found its name is unknown, but my guess is travel, as Las Vegas started getting more visitors from all over in the 1930s, and the Las Vegas Strip was built in 1941, which means drinks that started becoming popular elsewhere in the United States (like the Daiquiri in early-1900s Washington, DC) eventually made their way into burgeoning areas. Nevada needed to find ways to appeal to more visitors while also creating a new character of its own; hence, the classic Daiquiri most likely was reconfigured by a bartender here in the 1940s, giving birth to the Nevada cocktail. It is merely a Daiquiri with grapefruit juice added, and merely amazing. Put a little maraschino in it and you've got a Hemingway Daiquiri. Did Papa visit Vegas in the 1940s?!

2 ounces white rum (Bacardi Silver, Caña Brava, and El Dorado are great)

¾ ounce fresh grapefruit juice

¾ ounce fresh lime juice

¼ ounce simple syrup (1:1 sugar to water)

Dash of your favorite bitters

Garnish: lime wheel

Shake the ingredients with ice until chilled; strain into a chilled coupe glass and serve up, garnished with the lime.

AMERICANO PRESLEY
Brian Bartels

You didn't think Elvis had left the building, did you? This is a slight spin on the classic Americano cocktail, which is made with Campari, sweet vermouth, and club soda. Grapefruit juice is a terrific sibling to the exceptional Campari. As Las Vegas is known to inspire some irresponsible drinking behavior, having a low-alcohol beverage is a great idea—especially if it's going to be a long day of carousing. Campari is a lower-ABV aperitif, hovering around 24 percent in the United States, and sweet vermouth is 15 percent, making this a drink you can enjoy multiple times without feeling the higher level of alcohol. Elvis performed some of the most historic sold-out concerts in Las Vegas near the end of his career, and popularized quickie marriages in little chapels throughout the city with his 1964 film *Viva Las Vegas*. The famous catchphrase "Elvis has left the building" comes from when rabid fans at an Elvis show were hoping the King would be coming back for another encore, only to be told he had disappeared, so it's now okay to go home. Elvis put Las Vegas on the map of America. This Americano variation is an homage to his legacy. Feel free to sip, and, as Elvis says between songs . . . "Thankyouverymuch."

1 ounce Campari

½ ounce sweet vermouth (preferably Cinzano or Carpano Antica)

2 ounces fresh grapefruit juice

2 to 3 ounces chilled club soda

2 dashes Hella orange bitters

Garnish: grapefruit peel or orange peel (Or both! Double down. You're in Vegas, baby!)

Combine the Campari, vermouth, grapefruit juice, and club soda with ice in a chilled 10-ounce glass. Top with the bitters and garnish with the citrus peels.

I didn't feel there were too many laws prohibiting liquor access while I was in Utah (and yes, you are allowed to order a shot of liquor with your drink—but FYI it cannot be the same spirit as what's in your cocktail), but to Utah's credit, they handle their alcohol limitations very well, and with elevated decorum. Even the St. Bernard bartender at High West. One hundred percent sophistication.

Utah

I think the Mint Julep is the most American cocktail, for a few reasons:
1. It features bourbon (hard to get more American than that)
2. It's simple but full of flavor and tradition
3. Crushed ice. Ice is such a huge part of cocktail history. The crushed ice, for me, is telling of place; the hot humid southern states, etc., but also time.

—Holly Booth, bar director, High West (Park City)

HIGHER ELEVATIONS, POWDERY snow, rainbow trout, Rocky Mountain elk, and the beehive, which is the state symbol. (This was a surprising discovery, as I would associate bighorn sheep, rattlesnakes, and coyotes with Utah before bees. But that's the—pun intended—buzz these days.)

Sixty percent of Utah's population is Mormon, making it the most religiously homogenous state in America, with some slightly archaic drinking laws: The Zion Curtain is a velvet curtain where the bar functions behind the scenes of the restaurant. Some places even have a two-way mirror where bartenders mix drinks on the other side of the wall where guests dine. If there is less visible drinking, theory suggests there will be less alcohol abuse. Another unusual observation: bartender nametags. Walk into any bar in Utah and you will see every bartender wearing a nametag, with some even wearing painter's tape with names like "Hopscotch," "Baller," and "Cookie Pillow" written in Sharpie. "Why does everyone have a nametag?" I asked. Turns out it's a Utah state law. "A bar gets fined if their bartenders do not have names," said Cookie Pillow.

Next time you're in Salt Lake be on the lookout for Congregation Spirits, a new facility in the North Temple corridor, featuring a distillery, bar, and wood-fired grill, providing a "beverage campus" must-visit destination of whiskey, brandy, and gin, along with programs focused on cultivating ideas, relationships, and educational platforms for the community.

One of the popular new cocktails shared among the Salt Lake industry locals is the Wray Daq ("ray-dack"), a Daiquiri made with Wray & Nephew Jamaican rum. My friend Francine grew up in Jamaica, and when anyone was feeling ill, the family medicine was to spread Wray & Nephew, which is a high-proof rum, over their body, and Francine recalls her mother dousing her with half a bottle of rum every time she caught a fever. Sounds like Salt Lake City has been *catching* the fevers while *drinking* the Wray Daqs.

BAR SNACK

Eye toasts are the somewhat commonly known practice of looking the other person you are drinking with in the eyes, clinking your glasses, and then taking a sip or a shot of your drink. Tradition says that if you break eye contact bad luck will occur down the road. I might upset some people, but hogwash. One, we're all lucky, because we're alive. Two, carrying on someone else's traditions is great, but we shouldn't have to continue them if it makes us feel uncomfortable. Three, toasting and insisting someone look you in the eye—especially leaning in and encroaching on that person's private space—is unwarranted. Isn't it enough we have to clink our glasses while smiling and standing off-balance? I bring it up because I have long arms, and am therefore a klutz.

HIGH WEST WHISKEY
Wanship & Park City

Perhaps the most surprising fact about Utah's drinking history is Brigham Young actually produced a spirit called Valley Tan. Mark Twain mentions drinking Valley Tan on his trip through Utah in his book Roughing It, *where, Twain claims, "Mormon tradition says it is made of (imported) fire and brimstone."*

—Holly Booth, bar director, High West (Park City)

High West began its ascent to American whiskey fame in 2006, when it became Utah's first legal distillery since 1870. One year later, the company opened the Saloon in Park City, a cozy mountain village popular for fly-fishing, mountain biking, and the Sundance Film Festival. High West produces a healthy catalogue of award-winning whiskeys and remains committed to preserving the American West, donating 10 percent of after-tax profits to the American Prairie Reserve in Montana, an effort to establish the largest wildlife reserve in the lower forty-eight United States. *Whisky Advocate* named High West the 2016 Distiller of the Year. High West's saloon is well worth a visit. Everyone is as nice as a second slice of pie.

THE SHOOTING STAR SALOON
Huntsville, 1879

A mug of beer, a shot of whiskey, and leave the bottle. Dollar bills cover most of the walls, along with photos of Buck, the famous St. Bernard who used to watch over the saloon in the 1950s and who for seven years held the Guinness record for being the largest St. Bernard, at 298 pounds and 41 inches tall. Many locals love popping by for a drink and the famed Starburger, which is Polish knackwurst sausage sandwiched between two all-beef patties, with cheese. The Shooting Star's got everything you would need in a Wild West saloon, and the people inside are a healthy mix of friendly locals, biker groups, and bar industry professionals. Just observe the sign above Buck: "Never mind the dog. Beware of owner."

BAR-X
Salt Lake City

Bar-X holds a venerable place in Salt Lake City history, as it was the first bar opened the day after Prohibition ended. However, it doesn't have the same grungy, blue-collar dive bar vibes of its former self of ten years ago, as the space was resurrected with the right kind of nod to classic cocktail lounges, keeping things low-lit and spreading the holy glow of a Cadillac-length illuminated back bar. The staff produces great cocktails, the vibe is casual, and if you're lucky, you're stopping by to hear a local band playing an unforgettable cover of "Dead Flowers." If I had nowhere else to go, I would stay at Bar-X until they turned the lights up on me.

JELL-O

Yes, Utah consumes more Jell-O than anywhere else in the United States. Why do we need to know this? Because life is short. And you need to laugh at the absurdity every once in a while. Sadly, there is not enough evidence to confirm whether or not they are the free-world leaders in Jell-O shot consumption, but the proof is in the pudding.

UNDER CURRENT
Salt Lake City

Under Current is not *under* its sister spot, Current Fish & Oyster, but rather *next* to it (it's a trick!). There's a real cocktail program buzzing over the lengthy and beautiful marble bar, curated by Amy Eldredge, and it is b-a-n-a-n-a-s good! Under Current features fifty-nine cocktails on the menu—house originals and classics—and each classic lists the year it was created. The bar celebrates spirits, wine, cider, and beer—and yeah, it's not a trick: They have a pretty damn good-looking food menu, too.

SEA LEGS
Alejandro Olivares, Under Current, Salt Lake City

I believe that bourbon is a wonderful spirit to use in many cocktails. I really love Four Roses (Kentucky). They have been one of my favorite bourbons for a long time, and visiting their distillery a few years ago was one of my most memorable moments.

—Alejandro Olivares, bar manager, Under Current (Salt Lake City)

Two smoky spirits get a chance to shake things up in this very approachable Sour variation. Imagine if a Daiquiri just wanted to let its hair down and listen to "Immigrant Song" by Led Zeppelin—there we find Sea Legs and, hopefully, you.

1 ounce mezcal

1 ounce Islay Scotch (Under Current uses Laphroaig 10 year)

¾ ounce fresh lime juice

¾ ounce Giffard orgeat

2 dashes Scrappy's celery bitters

1 dash Angostura bitters

Glass rim: salt

Garnish: lime wheel

Shake the mezcal, Scotch, lime juice, orgeat, and celery bitters with ice until chilled; strain into a chilled half-salt-rimmed coupe glass. Top with the Angostura bitters and garnish with the lime.

ANGEL OF TOMBSTONE
Holly Booth, High West, Park City

Holly Booth is not only one of the nicest people on earth, she is a talented bar director for High West's celebratory saloon room in Park City, and can pretty much run an impromptu tour of what makes Park City, Salt Lake City, and the greater state of Utah so special ("Utah has pristine bodies of water for fishing, rolling hills and trails for hiking, and in addition to skiing, there are five national parks in Utah, so there's something for everyone") simply by how she speaks with true knowledge and appreciation for her surroundings.

1½ ounces High West Rendezvous rye whiskey

½ ounce Punt e Mes

½ ounce Nonino amaro

Garnish: Amarena cherry (a maraschino cherry also works)

Stir the ingredients with ice until chilled; strain into a chilled coupe glass and serve up, garnished with the cherry.

> **BAR SNACK**
>
> Many old-time saloons got in the habit of naming their places after familiar institutions, so in the event a patron was "detained" a little too long at "The Office Tavern," the patron could tell their loved ones they were at "the Office." The old timers were cheeky, cheeky, cheeky.

As far as SLC goes I try and convince everyone to check out Water Witch, a small neighborhood craft cocktail bar that I really enjoy.

—Alejandro Olivares, bar manager, Under Current (Salt Lake City)

Colorado is famous for its dramatic landscape, featuring river canyons, arid desert, and the snow-covered Rocky Mountains, where only the truly gifted dare ski and sip cocktails while dodging big horned sheep—who are notorious Negroni fans. Denver bartenders are very good at being communicative with each other—which is not only important, it's indispensible. Communication is one of our best tools we can ever use in the service industry. For instance, I walked into a bar five minutes after texting by buddy Mike Henderson, and they already knew I was coming. Sorcery!

Colorado

I have lots of favorite American distillers, but Leopold Bros. in Denver does some amazing stuff. They've got a unique three-chamber still they built to produce a one-of-a-kind rye whiskey that's still a few years out but is reportedly amazing even at two years. I still don't fully understand how that still works and I've probably seen it a half a dozen times.

—Mike Henderson, beverage development specialist, Breakthru Beverage Group (Denver)

COLORADO WAS A popular place to open a saloon in the nineteenth century. More than 270 saloons were known to have opened in Denver between 1858 and 1876, and Leadville, a mining town that everyone knew back then but rarely gets mentioned today, had 249 saloons in 1880.

Today, there are plenty of must-visit drinking destinations in Colorado, and I would know, as everyone from Colorado told me about them! The Buckhorn Exchange was the first restaurant bar to receive a liquor license after Prohibition, and arguably one of the first to have more than one million animal heads stuck on its walls, making it difficult to decide whether to keep looking around or consider the menu. There are great establishments throughout the Centennial State, such as Oak in Boulder, the Rabbit Hole in Colorado Springs, and Jimmy's in Aspen, which celebrates social camaraderie with the best of them. The Dogwood in Crested Butte, located in a cozy little former miner's cabin, gets plenty of recognition for its fresh-ingredient artisanal cocktails and adventurous appetizers.

My Brother's Bar in Denver has been around since 1873 and features one of the best burgers in the state, and Lady Jane, American Bonded, Morin, and Pony Up provide easygoing vibes with heightened cocktail proficiency.

Celebrated New York speakeasy Death & Co. opened its Denver cocktail bar in 2018, bringing elevated cocktails to the highest elevations, and doing it inside a beautifully designed space. My favorite cocktail there was the Curtis Park Swizzle, made with Singani brandy, amontillado sherry, fresh ginger juice, and absinthe. Swizzles are Sour-style drinks that originated in the Caribbean, often served in highball glasses: You pour in the ingredients and fill half the glass with crushed ice, then take a swizzle stick and spin from the top to mix the ingredients before topping with more ice.

Bread Bar sits in a former 1800s bakery, located at the foothills of the Rocky Mountains. It's only open on Friday and Saturday nights and Sunday afternoons. Vintage grain bins are stored on the shelves, along with the original four-seat bar, and the staff keeps the beer cold in an old-school icebox. All of the drinks are named after past residents of Silver Plume, a town of approximately 175 people. Bread Bar hosts live music and special events, and yeah, there's even a patio in the back so the dogs can hang out with everyone. Pretty awesome excuse for a pit stop while fishing or hiking in the mountains.

Lastly, it is illegal to throw snowballs around in Aspen, which means the scene in *Dumb and Dumber* where Harry is throwing snowballs at Mary couldn't have been real. That John Denver's full of shit, man.

BAR SNACK

Frank J. Wisner of Cripple Creek created the Black Cow in 1893, which we all now know and love as the root beer float. Legend has it he noticed the snowy mountain peaks off in the distances and felt they mirrored iced cream floating in soda. So even though Frank was surrounded by Colorado gold mines, he struck it rich in August 1893, which is a healthy reminder: National Root Beer Float Day is August 6.

COLORADO SPIRIT
WOODY CREEK DISTILLERS
Woody Creek

Not only is Woody Creek where Hunter S. Thompson lived and breathed for many handgun holidays (Thompson was known to host many a handgun party in his backyard), but Dr. Gonzo's neighbor, Woody Creek Distillers, took flight in 2013 and hasn't looked back since. Try the house gin in a unique and refreshing spin on a classic Cosmopolitan. If all of my cocktail and spirits colleagues are singing so much praise for a product, it's gotta be worth its weight in Dr. Gonzo typewriters.

COLORADO'S OLDEST BAR
THE BUFFALO ROSE
Golden City, 1859

Perhaps this assessment from the local historian Richard Gardner best captures this iconic American bar:

This isn't a story about wood, brick, steel, fire and stone—not simply a tale of the many businesses that have stood on the site or the colorful characters that have passed through these doors. No, this is the story of Golden City, of the American West and a rugged frontier spirit. It is a story about architecture and governments, railroads, cars, and motorcycles; shootouts, Olympians, entrepreneurs, and wars—it is a story of great economic expansion and profound depression, of drunken debauchery and of Prohibition. This is the story of The Buffalo Rose, but more importantly for the people of Golden, Colorado: it is our story.

COLORADO BUCKET LIST BAR
BRASS TACKS
Denver

Open since spring 2019, Brass Tacks is an all-day-long comfort spot for people looking to take a break from the daily grind. Just walking into the open space makes you feel like you want to hang there for a while—and it offers plenty of excuses to reinforce that sentiment: jukebox, game room with foosball and '80s movies, knockout food served late into the night (hey, egg and cheese sandwich), and dynamite drinks, featuring bottled cocktails, house originals, frozen Irish Coffee, and some creative takes on draft cocktails, like the peanut-infused bourbon and Coke and a watch the throne Paloma. Everything fits at Brass Tacks, coupled with the friendliest group of bartenders I've been around at 5,280 feet (or one mile, if that's easier to say).

COLORADO COCKTAIL BARS
WILLIAMS & GRAHAM AND THE OCCIDENTAL
Denver

Denver's LoHi neighborhood is one lucky little neighborhood, and the two cocktail bars I associate with its appeal happen to rest next to each other, owned and operated by Sean Kenyon, modern-day bar superhero. Williams & Graham has been carrying the torch for Denver's cocktail revolution since 2011. Upon entering the cozy little cocktail den through a bookcase, you'll find a friendly and informative staff waiting to serve up a bevy of classic cocktails and a wide variety of spirit selections. The Occidental, Williams & Graham's bad-boy next-door neighbor, has been unapologetically bucking the social norms since 2015. It's far less polished than the spot next door, and that's the point. But the cocktails are just as good. And there's pinball. And they serve Wisconsin cheese curds. Am I playing favorites? Punks don't have favorites.

COLORADO BULLDOG 2.0
aka the Colorado Buffalo, Mike Henderson, Denver

Sadly, the story of how the Colorado Bulldog came to be is unknown, but I can confirm one historical fact: Mike Henderson and I worked together in our formative years, and we definitely served our fair share of Colorado Bulldogs together at Paul's Club in Madison, Wisconsin, alongside Jim Meehan, author of *Meehan's Bartender Manual*, the definitive guide to building a bar and bringing one's bartender A game. Now Mike's running terrific bar programs throughout Colorado, and he created this version for the book you're currently reading. That little extra kick of cola is a nice feather in any American cap.

1¾ ounces vodka

1 ounce Galliano Ristretto (or another premium coffee liqueur)

¼ ounce cola syrup (recipe follows)

2 ounces half-and-half

Shake the ingredients with ice for 10 to 15 seconds; strain into a chilled cocktail or Martini glass and serve up.

Cola Syrup

Makes 1 cup

½ cup cola

½ cup pure cane sugar

Combine the cola and sugar in a saucepan and cook over medium heat, stirring occasionally, until the ingredients have integrated. Remove from the heat, let cool to room temperature, then transfer to a tightly sealed container and store in the refrigerator for up to 1 week.

BLACKBERRY SAGE SMASH
Sean Kenyon, Williams & Graham, Denver

This recipe comes from Mr. Colorado himself, Sean Kenyon, who helped put Colorado on the cocktail map with his wonderful bars Williams & Graham, the Occidental, and American Bonded. Sean is the truth. This cocktail was an early favorite at Williams & Graham, a trailblazer in the Denver cocktail scene.

4 fresh sage leaves, torn

4 blackberries

½ ounce fresh lemon juice

½ ounce simple syrup (1:1 sugar to water)

2 ounces Woody Creek rye whiskey

Garnish: fresh sage leaf and a blackberry

In a mixing tin, muddle the sage, blackberries, lemon juice, and simple syrup. Add the whiskey and ice and shake until chilled. Fine strain over fresh ice in a chilled double Old Fashioned glass and garnish with the sage leaf skewered atop the blackberry.

Studies have shown that there are two kinds of people on this planet: those who believe in extraterrestrial life, and those who believe in a half-salt rim on their Margarita. Though it is not commonly known, most extra-terrestrials prefer their Margaritas way up. (pause) It's okay if you didn't laugh at that. I'll be here all week.

New Mexico

IN 1912, NEW Mexico became the forty-seventh state in the union, and shortly thereafter earned a reputation for being an artistic haven. Painters, writers, and photographers flocked to the red-rock landscape, accented with a healthy number of historic churches, Pueblo and Spanish heritage, the Rio Grande River, and White Sands National Monument, a desert oasis unlike anything I had ever before seen.

Hatch chiles grow abundantly in the southern part of the state, almost as much as conspiracy theories out of Roswell (location of the alleged 1947 UFO crash) and Georgia O'Keeffe paintings, and hot air balloon fiestas are annual events in Albuquerque, which was known to be a booming railroad town back in the 1880s, when more than 150 saloons opened in a ten-year period.

An unusual practice started in 1958 Ski Valley, outside Taos: Ernie Blake, who owned the resort, convinced a terrified skier to make it down the treacherous hill by having her drink, a Gin Martini, delivered to her by his son. She had the drink, and then continued down the mountain with the utmost resolve. Blake then started a new tradition: He strategically placed Gin Martinis in glass porrons (basically, glass wine pitchers with a thin pour spout) on random stops throughout his hills. And why did he choose a Martini? "White wine makes the knees buckle," he told the *New York Times*. And so, the Tree Martini was born, and has been a part of New Mexico ever since. But don't tell the Margarita that, or maybe it already found out, since most of them are colored green, just like jealousy.

NEW MEXICO SPIRIT
KGB SPIRITS
Alcalde

Founded in 2012 but inspired by early-1800s New Mexico distilleries, KGB wields a nice portfolio of small-batch heirloom spirits. It's rare to find an American distiller making absinthe, and KGB's Brimstone was awarded a silver medal in the San Francisco World Spirits Competition in its first year of being bottled. The herbal, citrus-forward, peppery Hacienda gin is one of the few gins made from potatoes in the world.

NEW MEXICO'S OLDEST BAR
EL FAROL
Santa Fe, 1835

Everyone in Santa Fe reveres El Farol. The walls alone pay artistic homage to New Mexico's past, featuring arresting photography from local photographers capturing the people and landscape that make this area of America so special. El Farol serves traditional Spanish tapas, Flamenco dancers, live music, and classic Santa Fe Margaritas to sip between your samba sessions. Olé!

STATE FACT
The Turquoise Trail, a very pretty stretch of road from Albuquerque to Santa Fe, is always a welcome drive. I once parked my car and pet friendly horses out in the middle of nowhere. Southwest Native Americans consider the turquoise stone, or "skystone," a sacred talisman for health, happiness, and protection.

NEW MEXICO BUCKET LIST BAR
SILVA'S SALOON
Bernalillo

A welcoming atmosphere is a necessary ingredient for every American bar. The one thing that turns me off is a snotty bartender or host. Drinks should always be secondary to service. As a patron, I prize professionalism and courtesy. Those are qualities all bartenders should have.

—Natalie Bovis, the Liquid Muse, founder of the New Mexico Cocktails and Culture Culinary Festival (Santa Fe)

Silva's was founded the day after Prohibition's repeal by local bootlegger Felix Silva, and the remnants of the old days still decorate the walls and rafters, including one-hundred-year-old bottles of booze, old license plates, revolvers, vintage photos, a wooden hand giving a disembodied middle finger, and a phone booth, which was used for FBI investigations back in the day. It's a bar where you want to sip and chat with the locals until the sun begins to set, which is an important reminder that it's last call. Silva's closes at 7 P.M. every night, which keeps the riff raff out, but leaves time for all the memories and camaraderie.

NEW MEXICO BEVERAGE
SILVER COIN MARGARITA

The Silver Coin Margarita—silver tequila, Cointreau, lime juice, and simple syrup or agave nectar—is *everywhere* in Santa Fe. There is nothing complicated about the Silver Coin Margarita, and there shouldn't be—unless you can't make up your mind if you would like salt around the entire rim of your glass, or simply half of it. My good friend Sam Parker has a Parker Family recipe where he uses more triple sec than lime juice, which is totally fine depending on the ingredients. As Sam is apt to say, "Try not to have nine."

NEW MEXICO COCKTAIL BAR
THE COYOTE CAFE
Santa Fe

When one thinks of modern-day cocktails, creativity is often one of the most important factors to consider, and *creative* is a word I would associate with the Coyote Cafe. Not only is the restaurant serving some of the best food in Santa Fe, its owner and beverage director Quinn Stephenson—who started working in the original Coyote Cafe as a busboy in the '90s—is putting the pedal to the cocktail metal, with terrific house cocktails built for longevity. The smoked cherry Manhattan arrives in front of you in the blink of an eye and is served with a little razzmatazz (smoke!). I also love a place where a server approaches the service bartender and asks, "Pinot Grigio, if you please," and the bartender responds, "*You're* a Pinot Grigio." Well played, Geraldo.

STATE FACT

The White Sands National Monument has over 275 square miles of gypsum, white dunes that stretch across one's imagination of Star Wars planetary landscapes (the 1977 film shot scenes in the dunes). It's no wonder they call New Mexico "The Land of Enchantment." Carlsbad Caverns is a place to get lost in all day and leave with a whole new impression of the world, especially if you enjoy being incredibly close to tens of thousands of bats migrating at dusk.

BAR SNACK

Young people in 1880s New Mexico averaged approximately $1.67 a day in wages, when a meal in a hotel or boardinghouse cost seventy-five cents, and weekly rent in rooming houses was anywhere between five and eight dollars, so there was very little room for economic growth, which is why saloons started to offer free lunch counters.

SUMMER GODDESS
Natalie Bovis, Santa Fe

People don't use apricots enough in cocktails in general, and yet fresh apricot juice (or apricot puree, if you don't have fresh apricots from your local farmers' market) can be such a welcome mixer, especially since apricot trees are the first fruit trees to blossom in the spring. This drink tastes like the best parts of spring and summer, and with the addition of cinnamon, guess what—it kinda feels like it could win in any season.

2 fresh apricots, halved
(or ¾ ounce apricot puree
if you don't have fresh
apricots: Perfect Puree of
Napa Valley is great)

½ ounce simple syrup
(1:1 sugar to water)

2 ounces KGB Viracocha
vodka (or an alternate
American vodka)

¾ ounce fresh lemon juice

1 dash ground cinnamon

Garnish: lemon wheel

Muddle the apricots and simple syrup in the bottom of a mixing glass. Add the vodka, lemon juice, cinnamon, and ice and shake vigorously. Fine strain into a chilled Martini glass and serve up, garnished with the lemon on the rim of the glass.

THE JUDGE'S PALOMA
Brian Bartels

This Paloma packs some heat, as it not only pays homage to New Mexico's legendary chiles and spices by using Hella Bitters's wonderful smoked chile bitters but honors Judge Holden, one of the most terrifying fictional characters I have ever come across, featured in Cormac McCarthy's legendary 1985 western novel, *Blood Meridian: or The Evening Redness in the West.* Have you ever read a book that gave you goose bumps and you didn't know you were gripping it as though you were falling through the sky and it was your parachute? If not, read *Blood Meridian.*

2 ounces blanco tequila

1½ ounces fresh grapefruit
juice

¾ ounce fresh lime juice

½ ounce agave syrup

1 ounce grapefruit soda
(or regular club soda)

6 dashes Hella smoked chile
bitters (or Bitter End
Mexican mole bitters)

Garnish: lime wheel

Shake the ingredients with ice until chilled; strain over fresh ice in a chilled highball or rocks glass. Garnish with the lime.

BAR SNACK
Professional bartenders in the nineteenth century were expected to maintain a neat and tidy appearance at all times. Rolled-up shirts or short sleeves conveyed a half-completed impression that would likely drive away clientele. Most bartenders wore a white vest and white coat with black trousers, ideally tailored. None of them were allowed to drive to work in their UFOs.

One of my favorite memories of Arizona was when I arrived at my friends' house just outside Phoenix, a few hours after I stopped trying to take photos of all the roadrunners and that little thing called the Grand Canyon. They had so many citrus trees in their backyard I was eager to start bartending right then and there, peeling lemon, lime, and blood orange garnishes for the masses, which were only my friends Amy and Matt. It's important to have friends, and it's especially important to have friends who have so much citrus they need to squeeze fresh juice on a daily basis. The Land of Saguaros might be mostly desert mesas, but the citrus groves had me grooving and sipping Margaritas in no time.

Arizona

THE SUNSET STATE is famous for the Grand Canyon, Havasu Falls, Monument Valley, saguaros (aka cactus), palo verde, copper, bola ties, rattlesnakes, roadrunners, ghost towns, and Highway 10, one of the most pleasant American drives I have ever taken. It's a road that'll help you get lost in inspiration while feeling as if the clouds and blue skies are there only for you, and are ready to tell you exactly what you want to hear.

Tequila arrived through the silver gates of Nogales in 1936, so the next time you find yourself sipping on a Margarita, silently thank Arizona. It's no wonder the sun shines 85 percent of the year in Phoenix and Tucson.

Arizona has the highest level of UFO sightings per capita. There is still no answer to the "Phoenix Lights" incident on March 13, 1997, when a series of V-shaped lights appeared in the sky for 106 minutes. Speaking of the sky, Pluto, the ninth planet in our solar system (sorry, haters), was discovered in 1930 by Clyde Tombaugh at the Lowell Observatory in Flagstaff.

When Tucson isn't distracting me with its delicious carne asada options, I would recommend the wonderful Hotel Congress (a legendary music venue), Sidecar, Kon Tiki for epic rum drinks, and the Still, a distinguished speakeasy with an unmarked location, open only on Fridays and Saturdays—to access it, you need to send a text to make a reservation. And if stiff drinks and windowless bars are your thing, try the Buffet.

Phoenix holds the gold for cocktail bar options, such as the rum-friendly and sustainable seafood–loving Breadfruit & Rum Bar, Honor Amongst Thieves, the Womack, and Bitter & Twisted, which is housed inside the former Phoenix Prohibition headquarters. Good friends insisted we visit the Durant's, an iconic chophouse where you enter through the kitchen and into a dining room of red velvet banquettes. Everyone there is drinking Old Fashioneds and Martinis; it's like being in a live taping of *Mad Men*. We sat at the bar and ordered Gin Martinis served in goblet-size glasses, and upon the first sip, I felt transported back to the 1960s. But one of my favorite spots we visited in Phoenix was UnderTow, an underground tiki bar located in the bottom of a former Jiffy Lube station, designed to reflect a nineteenth-century clipper ship, where the "windows" of the ship reveal different aspects of tropical weather as you sit and sip on original Polynesian cocktails. Even though we were in Arizona, there wasn't a prickly pear with a bad attitude in sight.

BAR SNACK

Prickly pear cactus nectar often makes its way into Arizona margaritas, which is a health boost, as it's high in antioxidants, vitamin C, fiber, and carotenoids. Though prickly pear cactus nectar gets plenty of attention from tequila, give this wonderful mixer some rhum agricole or mezcal once in a while. They don't bite.

*The rhythm of a
night of service
at a bar comes in
pulsating waves;
for a bartender,
last call not only
represents the
end of the night,
but also a period
of transition—a
post-midnight
zone of contem-
plation when
they can ease
back into their
own head with-
out distraction
or obligation.
But the rush
of adrenaline
from being on
all night usually
requires a period
of decompression.
For many, that's
a shift drink or
two, or trying to
chase last call
at another bar
before it closes.*

—Brad Thomas
Parsons, author, *Last
Call, Amaro, Bitters*,
and *Distillery Cats*

Some of the best bars defy definition, which would make Valley Bar a must-visit to figure out what all the fuss is about. Depending on what night you visit, there could be live music, spoken word, a comedy set, or a group of college kids playing Skee-Ball and video games and shouting "Gucci!" at their high scores. The Rose Room—named after beloved first female governor of Arizona, Rose Mofford, public servant, All-American softball player, and all-around badass—holds an extensive cocktail menu featuring drinks referencing local politicians of varying infamy and repute. Pro tip: Sundays are all-night happy hour.

Opening in 2010 in downtown Tucson, 47 Scott subsequently became such a crowd favorite for its laid-back vibe, elevated comfort food, and dazzling cocktails it had to make extra room in the adjacent Scott & Co., a cozy, nondescript speakeasy. Both bars feature a healthy sampling of varying cocktail influences, postwar tiki notables, Golden Era cocktails such as the Bamboo (a complex low-ABV sherry and vermouth Martini) and the Paloma (featuring tequila and grapefruit juice and always welcome on a warm, sunny day), and house originals such as the Brick House Old Fashioned, made with bacon-washed rye whiskey, Demerara syrup, and bitters. When you're having cocktails from heaven next to a triple-stacked grilled cheese, there's not a lot to complain about in the world.

STATE FACT
Roadrunners are indigenous to the Southwest and are everywhere you turn in southern Arizona—but look fast. Roadrunners can travel up to seventeen miles an hour.

ARIZONA TEQUILA SUNRISE
Brian Bartels

Though the Tequila Sunrise most know today is credited to Sausalito, California, bartender Bobby Lozoff, who created the grenadine and orange juice–based version in 1969 and eventually served it to the Rolling Stones in 1972, the original Tequila Sunrise started a little farther east. Bartender Gene Sulit created the Sunrise at the Arizona Biltmore in the late 1930s when a hotel guest asked for a cocktail to be enjoyed poolside. Irving Berlin allegedly wrote "White Christmas" while spending time poolside at the Biltmore in the 1940s; no word on whether he was drinking a tequila cocktail at the time.

1½ ounces blanco tequila

½ ounce crème de cassis

¾ ounce fresh lime juice

1 to 2 ounces club soda

Garnish: lime wedge

Shake the tequila, cassis, and lime juice with ice until chilled; strain over fresh ice in a chilled highball glass and top with the soda water. Garnish with the lime.

ARIZONA SUNSET
Brian Bartels

This cocktail is meant to celebrate the sunny corners of everyday Arizona, as it sees plenty of sunshine. When I'm around the sun, I do enjoy some iced tea and lemons. Pair that with a dry, nutty sherry and some almond-forward orgeat and soon enough, I'm smiling. Are you smiling right now? Why do you have to be so gloomy all the time? Why can't you just be happy? You're embarrassing me in front of all my friends.

1⅓ ounces Lustau amontillado sherry

1 ounce cold unsweetened black tea

¾ ounce fresh lemon juice

½ ounce Giffard orgeat

½ ounce egg white

Garnishes: lemon wedge and a few twists of freshly ground black pepper (optional)

Combine the ingredients in a shaker and dry shake (without ice) for 15 seconds. Add ice and shake until chilled. Fine strain into a chilled coupe glass. Garnish with the lemon and pepper, if using.

BAR SNACK

Back in the day, "rotgut" was a poorly made or poor-quality alcoholic drink, and a word I knew at a very young age. (Thanks, Yosemite Sam, whom I always associated with Arizona.) Rotgut is also associated with bathtub gin, moonshine, and old Bugs Bunny cartoons. Did I just reference cartoons in a cocktail book? Ten points for me.

Yes, there are beautiful surfing beaches aligning the Pacific Ocean, along with giant sequoias, and I believe sensory depravation chambers are a big thing in San Francisco now, but there is so much more to California than we realize. There are avocados, avocado toast, almonds, walnuts, redwoods, northwoods, vineyards, wine mixers, mandarins, tangerines, sourdough bread, Mission burritos, Koreatown, Chinatown, Joshua Tree, and Coachella (selfieee!).

California

EUREKA! YOU'VE GOT a lot of great cocktail bars out there, California—and a lot of people to visit them. There are more than thirty-nine million people in California, which means one of every eight United States residents lives in the Land of Milk and Honey. The fortune cookie was invented here, the first motion picture theater opened in Los Angeles in 1902, and did you order this book on an Apple device? Invented in California, my friend. And you're probably wearing blue jeans, right? Levi Strauss, a German immigrant, came to California in 1873, bringing us the almighty American comfort garment.

California and its cocktail background—coupled with the rising tide of new cocktail bars and bartenders making waves throughout the Golden State—could be a book of their own. San Francisco has developed into the West Coast cocktail capital of America, the site of a revival on par with New York's. The early 1990s saw the introduction of Julio Bermejo's simple take on the classic Margarita, using 100 percent agave tequila with fresh-squeezed lime juice and agave syrup—no triple sec. Modern classics developed at land speed record in San Francisco: Marco Dionysos created the Chartreuse Swizzle; Jacques Bezuidenhout crafted the La Perla; the Irish Coffee at Buena Vista became a must-try; Tony Abou-Ganim came up with the Cable Car (spiced rum, triple sec, and lemon, with a cinnamon-sugar rim); and Thad Vogler's Bar Agricole illuminated the Bay City playing field with its Armagnac Old Fashioned.

Oakland doesn't get as much attention as San Francisco, but it should be noted that there are terrific bars and beverage destinations throughout the Town (howdy, Prizefighter), and they owe its cocktail history to people like Trader Vic and Don the Beachcomber—the Katy Perry and Taylor Swift of 1940s California tiki bar legend. Trader Vic created the Mai Tai in 1944, and it became the official cocktail of Oakland in 2009.

San Diego is the location for one of the most beautiful bars in the world. It's called Raised by Wolves. Google some images. It looks like a magical bar made for the set design of Tim Burton's version of *The Great Gatsby*. Second, this blessed beauty of a bar is located . . . in the Westfield UTC shopping mall. Just across from the Apple and Aesop stores. Once inside the blue door, visitors are staring at a seemingly well-kept retail store shelving notable bitters, spirits, and barware. After sitting down on a chair near a working fireplace, the wall spins like a trap door for 180 degrees to place you inside a pristine bar evoking a gilded era of cocktail majesty; with wolves on the walls, and a bubbling water fountain smack-dab in the center behind the bar, nearly as high as the ceiling. I haven't even talked about the delicious cocktails, have I? Because no doubt you have already put the book down and are headed there.

Second, not only does San Diego have the *Top Gun* bar (See? We can't escape Tom Cruise when it comes to bars and cocktail references), where Goose sings on the piano to Maggie, and Maggie says, "Take me to bed or lose me forever," San Diego has one of my favorite bar-restaurants in America: Turf Club. I was lucky enough to visit Turf Club once—once—and I feel like it's not enough. I can't wait to get back. Go there for the sexy red-light bar, and stay for the ice-cold gimlets, which you will sip in a booth while ordering steaks and vegetables and potatoes that are to be grilled in the middle of the room, while chatting with people from other tables who are all cooking their own food. Get a Martini, a Manhattan, or an Old Fashioned. Get anything. When I was there I met some sweethearts from Denver who offered me some of their Chartreuse. I'm not saying that would happen every single time, but at least I can give you hope. Please: Book a flight to San Diego. Go to Turf Club, then Raised by Wolves, then the Aero Club Bar, a dive bar with a nice selection of cocktails and one of the largest whiskey collections in the country. I will be your wing man any time you head to San Diego.

Los Angeles is responsible for creating the Brown Derby, the Harvey Wallbanger (purportedly named after a surfer who drank enough he bumped into the walls upon having the wild concoction), the Zombie (if you wanna get heavy, dig on this—but go easy, as it is boozy), and the now-ubiquitous Moscow Mule, putting vodka and ginger beer into symbiotic matrimony in the 1940s.

Los Angeles still has one foot in classic Hollywood sentiment, with terrific cocktail destinations such as Musso and Frank Grill (lionized in Quentin Tarantino's *Once Upon a Time in Hollywood*), West Hollywood's Dan Tana's, and Tonga Hut, L.A.'s oldest tiki bar, while modern-day Los Angeles has a bevy of worthwhile cocktail haunts. But each one takes forty-five minutes to get to by car, so please be responsible and don't drink and drive. The NoMad opened a bar in downtown L.A. that equals its New York majesty—and this one has a pool and bar on the rooftop; Ever Bar assembles creative riffs on classics in a relaxed setting; the Spare Room balances house cocktails with nearby bowling lanes and Jimmy Kimmel's headquarters across the street; the Normandie Club in Koreatown is a favorite for industry people and always delivers on its selections, even celebrating riffs on the classic Martini. Harvard & Stone is a great cocktail bar and intimate music hall, which deftly avoids categorization. Enter any night of the week and you might find a cocktail competition taking place, a spirits tasting, live music, a burlesque show, or all of these things combined! The R&D Bar in the back of the space has weekly menu changes and features some amazing themed cocktail menus. One of my personal faves was the *Dumb and Dumber* cocktail menu, with He Must Work Out, Mary Samsonite, Those Your Skiis?, Both of Em?, and So You're Sayin' There's a Chance. Hopefully, you're saying there's a chance you'll make it here for a great night.

BAR SNACK

"The Bartender's Handshake" refers to a shot of Fernet-Branca. So a few years back, San Francisco bartenders—often tribal and community-based by nature—would visit one another's bars, many of which were located in the cocktail epicenter of the city, the predominantly Italian North Beach neighborhood, and Fernet shots were poured to celebrate small reunions. Made in Milan, Fernet became the official spirit of San Francisco (more Fernet is consumed here than anywhere else in the United States), as its inhabitants followed the example of their loyal barkeepers. I know the more I keep talking about Fernet, the more Fernet sounds like the foreign exchange student who's wearing too much cologne and seems twenty years older than anyone else at the party, but Fernet is a uniquely flavorful spirit, and some people can't see past the visual aspect of Fernet in a glass. Fernet is very dark and viscous, and some might say it looks like a heartbroken spider that has crawled into a bottle and cried for weeks on end. Take a sip of Fernet, and take a sip of San Francisco, which in the nineteenth century was regarded as one of the most lawless cities in America. You fiend.

CALIFORNIA'S OLDEST BAR
POZO SALOON
Santa Margarita, 1858

I don't like sitting at a desk—I like keeping in motion, and a little bit of chaos, and that's bartending.

—Steven Liles, bartender at Smuggler's Cove, in Imbibe magazine

Not only does it look like a place where Jesse and Frank James would stop and have a sarsaparilla or two on the run from Johnny Law, it actually is a spot where the famous robbers once stopped. Operating since 1858 just outside of San Luis Obispo, the bar has developed a new following for bringing in live music.

CALIFORNIA COCKTAIL BAR
THE VARNISH
Los Angeles

The number of craft cocktail bars opening in Los Angeles over the past ten years has been dizzying enough that you might get lost in the shuffle and not recognize the dealer, which was the Varnish, a bar that has been loved since it opened its doors in 2009. In an era in which every new bar needs to outdo the next with media relevancy, the Varnish continues operating with subtle nuances that punctuate to desired effect—which keep it classy—and it's still standing, and it's still telling stories.

. . . .

I recommend two important California bars: Specs' Twelve Adler Museum Café in San Francisco is historic perfection, filled with curiosities and enough visual interest to let you linger over your Anchor Steam. And the Tiki-Ti on Sunset Boulevard in Los Angeles, for the unbroken family chain of cocktail history.

—Martin Cate, co-owner, Smuggler's Cove (San Francisco)

CALIFORNIA SPIRIT
ST. GEORGE SPIRITS
Alameda

Located in East Bay, St. George has the respect and attention of just about every industry professional I know and have interviewed for this book. The company produces three different gins, an American whiskey, a green chile vodka with four different kinds of peppers, an absinthe, Nola coffee liqueur, a sensational raspberry liqueur and brandy, a terrific American amaro (Bruto), and a healthy list of other spirits. St. George puts only the best versions of its product into its bottles. The website quotes Thomas Alva Edison, one of my heroes: "I have not failed. I have just found 10,000 ways that don't work." St. George's response? "If we can get one lightbulb in 10,000, we'll drink to that."

BUCKET LIST BAR
SMUGGLER'S COVE
San Francisco

Though located on an unassuming city block, Smuggler's Cove is the truest expression of disappearing into time—chronologically speaking, the 1950s. It is an environment that evokes a bygone era, but it handles the nostalgia so well you can't help but drink up the sentiment. It literally feels like your problems disappear when you cross the threshold. There are star-tenders in your midst at Rebecca and Martin Cate's famous tiki temple, and the beautiful part about it is that none of them carries a whiff of attitude, an impressive feat when balancing more than four hundred different rum selections and a cocktail menu of tiki-torch-bearing majesty.

Kevin Diedrich (P.C.H.) is one of my favorite American bartenders. I have seen him work in a variety of bars over many years, and it never matters the setting or the crowd, he is the epitome of calm, professional, highly skilled, and, most importantly, friendly. And he makes a mighty fine drink to boot.

—Rebecca Cate, co-owner, Smuggler's Cove (San Francisco)

CALIFORNIA COCKTAIL BAR
PACIFIC COCKTAIL HAVEN
San Francisco

It's very easy to remember my first visit to P.C.H.: It was slightly rainy, definitely cold, dark (it was nighttime, so that makes sense), and there was a glowing neon "P.C.H." and pineapple images spread throughout the narrow space near San Francisco's Union Square. But the most unforgettable part was the warm welcome from everyone working in the space, and how comfortable they made me feel upon getting settled, and how well-informed the staff were on the history of cocktails—notably the history of San Francisco's cocktails and modern-day evolution. It's a testament to creator Kevin Diedrich's diligence in creating a wonderful bar program.

The cocktail is the most American cocktail. Without America, the whole concept probably wouldn't exist. People in the south'll probably say Sazerac, northerners the Martini or Manhattan, and no one would argue with an Old Fashioned, but really the most American cocktail is the cocktail itself.

—Todd Carnum, bar manager, Interval at Long Now (San Francisco)

CALIFORNIA COCKTAIL BAR
POLITE PROVISIONS
San Diego

Erick Castro, of the famed *Bartender at Large* documentary series and cofounder of Bartender's Weekend, a three-day industry networking event, opened the Polite Provisions cocktail playground in 2013, and the city of San Diego had a new and wonderful problem on its hands: Polite Provisions immediately became the place everyone wanted to go. If you're looking for obscure ingredients finding their way into the same glass and elevating your taste buds into the stratosphere, then look no further. There's a drink for everyone here! Just looking at the menu will make you smile.

CALIFORNIA BEVERAGE
MOSCOW MULE

Hard to believe, but in the early 1940s vodka was a weak-selling spirit until Jack Morgan, the owner of the Cock 'n Bull restaurant in Los Angeles, and friend John Martin, of Heublein, collaborated on a drink to help each other achieve a greater balance in the universe. They took vodka, lime juice, and ginger beer and called it the Moscow Mule, placing the ingredients in copper mugs with an image of two mules yukking it up. There are many bars today that feature Mule variations, using varying spirits and producers of ginger beer, along with some homemade recipes, all of which are easy to build. To this day, I stand behind Fever-Tree ginger beer, which has enough spice and kick to keep this scrawny huckleberry honest all day long. Serve it with one of California's many terrific artisinal distilleries, such as Young & Yonder, Re:Find, or Mulholland Distilling, a double charcoal-filtered vodka with a minty, peppery finish.

TOMMY'S MARGARITA

Julio Bermejo, San Francisco

This twist on the classic Margarita was immortalized in the early 1990s by Julio Bermejo at Tommy's Mexican Restaurant, a shrine to tequila. It's amazing how much the tequila's characteristics reveal themselves by substituting agave for the usual triple sec, and using an aged tequila—like reposado or añejo—is like taking the engine of a Ferrari and putting it in, well, an electric car, of course!

2 ounces reposado tequila

1 ounce fresh lime juice

1 ounce agave syrup

Garnish: lime wedge

Shake the ingredients with ice until chilled; strain over fresh ice in a chilled rocks glass and garnish with the lime.

POP QUIZ

Devon Tarby, Los Angeles

To know Devon Tarby (of Proprietors, LLC) is to know someone who looks at life with the right kind of love, and though she can rock a wicked mean Southie Boston accent, kid, she emanates joy from every pore, and life is always better when she's around—especially when she's creating wonderful drinks like the Pop Quiz. For the Old Fashioned lover in all of us, this provides a malty, caramel mouthfeel, with root beer and chocolaty notes that'll make you Snoopy dance whether it's before or after a meal.

2 ounces bourbon

½ ounce Ramazzotti amaro

⅛ ounce (or 1 teaspoon) simple syrup (1:1 sugar to water)

2 dashes Bittermens mole bitters

Garnish: orange peel

Stir the ingredients with ice until chilled; strain over fresh ice in a chilled rocks glass and garnish with the orange.

BROWN DERBY

Brian Bartels

This cocktail was created in 1930, which was clearly smack dab in the middle of Prohibition, which of course means this cocktail was not created at the Vendome Club in Hollywood, which opened in 1926, because all of that would be illegal, and nothing illegal happens in Hollywood.

2 ounces bourbon

1 ounce fresh grapefruit juice (pulp-free)

½ ounce honey syrup (recipe page 89)

Shake ingredients with ice until chilled and strain into a chilled cocktail glass.

Hawaii

"Aloha" is derived from the Polynesian word "alofa," which means love, compassion, and mercy. It makes perfect sense that it's used as both "hello" and "goodbye," as it keeps the good juju through all correspondence.

THIS TROPICAL ARCHIPELAGO has been "hangin' loose" since 1959, when Hawaii became the fiftieth state in the United States. Our Aloha State was formed by underground volcanoes that erupted thousands of years ago, and now make up the eight main islands of Hawaii (which actually has 132 islands in total; the other 124 islands total only about three square miles of land, and are not fit for human habitation).

We owe much of our current mainland tiki culture craze to Hawaii: vanda orchids, malleable paper umbrellas, and the occasional cocktail served in a fresh coconut. Contemporary tiki culture in Hawaii seems to have one foot in history and one foot in modern techniques and recipes, which is a good thing, given that tiki culture started in Hollywood, California, of all places, but eventually found its way to Hawaiian getaways through the Mai Tai cocktail, which debuted in Oakland, California, in 1944 at Trader Vic's.

Cocktails in Hawaii got a boost with Donn Beach, who brought his creative cocktail influence to Polynesia in the late 1940s, establishing Hawaii as a vacation destination when "boat drinks" and exotica music took off in midcentury resorts. After World War II, when things started settling down in the South Pacific, Donn Beach turned Waikiki Beach into a tourist destination for travelers. Donn embraced some elements of Hawaiian tradition in his tiki designs for the island, and the two worlds ended up making worthy impressions through Donn's commitment to fresh ingredients and juices, which were readily available in Hawaii's tropical climate.

Coco Lopez coconut cream found commercialization in 1954, and frozen drinks would soon follow, but the world of tiki and boat drinks turned a corner with Hawaiian Village Hotel bartender Harry Yee in 1955. He was the first bartender to put an orchid into a cocktail, accidentally landing on this

*My first cocktail
was a vodka
and Slice on a
Hawaiian beach.*

—Julie Reiner (born
in Honolulu), owner,
Leyenda and Clover
Club (Brooklyn, NY)

future Instagram-friendly garnish. In the 1950s, Hawaiian bartenders would garnish their cocktails with sticks of sugarcane, but the drinker would put the sugarcane in an ashtray, making a sticky mess. "I wasn't thinking about romance," Yee later said. "I was being practical."

Elvis Presley filmed *Blue Hawaii* in the early 1960s, and the cocktail being ordered in the movie was the Mai Tai, only adding to the lure of faraway exotic island locations.

Then, sadly, cocktails lost their way in the 1970s and '80s, as commercial mixes replaced fresh ingredients, and tiki faded. Even in Hawaii, which could still claim the beaches, palm trees, coconuts, and coffee (arguably the most celebrated beverage of Hawaii), most cocktail programs traveled the unfortunate path of artificial ingredients. Until people like Jeff "Beachbum" Berry came along and helped revitalize the legacy of Donn and Vic, going so far as to reach out to the former bartenders who worked for them, and we were allowed to recapture the true essence of tiki culture from the 1950s in places like Los Angeles, San Francisco, Chicago, and New York.

And the best news: Thanks to our modern-day bar superheroes, who wear aprons instead of capes, and whose superpower is researching history, Hawaii regained its tiki traction. Nowadays, places like Bevy retain the tiki glory, while creating new recipes and memories for locals and travelers alike; Monkeypod Kitchen in Ko Olina provides surf décor, tiki torches, and live entertainment as you sip on flavor-bursting balanced tiki originals; and the Royal Mai Tai at the Royal Hawaiian Hotel, where Trader Vic himself adjusted his original Mai Tai recipe with fresh orange and pineapple juices in 1953, is now back on the menu after unnecessarily languishing in obscurity. But if you're a purist, there's no better place than the Hilton Hawaiian Village, where bartender Harry Yee started the Blue Hawaii revolution in the 1950s, and which still claims its link to history, with head bartender Joe, who was hired as a busboy by Harry Yee in 1970 and still creates the original Blue Hawaiis, Banana Daiquiris, and Tropical Itches (rum, bourbon, Curaçao, passion fruit, pineapple, and lemon juices and garnished with a long back scratcher, naturally) while applying contemporary creativity with a menu celebrating products popping up on many American bar shelves, such as Fever-Tree, Casamigos tequila, and Suntory whiskey, along with local products, such as Kō Hana rum out of Oahu.

The islands are famous for pineapple, which is one of my favorite ingredients in cocktails, and though Jim Dole founded the Hawaiian Pineapple Company in 1901, nothing eclipses fresh pineapple juice. Rest assured, if we are near a blender, or ice, or there is reggae playing, you and I are having a drink with pineapple, my friend. Common side effects: too much smiling, too much fun.

BAR SNACK

Ever notice a certain melodic, transportive, and atmospheric sound coming from the bar where everyone is wearing Hawaiian shirts, and suddenly you feel like you're in a jungle? You are probably hearing Exotica music, aka Polynesian Pop. Exotica aptly captured the tiki movement in places like the Hawaiian Village Hotel in the 1950s, featuring seminal artists like Les Baxter, Martin Denny, and Yma Sumac. But there's still plenty of room for Don Ho's "Tiny Bubbles," and my personal favorite, "Shells," a hypnotic song sung by Scrappy Olivieri, a very obscure but wonderful singer. Mesmerizing.

HAWAII SPIRIT
KŌ HANA
Oahu

Though not often associated with the production of rum, Hawaii produces a lot of sugarcane, and Kō Hana utilizes this accessibility with the most noble of distilling techniques. Most rum is made with processed molasses, but Kō Hana observes a grass-to-bottle practice with its distillates, and the result is often revelatory—but the process is never easy, as creating agricole rum requires harvesting, pressing, and fermenting the sugarcane juice immediately, before it turns. (*Agricole* means "agriculture" in French.) The rums inhabit a fruity, fresher structure with notes of banana, lychee, and earthy white truffle.

HAWAII'S OLDEST BAR
SMITH'S UNION BAR
Honolulu, 1935

It seems odd that the oldest bar in Hawaii sounds like a bar that could be in any other small town in the eastern part of the American Midwest, but Smith's Union Bar is right there, in downtown Honolulu's Chinatown, waiting to serve you, whether you're a local, a friendly tourist, traveling on business, a wartime hero, a gangster, or just passing through on assignment, you old sailor, you. And yes, there are also ukulele jam sessions to go with First Fridays block parties and the regular karaoke. I know you were worried that wasn't included in the brochure.

STATE FACT
While moonshine tends to be associated with West Virginia and southern states, Hawaii has brewed its own version of moonshine for thousands of years. The drink, called "swipe," is simply pineapple moonshine, and, much like moonshine on the main land, "swipe" was outlawed twice, once in 1818 and then a century later by the national government.

HAWAII BUCKET LIST BAR
BEVY
Honolulu

Located in the bustling, hip neighborhood of Salt Kaka'ako, Bevy has been serving happy islanders since 2013 with fresh local produce, lava rock wall installations, and Prohibition-era ambience, formulas that work well when paired with award-winning cocktails by mixologist Christian Self. Bevy serves a wide variety of house originals next to classics and large-format punches for groups, along with a daily cocktail special. Word on the island is they serve the best Mai Tai around, giving it a Thai spin by incorporating lemongrass and ginger foam. On top of its terrific cocktails, the place is even more exciting during happy hour, when the prices will make you say "Cowabunga" before you ever hit the waves.

HAWAII COCKTAIL BAR
BAR LEATHER APRON
Honolulu

James Beard semifinalist Bar Leather Apron serves an extensive selection of Japanese whiskeys, specialty Highballs, classic and contemporary cocktails, and original concoctions influenced by Hawaii. One of its biggest draws is how local produce is incorporated into the beverage program, which helps in creating drinks such as the Mari's Garden, made with Fords gin, fresh cucumber and watermelon juice, yuzu, celery bitters, and soda (all the produce in the drink comes from, naturally, Mari's Gardens aquaponics farm in Oahu.)

BAR SNACK
If someone offers you a flower lei, it is considered rude to not accept it.

BLUE HAWAII
Brian Bartels

Created in 1957 by bartender Harry Yee, the Blue Hawaii is without a doubt one of the most aesthetically pleasing cocktails for the eye to behold. Some claim Yee held up each cocktail to ensure the drink's color matched the aquamarine Pacific in the distance. On top of this, the garnish is simply transformative, which is probably why the cocktail was so popular in wintry parts of America, often served in supper clubs in Minnesota and Wisconsin. It's simply fun in a glass.

¾ ounce white rum

¾ ounce vodka

1 ounce blue Curaçao
    (Giffard makes a great
    one—Curaçao Bleu)

2½ ounces pineapple juice

½ ounce fresh lime juice

½ ounce fresh lemon juice

½ ounce simple syrup
    (1:1 sugar to water)

Garnishes: pineapple wedge,
    cocktail umbrella, mara-
    schino cherry

Shake the ingredients with ice until chilled; strain over, ideally, crushed ice (but any ice will do) in a chilled Hurricane glass and add the garnishes.

FOOL'S GOLD
Jen Ackrill, Top of Waikiki, Honolulu

Gaz Regan selected the Fool's Gold for his 2015 "101 Best New Cocktails" for being "weird and wonderful," and I picked it for this book because the ingredients are not easily acquired (not unlike visiting Hawaii), and tracking them down is an adventure in itself—and once you do, you're in for a delicious reward.

1 ounce St. George Dry
    Rye gin

1 ounce Buffalo Trace
    bourbon

¾ ounce Bittermens Amère
    Nouvelle

¼ ounce Giffard Banane
    du Brésil

Garnish: lime peel

Stir the ingredients with ice until chilled; strain into a chilled coupe glass and serve up, garnished with the lime.

BAR SNACK

Pineapples are not only hard to handle and easy to slice (with a sharp blade), they are the international sign of hospitality. Hundreds of years ago, Native Americans would place a pineapple outside their homes when receiving visitors. Colonials followed the Native American tradition: Any guest who was invited to a party where pineapples were featured knew the host had spared no expense. It has now become common for service professionals to have a pineapple tattoo some-where on their body. If you're ever in a bar or restaurant and see your fair share of pineapples, or meet a person (hey, Elena Silva) with a pineapple tattoo, you will have a thoughtful friend for life.

Epilogue

THERE HAVE BEEN plenty of wonderful cocktail books arriving on shelves in the past few years, which is a terrific sign that we are evolving. Bartenders are taking the knowledge of these cocktail books and ushering them into their own bar programs throughout the country. Score. Ten points for all of us. I am reminded of my first time visiting Tales of the Cocktail in New Orleans, when I was having a drink with Jim Meehan at the Hotel Monteleone bar. At least five different people approached him in the first twenty minutes of our drink to ask if it was really him, and if so, they wanted to let him know how important his *PDT* cocktail book was to them, how it enabled them to create their own programs in other parts of America, where craft cocktails, quality ingredients, and thoughtful, influential approaches to our work environment did not yet exist. It was clear to me that the world of bars and bartending was changing right there before my eyes, and it led me to writing this book as a celebration of how big a country we are and how varied our styles and nuances play across the bar stage. Every night is a performance. Some of us are players. Some are proficient technicians. Some buy a ticket and take the ride. But we are all connected by the unifying, indispensable, limitless wealth of camaraderie. Nothing beats meeting a good friend for a drink and a healthy conversation in a warmly-lit public house.

Writing this book was one of the most challenging mountains I ever dared to climb, but it was worth every step of the process. I got to see parts of America I had never visited before, visited legendary bars and bucket list destinations I had only heard in celebrated passing, and met some wonderful new friends who I hope to stay in touch with forever. There are many great people doing wonderful things throughout the country. As Ma Bartels would say, "Where do they all come from?!"

Growing up, I was most inspired when I could open a book and discover a new world, story, or characters waiting for me inside. I hope this book achieves a little bit of that sentiment. I'm grateful for the opportunity to write about what inspires me, and will always chase that horse no matter how fast or far it goes.

Where are we headed for the future of cocktails? That road is not unlike the ending of *Back to the Future*. "Where we are going," says Doc Brown, "We don't need roads." And Doc and Marty get into the Delorean and take off into the sky, right? Well, maybe we all don't need roads in some of the places we are going. But we certainly need ice.

It is an honor and privilege to know everyone included in this book, and this profession.

I wish you all the good fortune of finding something you love, and letting it take roots.

Recipe List

EACH OF THE recipes found throughout the book are listed here, organized by region and then spirit type. Whether you are looking for a taste of your home state, or a way to use your favorite spirit, you can find a winner in these lists.

RECIPE LIST BY REGION

RECIPE LIST BY SPIRIT

Acknowledgments

AMERICA IS A big, beautiful country, and it's worth visiting over and over. So before I continue, I would like to thank the people I met along the way, everyone kind enough to provide me with time and attention to appreciate this wonderful land.

First to my family: thank you and love to my parents, sisters and brothers, aunts and uncles, cousins, nieces, nephews and every one of your pets. I am lucky to be a Bartels. Special message to my nieces and nephews: it's *always* a good time to pick up a nearby book and read more about the way the world works.

Thank you to my agent, Rica Allannic, of David Black Literary Agency, who helped set the wheels in motion. You're very good at what you do. I tell everyone.

Thank you to Abrams, for believing in this book and helping me every step of the way. Humble, huge thanks to my editor, Laura Dozier, who was patient, communicative, and even went so far as to work on this book while on vacation! I am grateful for your guidance. You. Simply. Rock.

Thank you copyeditor, Liana Krissoff. You fact-check with the best of 'em—and that's a fact you don't need to check!

Mike Burdick. The Golden Glove of illustration. Thank you so much for contributing your talented artwork throughout the book. I know you worked your butt off on these illustrations. I am forever grateful.

Thank you beyond the printed words captured in this book for all the bartenders, bar managers, owners, writers, and industry professionals who shared your experiences, stories, and research. You have a pal for life, and I will always be happy to return the favor should you ever need help.

Thank you for everyone who took the time to answer my questions. Dale DeGroff, Audrey Saunders, Julie Reiner, Gaz Regan, Jocelyn Smith, Mary Miller, Derek Brown, Allen Katz, Sara Camp Milam, Toby Cecchini ("Check-eee-knee")(Go Pack!), Brooks Reitz, Tom Cruise, Rebecca and Martin Cate, Brandon Peck, Leishla Maldonado, Emily Morton, Morgan McKinney, Jeffrey Morgenthaler, Josh Graham, Miles Macquarrie, David Embury, Jacob Grier, Don Lee, Ivy Mix, Amy Kovalchick (Princess of Pittsburgh and as true as the light of day; love to you and Pam), Sara Camp Milam, Wild Bill at the Collins, Samuel Bishop, Tanner Scarborough, Aaron Post, Michael Toscano, Anu Apte and Chris Elford, Kevin King, Nick Tillinghast, Toby Maloney, Hunt Revell, Joy Buehler, Brad Goocher, Greg Boehm and Cocktail Kingdom, Keith Hamm, Alex Negranza, Marcus Owens, Troy Rost, Todd Carnum, Mike Henderson (The Duke of Denver), Rachael and Feizal at the Atomic, Bobby Huegel, Murray Stenson, Natasha David and Jeremy Oertel, Tyler Davidson, Jace Poliquin, Joseph Stinchcomb, Jackson Cannon, Dan Oskey, John Dye, Caroline McCarty, Natalie Bovis, Ryan Maybee, Robert Simonson, Brandon Peck, Holly Booth, Remi Courcenet, Sara Lynch, Jen Ackrill, Christian Huisman, Dermot McCormack (next Mick Jagger joke's on you, pal), Jared Sadoian, T. J. Siegal, Cynthia Turner, Eric Ho, Cody Horan, Sarah Crowl-Keck, Dan Oskey, Leo Robitschek, Emma Janzen, Justin Lavenue, Briana and Andrew Volk, Jermaine Whitehead, Fred Comegys and the Comegys Family, Sean Enright, Julio Bermejo, Sam Treadway, Ryan Sparks, Devon Tarby, Alejandro Olivares,

Sarah Maillet, Meaghan Dorman, Sean Kenyon, Jen and Mark Sabo, Chris Bender, Jill Cockson, Aaron Polsky (Happy Birthday, bud!), Brian Nixon, John Lermayer and Chris Hopkins, KaBoom (aka Katie), Ivy McLellan, John Dye, Charlie Rausch, Tobin Ludwig (Hella4Life), Brian Kelley, Gary Crunkleton, Paul Clarke, Tristen Hoffer, Thor Messer, Andre Darlington, Nourish Knoxville, Misty Kalkofen, Paul Calvert, Christopher Marty, Sophia Kim, Erick Castro, Maggie Hoffman, Julie Haase, Marco Zappia, Brittany Fells, Ryan Gullett, Todd Appel, Travis Hernandez, and A-K Hada.

Thank you to every place I was ever lucky enough to work, and to all the wonderful investors throughout Happy Cooking Hospitality and the Settle Down Tavern, who entrusted us with making noteworthy neighborhood destinations for not only terrific food, hospitality, and warmth, but creative, inspired cocktails.

Thank you to friends who hosted me on my travels. Laura and Brian Grover, Simon Kelly and Francine, Matt and Amy, Natalie and Jeremy, and the Michigan Lauers (next Coneys are on me). You were there. You saw what happened. Don't tell anyone. I am humbled by your kindness and generosity.

Thank you to pals, near and far, but always around:

Thank you with chaotic gratitude to the following friends and loyal souls: Brad Thomas Parsons (It's too early for ponies, but never too late for a cold one with Uncle Marty), Nick and Rotem, Will and Erin Enright, Tess and Kevin Denton Rex, Abi and Eric Medsker, Kottke, Shoko and Rob Moose, Tracy Swanson, Will "Sweet Berry Wine" Blomker and Eva, the Piasio Family and Dimes, Kevin MAN Mahan, the Benedetto Family, the Chicago Quartaros, (Jessica, Gail, Shannon, Lauren and Meow-lissa), McNeil, Maybe Quinn Chandler and definitely Shawna, Dario, the Baumanns, the Millers, the Tomahawk Theilers, Compeeeee, the Showtime Tarpeys, Eliot, Rob, Ted and the Great Dane Family, Lulu Martinez (thanks for all the help and support!), and my Settle Down Tavern family, Ryan Huber and Sam Parker, and their loved ones, whose families are extended Bartels Family members for life.

Thank you to Emily Timberlake, dear friend and talented defender of justice, who helped plant this wonderful seed of the United States inside my head.

Lastly, thank you to my brother Gabriel Stulman, his wonderful wife, Gina, and the Happy Cooking Hospitality Family for putting up with me while writing this puppy, but not only that—putting up with me for ten beautiful years. Happy Cooking gave me what I was looking for when I moved to New York: opportunity. It's been amazing to build such special places for people to visit and celebrate all the wonderful food, fun-loving cocktails, and any reason to be thankful for community. I will be a part of Happy Cooking for the rest of my life, and carry the torch of their influences wherever I roam.

If I missed anyone, come say howdy at the Settle Down Tavern in Madison, Wisconsin, a friendly, old fashioned neighborhood hangout, where I will be bartending for the first time in a while. I can promise two things: I will be clumsy and I will try to hide it, like a 1920s sideshow magician who always wanted to be a 1980s B-movie sorcerer.

Happy trails,

BB

About the Author

BRIAN BARTELS was raised in Wisconsin. His first book, *The Bloody Mary*, was nominated for an IACP Award. For the past ten years he was a Managing Partner and Bar Director for Happy Cooking Hospitality in New York, and is an owner of the Settle Down Tavern, the greatest bar and grill since *Game of Thrones* ended, located in downtown Madison, Wisconsin. (Dragons drink for free). He's been featured in *Imbibe*, *Wine Enthusiast*, and the *New York Times*. His writing has appeared in *Fiction Writers Review*, *PUNCH*, *VinePair*, the *Missouri Review*, *Hobart*, and *China Grove Press*. He lives in the United States, and loves America, like, a lot.

WWW.BRIANBARTELS.COM

Bibliography

These titles—and a healthy amount of other resources—were instrumental in helping share the message of our drinking history throughout the United States. It's an honor to include them and the wonderful writers who worked so hard for them to arrive in bookstores everywhere.

Arnold, Dave. *Liquid Intelligence: The Art and Science of the Perfect Cocktail.* New York: W.W. Norton & Co., 2014.

Berry, Jeff. *Beachbum Berry's Potions of the Caribbean: 500 Years of Tropical Drinks and the People Behind Them.* New York: Cocktail Kingdom, 2013.

Boothby, William T. *The World's Drinks and How to Mix Them.* San Francisco: Boothby's World Drinks Co., [1908] 1934.

Brown, Derek, with Robert Yule. *Spirits, Sugar, Water, Bitters: How the Cocktail Conquered the World.* New York: Rizzoli, 2019.

Bullock, Tom. *The Ideal Bartender.* St. Louis: Buxton & Skinner Printing & Stationary Co., 1917.

Carlin, Joseph M. *Cocktails: A Global History.* London: Reaktion Books Ltd., 2012.

Cate, Martin and Rebecca. *Smuggler's Cove: Exotic Cocktails, Rum, and the Cult of Tiki.* Berkeley: Ten Speed Press, 2016.

Charming, Cheryl. *The Cocktail Companion: A Guide to Cocktail History, Culture, Trivia and Favorite Drinks.* Miami: Mango Publishing Group, 2018.

Cheever, Susan. *Drinking in America: Our Secret History.* New York: Twelve, 2015.

Clarke, Paul. *The Cocktail Chronicles: Navigating the Cocktail Renaissance with Jigger, Shaker & Glass.* Nashville: Spring House Press, 2015.

Curtis, Wayne. *And a Bottle of Rum: A History of the New World in Ten Cocktails.* New York: Broadway Books, 2007.

Darlington, Andre and Tenaya. *The New Cocktail Hour.* Philadelphia: Running Press, 2016.

DeGroff, Dale. *Craft of the Cocktail: Everything You Need to Know to Be A Master Bartender, with 500 Recipes.* New York: Clarkson Potter, 2002.

Embury, David A. *The Fine Art of Mixing Drinks.* New York: Mud Puddle Books, 2008.

Farrell, Shanna. *Bay Area Cocktails: A History of Culture, Community and Craft.* Mt. Pleasant: American Palate, 2017.

Food & Wine. *Cocktails (multiple volumes).* New York: Food & Wine Books.

Ganong, Niki. *A Field Guide to Drinking in America.* Portland: Overcup Press, 2015.

Grimes, William. *Straight Up or On the Rocks: A Cultural History of American Drink.* New York: Simon and Schuster, 1993.

Haigh, Ted. *Vintage Spirits and Forgotten Cocktails: From the Alamagoozlum to the Zombie, 100 Rediscovered Recipes and the Stories Behind Them.* Beverly: Quarry Books, 2009.

Imbibe Magazine. *The American Cocktail: 50 Recipes that Celebrate the Craft of Mixing Drinks from Coast to Coast.* San Francisco: Chronicle Books, 2011.

Jensen, Jamie. *Road Trip USA: Cross-Country Adventures on America's Two Lane Highways.* Berkley: Moon Travel Guides, 2018.

Kaplan, David, Nick Fauchald, and Alex Day. *Death & Co.: Modern Classics Cocktails, with More Than 500 Recipes.* Berkeley: Ten Speed Press, 2014.

Katz, Josh. *Speaking American: How Y'all, Youse, and You Guys Talk.* New York: Houghton Mifflin Harcourt, 2016.

Lapis, Diane and Anne Peck-Davis. *Cocktails Across America: A Postcard View of Cocktail Culture in the 1930s, '40s, and '50s.* New York: The Countryman Press, 2018.

Lender, Mark Edward, and James Kirby Martin. *Drinking in America: A History.* New York: The Free Press, 1982.

McDevitt, Cody, and Sean Enright. *Pittsburgh Drinks: A History of Cocktails, Nightlife & Bartending Tradition.* Mt. Pleasant: American Palate, 2017.

Meehan, Jim. *The PDT Cocktail Book: The Complete Bartender's Guide from the Celebrated Speakeasy.* New York: Sterling Epicure, 2011.

_____. *Meehan Bartender's Manual.* Berkeley: Ten Speed Press, 2017.

Milam, Sara Camp, and Jerry Slater. *The Southern Foodways Alliance Guide to Cocktails.* Athens: The University of Georgia Press, 2017.

Morgenthaler, Jeffrey, and Martha Holmberg. *The Bar Book: Elements of Cocktail Technique.* San Francisco: Chronicle Books, 2014.

Munat, Ted, with Michael Lazar. *Left Coast Libations: The Art of West Coast Bartending: 100 Original Cocktails.* Left Coast Libations, 2010.

Pacault, F. Paul. *Kindred Spirits 2.* Spirit Journal, 2008.

Parsons, Brad Thomas. *Bitters: A Spirited History of a Classic Cure-All, with Cocktails, Recipes, and Formulas.* Berkeley: Ten Speed Press, 2011.

Regan, Gary. *The Joy of Mixology: The Consummate Guide to the Bartender's Craft.* New York: Clarkson Potter, 2003.

Robitschek, Leo. *The Nomad Cocktail Book.* Berkeley: Ten Speed Press, 2015.

Saucier, Ted. *Bottoms Up.* New York: The Greystone Press, 1951

Simonson, Robert. *A Proper Drink: The Untold Story of How a Band of Bartenders Saved the Civilized Drinking World.* Berkeley: Ten Speed Press, 2016.

Sismondo, Christine. *America Walks into a Bar: A Spirited History of Taverns and Saloons, Speakeasies and Grog Shops.* United Kingdom: Oxford University Press, 2011.

Steinbeck, John. *Travels with Charley in Search of America.* New York: Viking Press, 1962.

Stern, Jane and Michael. *Road Food.* New York: Clarkson Potter, 2017.

Stewart, Amy. *The Drunken Botanist: The Plants That Create the World's Greatest Drinks.* Chapel Hill, NC: Algonquin Books, 2013.

Thomas, Jerry. *The Bartender's Guide: How to Mix Drinks.* New York: Dirk and Fitzgerald, 1862.

Thompson, Toby. *Saloon: A Guide to America's Great Bars, Saloons, Taverns, Drinking Places, and Watering Holes.* New York: Grossman Publishers, 1976.

Wondrich, David. *Esquire Drinks: An Opinionated and Irreverent Guide to Drinking.* New York: Hearst Books, 2002.

_____. *Imbibe! Updated and Revised Edition: From Absinthe Cocktail to Whiskey Smash, a Salute in Stories and Drinks to "Professor" Jerry Thomas, Pioneer of the American Bar.* New York: TarcherPerigree Books, 2015.

_____. *Punch: The Delights (and Dangers) of the Flowing Bowl.* New York: TarcherPerigee Books, 2010.

Index

Note: Page numbers in *italics* indicate recipes, and page numbers in parentheses indicate non-contiguous references.

Index 268

Editor: Laura Dozier
Designer: Eli Mock
Production Manager: Denise LaCongo

Library of Congress Control Number: 2019939755

ISBN: 978-1-4197-4287-3
eISBN: 978-1-68335-835-0

Text copyright © 2020 Brian Bartels
Illustrations by Mike Burdick

Cover © 2020 Abrams

Printed and bound in China

10 9 8 7 6 5 4 3 2 1

Abrams Image books are available at special discounts when purchased in quantity for premiums and promotions as well as fundraising or educational use. Special editions can also be created to specification. For details, contact specialsales@abramsbooks.com or the address below.

Abrams Image® is a registered trademark of Harry N. Abrams, Inc.

ABRAMS The Art of Books
195 Broadway, New York, NY 10007
abramsbooks.com

Up / Coupe

Rocks / Old Fashioned

Pint

Wine Glass

Up / Martini

Shot Glass

Rocks Glass

Highball

Collins

Beer Mug

Hurricane Glass

Coffee Mug

Bloody Mary

Tiki Mug